A Great Cloud of Witnesses:

The Catholic Church's Experience in the Holy Land

Sir Jeffery M. Abood

Dedicated to Our Lady, Queen of Palestine

Good Shepherd Parish, Jericho

"never was it known that anyone who fled to thy protection
implored thy help, or sought thy intercession
was left unaided."

Sir Jeffery M. Abood

Knight Commander

Equestrian Order of the Holy Sepulchre of Jerusalem

Pending Copyright © 2015 by Jeffery Abood
All rights reserved. No part of this publication may be reproduced in any form or by any means, except for brief quotations in printed reviews, without the prior permission of the author/compiler. Contact: jabood@att.net All articles/photos have been reprinted with permissions. Some articles have been edited for length. Many of the articles included here were previously compiled and published in a 3 volume educational series used as a resource by the Equestrian Order of the Holy Sepulchre of Jerusalem. The views and opinions expressed in this book are those of the individual authors and do not reflect the official policy or position of the Order.

Cover Photo: Athena Brown

PATRIARCHATUS LATINUS - JERUSALEM

بطريركية القدس للاتين

Prot. No. (3) 1059/2014

November 26, 2014

Dear Friends,

It is always encouraging when someone from the outside takes a keen interest in the life and times of Christians of the Holy Land. It is reassuring to know that we are not forgotten. This resource booklet takes the initiative to provide articles that give knowledge and perceptive insights into the historical and present-day Holy Land cultural, religious and social context. In general, the booklet's articles provide a wealth of information and insight on subjects written from a human interest perspective describing "the roots and issues", education endeavors, religious freedom, relations among Christians, pilgrimages and dreams and hopes, subjects often overlooked in general media coverage.

The publication does a valuable service in providing a compendium of articles that offer enlightenment and inspiring reflections ranging from on the past and present life of Christians in the Holy Land. I encourage you to read these informative articles and pray that they will be a springboard from which you can dive into a deeper understanding of past history and contemporary issues, thereby becoming a greater advocate of truth and justice in the pursuit of a sustainable peace in this once Holy Land that is now devastated by hatred, fear and violence.

My sincere thanks to Sir Jeffrey Abood for undertaking and completing this project, and to you, the reader, for your concern, prayers and support of Christians in the Holy Land.

May Divine favor and blessings remain with you always!

In Christ our Savior,

+Fouad Twal, Latin Patriarch

"I am inspired to know that you are taking to heart a future for our community, and to recognize that you, our brothers and sisters in Christ have not forgotten the faithful of the Holy Land. It is an assurance that we are not alone and isolated."

His Beatitude Fouad Twal, Latin Patriarch of Jerusalem

"The Arab Christians are the Living Stones of the Holy Land. They are the first believers in our Lord Jesus Christ, but they feel they are the forgotten faithful."

Bishop Dr. Munib A. Younan, Bishop of the Evangelical Lutheran Church in Jordan and the Holy Land, President Lutheran World Federation

"We are different Christian denominations, but all Palestinians. While we have our own religion and heritage; we are a principal part of the fabric of our homeland and the Arab Palestinian people."

Theodosios Atallah Hanna – Greek Orthodox Patriarchate of Jerusalem

Table of Contents

2	A Great Cloud of Witnesses
4	Christians of the Holy Land: An Overview
31	A Background: Israel, Palestine and the Christian Communities
45	The History: Yesterday's Roots and Today's Issues
55	The Papal Voice
78	Living as a Christian in the Holy Land
114	Obstacles to Peace
155	A Right to Education
175	Religious Freedom
189	Christian Relations in the Holy Land
204	Christians in Israel
234	Christians in Gaza
289	Pilgrimages
296	Moving Forward: The Hope for Peace

"Don't be satisfied with what you read in the newspapers. Dig deeper. There you will find the truth."

His Beatitude Latin Catholic Patriarch Fouad Twal

A Great Cloud of Witnesses:
The Catholic Church's Experience in the Holy Land

Hearing our own voice.

Seeking to understand the Holy Land and the Christian's life in it, can at the outset, seem a confusing, possibly even daunting task. There are any number of voices seeking to influence one's perception of the Christian situation in Palestine and Israel. Yet, it is the voice of the Church that speaks the clearest.

Each day, the Catholic Church in the Holy Land, in her social service agencies, hospitals, schools and parishes, witnesses the human consequences of the ongoing troubles that plaque the land of Jesus' birth. They have gone on record as a way of sharing those experiences with the larger Church.

What you will find contained herein is the voice of the Church in its' own words. It is not the voice of politicians or pundits or ideologues. It is the uncensored authentic voice of the Church in the Holy Land and it continues to faithfully call out to us. This is a compilation of the words of Popes, Patriarchs, Cardinals, clergy, teachers and the everyday Catholic in the street. It is uniquely, the Christian experience. It has been consistent, truthful and unfortunately, too often ignored.

This is a humble attempt to help change that.

In doing so, this book has brought together for the first time in one place, a series of official Church statements, documents, articles, and interviews collected from over a seventy year time span. And while some of the articles are older, the larger issues they address have never been resolved. All of these articles are solely from the Christian perspective and address issues specific to the Holy Land.

When most people think of the Holy Land, they think of Israel and Palestine. Many also believe that whatever transpires there is simply a matter concerning Jews and Muslims. Yet, there is a very significant community whose voice is too often left out, not only of much of the dialogue, but also of many of the possible solutions regarding the Holy Land. That voice is the voice of the Church and its' people.

It is a voice that many are not generally familiar with. If you say there are Catholics living in Gaza; it can sound strange indeed to someone unfamiliar with the Churches history and presence there.

As the Christian population in the Holy Land has decreased from historically around 18% to less than 2% today, it is imperative we correctly understand the situation of our brothers and sisters living there.

In order to better understand their lives in this troubled land, it is the voice of the Church, that can provide us with a solid base on which to form our perspectives. It is a voice free of "spin", agenda or politics. As Archimedes said, "Give me a place to stand and I can move the earth". The Church has provided us with that place to stand, so that we can make a positive difference.

The Christians in the Holy Land have a saying, that "we live in a land that has experienced the Resurrection, so as Christians, we always have hope". Part of that hope is us. Our prayer is that the reader will hear what the Church is saying and join their voices to those of this "great cloud of witnesses".

Christians of the Holy Land: an Overview

"Catholics of the world must offer their prayer and expressions of solidarity...to the Christian community of that blessed land. Despite their countless difficulties, these Christians offer day by day, and in silence, an authentic witness to the Gospel."

Cardinal Daoud, Prefect of the Vatican's Congregation for Eastern Churches, 2007

The Crowning of Thorns

+ **Fouad Twal, Patriarch**

February 15, 2013

Dear Brothers and Sisters,

1. Here we are at the beginning of Lent, two days after Ash Wednesday, as is a tradition in Jerusalem at the Church of the Convent of Ecce Homo. We commemorate the crowning of Jesus Christ with thorns. We have begun the forty days of Lent which leads us to Easter. In a burst of love which we shall never fully grasp, Jesus, the Son of God, gave his life for the glory of God and the salvation of the world. Today we depart from the gospel narrative to contemplate, to meditate, to delve into the third sorrowful mystery, the mystery of the rosary, the crowning with thorns.

2. Jesus was crowned with thorns, Jesus was insulted, humiliated, subjected to ridicule, general mockery, laughter and all possible forms of public and personal humiliation: this is what is marked out in this third mystery. Jesus suffered in his body, in his heart. It is in Gethsemane also that the tribulation penetrates His most holy soul.

With the crown of thorns, with what precedes and what follows, with all that extracts from Christ tears and cries, God the Father suffers with his Son. This sacrifice reveals the Father's love, willing to give up the life of his Son, to save the life of each of us, as we are. Through the sufferings of Jesus, He said "I love you." The love of Christ is stronger than the pain it inflicts on his humanity. This love confers on Him His true royalty. These thorns encircle the forehead of the Redeemer as a crown of glory, because this crown, this and no other, Jesus accepted with love. Jesus wanted the kingdom of love, a kingdom not of this world.

3. As Christians, we too are called to bear our crown of thorns, that is to say, willing to suffer for Christ's sake and to share in his suffering (1 Peter 1: 21). Jesus said that anyone who wants to follow him must carry his cross (Luke 9: 23). Become a disciple of Jesus, not only by following, but also by carrying in our bodies "what is still lacking in Christ's afflictions " (Col 1: 24).

Here in the Holy Land, and the Middle East in general, we too are stifled by the thorns of war, violence, extremism, instability, migration, and injustice. Here in the Holy Land, Jesus continues to suffer where believers are divided, where injustice reigns, where migrants and refugees are mistreated.

We carry a crown of barbed wire, a tunic of concrete and graffiti. And we Christians form another Calvary Church of the Via Crucis which has not yet been completed.

For us, trying to live as disciples of Christ on the Land of Salvation, is to agree to take on ourselves, as Simon of Cyrene, a part of the cross of Jesus. It is to be willing to take upon ourselves, unworthy descendants of Veronica, a portion of that sputum that dirtied the face of the Lord. In each of us lives another Simon of Cyrene and a beautiful Veronica who dares to reach out to the neighbor. I am proud of our Church in Jordan where Caritas-Jordan is doing miracles for hundreds of thousands of Syrians refugees.

4. We are not allowed to lose faith and hope. Our vocation is between Calvary and hope. And "hope does not disappoint" (Rom 5: 5). We proudly wear the crown which is the identity of our vocation, and which associates us with the passion of Christ. It involves the vocation of personal conversion of hearts, that the old man dies. It involves suffering that purifies the heart and feelings; the more love grows, the more it accepts pain as a companion. But the glance on the Crucified One gives strength, patience, sometimes obedience leads to the humiliation, contempt for human dignity, or until death. Do not forget that the Master is also passed by and he forgave. He conquered.

5. We know that only Jesus, having gone through the tribulation and death to resurrection, can bring salvation and peace for all the people of this region of the world (cf. Acts 2: 23-24. 32-33). He alone is the Christ, the Son of God, that we proclaim! Let us therefore repent and convert " that your sins may be blotted out, 20 that times of refreshing may come" (Acts 3: 19-20a).

6. We wear this crown, hoping, one day, to have the joy of living in the Kingdom of Heaven. The crown of thorns will turn into a crown of glory.

Do not forget that we are co-heirs with Jesus and he will share his glory with us through the Holy Spirit Who crowns us with the grace of God, a glorious crown offered by a good and merciful God, an incorruptible crown which will last eternally (1 Peter 5, Jas 4 and 1.12).

During Lent, we learn to unite in prayer, in love with the person of Christ and with all human beings who suffer, and learn to meditate on the signs of the Passion and all that he suffered for us. The Blessed Mary, who accompanied Jesus in the crowning of the passion tells us that the Rosary is also a crown: a crown of prayers.

Dear Brothers and Sisters, may Blessed Mary guide us and keep us throughout Lent until the Holy Easter.

Amen.

Holy Land: The Situation of Christians in Jesus' Homeland

Cardinal John Foley tells how the Christians live between Muslim and Jewish fundamentalism

BY WLODZIMIERZ REDZIOCH - FEBRUARY 2010 *"INSIDE THE VATICAN" Magazine*

In your capacity as Grand Master of the Knights of the Holy Sepulcher, you are particularly concerned about the Catholic Church in the Holy Land. What is the present situation of Christians in Jesus' homeland?

CARDINAL JOHN FOLEY: The paradox is that for Christians living in the Holy Land it is terribly hard to reach Bethlehem, Jesus' birthplace. Getting to Bethlehem is easier for tourists than for the local Christians: lots of permissions are needed and there are lots of check points. At Christmas, the Patriarch of Jerusalem celebrates Midnight Mass. There were many people present, though not so many as in the previous years, owing to restrictions.

How do Christians live in the Holy Land?

CARDINAL FOLEY: Let's quote some figures first of all: 60 years ago, 18% of the people who lived in the Holy Land (i.e., of Israel and Palestine) were Christians; now Christians have gone down to 2%.

A great number of Palestinians, even Christian Palestinians, have emigrated to Jordan, but most of them have gone to America and several European countries. Fortunately, Christians are looked at with favor in the countries that receive them, as they have a good education and are not regarded as extremists. Needless to say, the emigration of Christians is a great loss for the local Church.

Living conditions are worse in the Palestinian territories on account of the wall. The wall divides the Palestinian camps and towns from Israel and even internally, and makes it difficult for the population to reach their jobs, schools, hospitals, etc. So life is hard for everybody in the Palestine region, especially for Christians. The situation is by far the worst in Gaza, an outdoor prison. But there are very few Christians there.

The struggle for the building of a Palestinian state was at first nationalistic, but now it has turned into a religious struggle: the Palestinians have embraced the cause of Islam. How does this affect the situation of Christians?

CARDINAL FOLEY: The Palestinian cause should not be seen as an Islamic cause: Palestinian society is made up of Muslims, but of Christians too, both Orthodox and Catholics. There were lots of Christian Palestinian leaders in the past; even nowadays there are some. But Christian Palestinian leaders have no connection with violent or extremist groups. An important fact must be remembered: the Palestinians are accustomed more than other Arabs to living in a multi-religious society. In the past believers of different faiths used to live together in peace. An example of this peaceful coexistence is that Catholic schools are open to Muslim students. During the Holy Father's visit to the Holy Land, the king of Jordan, the Israeli prime minister and the president of the Palestinian Authority acknowledged the great contribution of the Catholic schools to peace and coexistence.

So Christians find themselves between Muslim and Jewish radicals. Everyone knows about the difficult situation of Christians in the Palestinian territories, but very little is said about Jewish fundamentalism (Orthodox Jews who spit at Franciscans and burn the New Testament) and of the imposed restrictions on Christians by the State of Israel...

CARDINAL FOLEY: When I first visited the Holy Land way back in 1965, I passed through Mandelbaum Gate, at the time marking the Israeli-Jordanian border and entered the Orthodox district of Measharim. I was carrying a suitcase, but it was a Saturday, Orthodox Jews began to throw stones at me.

Isn't Israel now ruled by fundamentalists like those who threw stones at you?

CARDINAL FOLEY: This is a big problem facing the Netanyahu government (I would like to say the Israeli prime minister studied in my hometown of Philadelphia. I know the high school he went to and we talked about it in one of our meetings). He won the election appealing to the most extremist circles; now he presides over a government that intends to find a way out of the Palestinian conflict on the one hand and to meet the demands of the extremist parties on the other hand. Let us remember that Minister Avigdor Lieberman before the election suggested that all the Palestinians should be expelled and sent to other Arab countries.

The political context explains the difficulties confronting Catholic priests and religious since members of the Shas Jewish fundamentalist party too control the Israeli Interior Ministry. Israel is determined to cut down the length of residence permits for Catholic clergy to one year...

CARDINAL FOLEY: We would like Israel to guarantee movement for priests and seminarians. These are now afraid of leaving Israel in case they should not be allowed to return. Let's hope that Israel will be induced to right this great injustice.

Restrictions on residence permits are not only an injustice, but also violate the 1993 Fundamental Agreement between Israel and the Holy See...

CARDINAL FOLEY: In my opinion the complete disappearance of the Christian community in the Holy Land would be a tragedy even for the State of Israel. Though remaining a Jewish state, Israel would be more credible accepting and respecting believers of other religions. This brings in, not only the question of the Israeli-Palestinian border, but also the question of the rights of minorities.

Eminence, you are the Grand Master of an Order which originated in Palestine. What do the Knights of the Holy Sepulchre do for Christians in the Holy land nowadays?

CARDINAL FOLEY: Members of our Order have two goals: deepening their spiritual life, which they also do through pilgrimages to Jesus' homeland, and helping Christians in the Holy Land.

Since the year 2000, we have sent more than $50 million for the maintenance of parishes, schools, hospitals and other institutions. In other words, our concern is to guarantee the presence of Christians, i.e., of "living stones" in the Holy Land.

Do you cooperate with the Latin Patriarchate of Jerusalem?

CARDINAL FOLEY: We send most of our aid through the Patriarchate. They lay down a scale of requirements and projects they intend to carry out; we do our best to help them. For example, we helped the Patriarchate to enlarge its seminary, since there is an increase in vocations.

It must be remembered that when Pius IX restored the Latin Patriarchate of Jerusalem, he also restored the Order of the Knights of the Holy Sepulcher with the aforesaid purposes.

They say there will be peace in the world when there is peace in Jerusalem: what can we do to help Israel and the Palestinians to find a definite solution to their conflict?

CARDINAL FOLEY: We have no military or economic power to press the parties involved in this conflict. We make a different kind of contribution: as I said before, we have schools and social institutions to contribute to mutual understanding and reconciliation. The Holy See, on the other hand, has its' own representative in Israel, the nuncio, Archbishop Antonio Franco, who has his office in Jaffa (the international community does not recognize Jerusalem as the capital of Israel) and who serves as apostolic delegate in Jerusalem, one of whose tasks is to make sure that the rights of Catholics in the Holy Land are respected.

What can individual believers do?

CARDINAL FOLEY: In my opinion it is very important for Catholics to go on pilgrimage to the Holy Land and visit places made sacred by Jesus' presence; they should also meet local Christians and know about their problems. The organization of pilgrimages should also include encounters with the local community, i.e., the "living stones" of the Holy Land: this is a way to give them hope again.

Our Situation in the Holy Land

By H.E. William Shomali, Auxiliary Bishop of Jerusalem

Speech given at HCEF International Conference, Oct. 2011

Introduction

Historical Palestine is a small country, only 25000 km2, but rich in history. It is the religious cradle of the Judeo-Christian world and a center of Islam. There, live two peoples, with two languages, and practicing three monotheistic religions. This small geographic area continues to handle a serious conflict for nearly one century. This conflict explodes every 10 or 12 years, and we cannot expect that it will be resolved in a short time, because of other major problems (Israeli settlements, return of refugees, the borders of the future Palestinian state and especially the question of Jerusalem). We live in a tense situation which causes both Israelis and Palestinians much frustration and bitterness. Sometimes, both become more reasonable. The exchange of prisoners last week was a good signal sent by both sides meaning that it is still possible to achieve something positive.

We also know that same causes lead to the same effects. Violence can explode at any time, and it can include the Holy Land and the entire Middle East. An example is the current tension between Turkey and Israel after the massacre of nine Turks on board a ship on the coast of Gaza. Tension can unleash a war. Another example: every time Fundamentalist Jews congregate and come up to the esplanade of the Temple Mount, it leads to a lot of tension that may one day ignite the entire region. The second Intifada began there. The Temple Mount remains a "casus belli"(cause of war) between

Muslims and Jews, something that is difficult to resolve through negotiations.

In this part of the world lives a vibrant Christian minority, but its number continues to shrink.

Two important questions arise:

- How can this Christian minority live or survive?
- What hope have they for the future?

For reasons of methodology and time I will limit my talk mainly to Palestinian Christians.

I-   Economy

The Palestinian Territories is a poor country. If we compare its situation with other neighboring countries in terms of gross domestic product (GDP) per capita and taking into account purchasing power parity (PPP) per capita, we will have the following results from the World Bank:

Country	Year	GDP (or PPP per capita)	Classification of 192
Palestine	2011	$2,900	168\226
Jordan	2011	$5,400	142
Israel	2011	$29,800	45
Italy	2011	$30,500	42
France	2011	$33,00	39
USA	2011	$47, 200	11
Qatar	2011	$179,000	1

Gaza is a bit apart from other Palestinian territories, because of the blockade and restrictions imposed that make humanitarian conditions deplorable and prevent the improvement in the situation. Restrictions affect the importation of raw materials. Poverty remains very high in the Palestinian territories:26% of Palestinians live in poverty. The World Food Program(WFP) indicates that 33% of Palestinians are currently in a state of food deficiency.

A- Resources

In addition to foreign aid, particularly European and American aid which reached one billion dollars a year, there are five main resources of the Palestinian economy:

1. Stone industry: The industry provides the Palestinian economy $700 million a year. A fifth of the product is consumed in Palestine; the rest is mainly exported to Israel.

2. Religious tourism: Religious tourism has a strong potential for the future. The holy places are sacred to the three religions and can attract millions of pilgrims if there was peace and especially if Muslim pilgrims could obtain visas. In this case, the numbers could triple for hotels, restaurants, and buses because the number of pilgrims would rise from 3 million pilgrims a year today to 10 million as we dream. In addition to guides, hotels and restaurants who profit from the tourism industry, are the artisans. They make sacred objects from olive wood and mother of pearl. This craft industry brought into the country in the 14th century by the Franciscan friars now provides jobs for hundreds of Christians.

3. The third resource is from **professions and jobs** in the public and private sectors. Wages are generally low. An employee normally receives between 300 and 1,000 Euros a month. The great advantage of being an employee is the health insurance coverage which only 20% of the population has access, and others must arrange for coverage as they can. If the need to undergo surgery arises, they literally must beg to pay the cost.

4. Taxes and foreign aid: Palestinian Authority's annual budget is $3.7 billion. Part of it is constituted by the taxes that Israel collects from Palestinians import and gives back to Palestinians. Since Oslo peace accords signed between Israel and the Palestinians in 1994, Israel has been collecting taxes on behalf of the PNA every month. Israel usually transfers 100 million U.S. dollars every month into the PNA budget. The PNA uses the money to pay salaries of 148, 000 security and civil employees. Only $400 million are yearly collected in income and sales taxes within the West Bank and Gaza. The total income from taxes amounts to 1 billion 600 million dollars. Why are domestic tax receipts so low? Because the economy is in constant recession and "operates well below its potential," according to the World Bank.

What debilitates and cripples the Palestinian economy is Israel's heavy, systematic restrictions on movement within the occupied territories – hundreds of roadblocks and military checkpoints that delay, prolong and sabotage normal economic activity and, hence, potential tax revenues. Even with all those revenues coming from taxes, there is still more than two billion shortfall in the Authority's budget that should be filled by foreign help. In fact, 1 billion 800 million come as help from Europe, USA and Arab countries.

5. There is also a light industry: textiles, furniture, paper, paints, plastic manufacturing, medicine, food such as bread and pastries; and building materials. Bethlehem also produces araq and wine. Cremisan wine is famous throughout the region.

B-   Some difficulties

1. Walls and barriers: Israel seems to have invalidated the border issue by building a wall 700 kilometers long, apparently for safety and security, which is partly true, but it is above all to create the new border between Israelis and Palestinians. This wall swallowed almost half of the Palestinian territories and includes illegal settlements which were built after 1967. The walls and barriers are a nightmare for everyone. It is not easy to get a permit to enter Israel. Exceptions are made as in cases of illness, or pilgrimage during major feasts. Even with a permit, workers going to Israel are faced with the difficulty of crossing the checkpoint, losing so much time for passage. Some would get up at 2 o'clock in the morning to line up at the checkpoint to be the first to cross when it opens at 6:00 A.M.

Many Christian and Moslems are willing to go to pray in Jerusalem, the holiest city for Christians and one of the three holiest in Islam. Christian worshippers need a permit to enter the Holy City. It is given at random. But people are happy if they obtain one which lasts one month. During their feasts, Moslems are allowed just for one day. Generally those who are above 45 years are allowed to enter without permits.

2. Travel: Furthermore, the Palestinian territories do not have their own airport and Palestinians cannot travel from Tel Aviv, but from the Amman airport in Jordan. Trips become longer and more expensive with difficulties in obtaining visa for the host country. What a waste of time to prepare for a trip. It's heroic! The most surprising thing is that you get used to the abnormal that becomes normal.

3. Real Estate construction: This problem is unique to Jerusalem and Israel. The total population of Jerusalem is approximately 800,000 inhabitants, of which 36% are Palestinians and 2% are Christians. Normally, the Palestinians should get a third of the building permits from the municipality. But in reality, they only get 8%. This has made house rentals more expensive and the price of land for construction has escalated. An apartment of 100m2 would cost in the same neighborhood of Jerusalem about 400,000 dollars. That is why many Jerusalemite families will live in Bethlehem or Ramallah to find reasonably priced housing accommodation at the risk of losing their social security and health insurance, and even their Jerusalem identity card. Many give up on marriage because of housing shortage.

Despite segregation in the housing sector which caused a serious crisis on the Palestinian side, the Latin Patriarchate, after years of hard work, received from the municipality of Jerusalem, permission to build 72 apartments in the south area of the city in Beit Safafa, two kilometers from the Bethlehem checkpoint. This project will assist young couples and families. The success of this project has encouraged others to duplicate this undertaking. Without such projects, young people of Jerusalem will be forced to emigrate.

4. Family reunification: This is a serious problem. If the wife is Jordanian and the husband is Palestinian, the wife cannot come and live in the Palestinian territories without permission to enter Palestine. The same is true for a Palestinian woman whose husband is in Jerusalem or Israel. Thousands of such cases exist. Moreover, all Palestinians, who were outside of Palestine during the 1967 war and who have not been registered by the Israelis have lost their and their children's right of residence in their country of origin. Among them are thousands of Christians

5. Hatred and ignorance of each other: Because of wars, violence and retaliation between the two peoples; because of the barriers and walls that have enclosed the Palestinians in a large ghetto; because of the large number of prisoners in Israeli prisons and suicidal actions committed by Palestinians in Israeli cities, hatred and ignorance of the other reign in the Holy Land. If a Palestinian child is asked what he knows about the Holocaust, he will deny it or say that the Jewish people well deserved it. If an Israeli child is asked what the word "Nakba" means, he can say he knows nothing. Everyone has his own memory of the past and retains only his own sufferings, being unwilling to open up to the suffering of others.

6. Emigration: All the foregoing reasons, including unemployment, insecurity and being a minority living with two large majorities have pushed many of our Christians to emigrate to the West. In the English census of Palestine in 1922, the Christians of Jerusalem were 14.700 while Muslims were 13.400. In 1948, Christians were 29.000, and Muslims 40.000. The Nakba of 1948 decimated the Christian population of Jerusalem, that the 1967 census showed the number of Christians down to 12.646. Today there are approximately 10,000 to 12,000 inhabitants in a total population of 800,000. The number of Palestinian Christians of the diaspora is half a million, while those who remained in Palestine are 50000. In Israel there are 180,000.

7. Water: There is severe water shortage in the Holy Land. The rainy season lasts three months. The result is an average of 500ml per year. Fortunately there is groundwater which is totally controlled by the Israelis, and the Palestinians are entitled only to a limited portion of this groundwater. It is a paradox, and yet true: what was returned to the Palestinians in Area A and B is the land while the air and what is underground belong to the Israelis who have the right to fly over all of Palestine and control groundwater. The water shortage is a recurring crisis each year during the summer.

II- Politics

Speaking of the economy and the difficulties of daily life, we inevitably hit the political problem. But we want to explore the merits of this problem in its several dimensions.

Why is this conflict so difficult to resolve?

It is difficult because the nature of the dispute, before being political and military, it is ideological with a religious background. Nothing is worse than a politically related religious ideology. The issue revolves around this question: Who owns the Holy Land? There are two answers, two visions of the history of this country, and therefore two possible solutions.

I will limit myself to two points:

1- The territorial issue

The Israelis believe that all Palestine is Jewish by God's promise to Abraham and his descendants. They assume that all Jews living in the Holy Land or in the Diaspora are genealogically descendants of Abraham. We will not discuss the theological problem. We will only talk about the consequences of this ideology. If the Holy Land belongs to the Jews, the term "occupation", used by the United Nations to describe the effects of the 1967 war is wrong. Therefore, Israelis replace it with the word "liberation". They officially call the occupied territories the "disputed territories". Obama's speech last May recognized the borders of June 4, 1967, but he is not prepared to put his words into practice and to recognize the right of Palestinians to an independent state at the Security Council. On the contrary, he threatens to oppose by the U.S. veto.

2- The Jerusalem Issue:

It is a territorial issue. For Palestinians, Jerusalem is an integral part of the occupied territories. For the Israelis, it is the exclusive and indivisible capital of Israel forever. The idea of making Jerusalem a capital of two states is not accepted by the Israelis. The issue of Jerusalem is one of the greatest problems of the world. The hardest part of the problem is the conflict between Muslims and Jews for the possession of the Temple Mount, now under Muslim control, which they call al-Aqsa or Al Haram Al Sharif. This holy place is a flash point of the ongoing tensions between the two communities. In part there is also an apprehension that some Jews wish to build the Third Temple.

III- Religion

The Message to the People of God and the 44 Recommendations of the Synod of Bishops of the Middle East are a Charter for us. The Synod did not claim to find a solution for all problems of Christians but it provided a necessary light to look at the reality through the eyes of God. An example may illustrate this: to make Christians stay in the Holy Land, we must persuade them that their permanence and cohabitation with Moslems in Palestine is a true vocation to live and to witness of our faith in the land of Jesus.

Freedom of religion and freedom of conscience: Religious freedom exists in the Holy Land. We do not suffer from any problems. We can build schools, churches and display religious symbols in Palestine, Israel and Jordan. Furthermore, freedom of conscience is missing. Someone who changes his faith is scorned by the community. A Muslim who converts to Christianity may risk his life. A young Christian woman who flees home to marry a Muslim is abandoned by her family, never to be seen again, cast to oblivion and considered dead. When this happens, it is a real tragedy for the family. It is the talk of the whole village, putting blame on the parents who failed to properly educate their daughter.

Relations with Muslims: Comparing our situation in Jordan and Palestine with what is happening in Egypt, Iraq or Saudi Arabia, our relations with Muslims are really good. Although there is occasionally little tension, it is wrong to talk about anti-Christian persecution. What we expect from the dialogue with Islam are: to dispel prejudices; foster mutual knowledge and esteem, friendship; dialogue on secondary issues such as the environment and climate change; highlighting common values such as prayer, fasting, almsgiving and pilgrimage. Together we have a common history and a common language. There are places of daily dialogue in our schools, our hospitals, at the university in addition to annual conferences. We must not underestimate the interactions of life, such as dialogue in the street, good neighborhood, invitations to a Ramadan Iftar and exchange of visits during the holidays. But what happened in Egypt in the last days is appalling. The religious freedom for Copts in building churches is limited. They suffered when they saw their church put to fire in a small village of the upper Egypt, 440 miles north of Aswan city, nearest big town. They went to the street to protest. What happened was unexpected. The clashes with the army left 25 dead and 200 wounded. The solution is that Egypt changes the rules and follows one standard in the construction of mosques and churches.

Relations with Jews: We have no serious problems in interreligious dialogue with Judaism. What we have in common, such as the Bible, the Jewish origins of our liturgy and the first church give us a solid platform for a serious dialogue based on mutual respect. But we must highlight that political issues often poison interreligious dialogue. It is disconcerting that most of the time dialogues do not happen between local Christians and Jews in Israel but in other countries between foreign Christians and Jews of the Diaspora.

Let me conclude that –Despite the continuing conflict that does not seem to have a promising solution in the near future, we must "hope against all hope" (Rom.4:18), and pray that the Lord transforms this death situation into a life situation where all the inhabitants of the country, Christians, Muslims and Jews can live harmoniously. The fate of this community and its survival depends on the evolution of the peace process but also on the ability of our Christians to live as free and equal citizens in the midst of two majority blocks: Islam and Judaism. It also depends on their ability to find within their faith a force to remain Christians, to be proud of it and to offer a beautiful testimony to others of their faith. We pray every day for peace, knowing that the Lord is the master of history and that peace is a gift from Him and not the result of diplomatic efforts that have altogether failed. The Lord knows to surprise us and generously gives more than our expectations. In fact, Jerusalem is the city of great surprises. This is where the Lord has risen on the third day when nobody believed. Relying on this, let us together continue to pray and hope.

Lives of the Christians in Jerusalem

In his role as Grand Master of the Equestrian Order of the Holy Sepulchre, Cardinal Edwin O'Brien visited the Holy Land in early December. In an interview he noted that the Christian population now numbering about 2%, is down significantly in just a few years.

Israel's plans, for 30,000 new settlements, he said, will complicate things even further for the Palestinians. The situation is uncomfortable for Christians and others, he said, "most of the people have fled because of the pressures there. There are no jobs, they can't travel, great repression in that part of the world and it's a shame." "The more that that land is taken away from them and settlements, permanent settlements are built up, it's going to be virtually impossible to envision a free Palestinian state."

The role of the Knights of the Holy Sepulchre, he said, is "precisely to help that small, but vivid Christian community. More than 30,000 members of the Order of the Holy Sepulchre dedicate their time, knowledge and resources. Their donations help fund 45 schools and more than 60 parishes and several orphanages in the Holy Land.

One of the biggest challenges, he believes, is actually having an open debate about the conflict between Israel and Palestine: "For some reason we can't openly debate these things in the United States where we're afraid to be accused of anti anti-semitism, but the discussion in Israel among the Jewish people is much livelier."

Still, O'Brien believes pilgrims from abroad provide emotional support for the Christian community, not just money. "The midnight

Mass is something that is known worldwide, that's a sign for Christians that there is still life in the Church, there is concern for them on the part of the Church Universal," he added. Through his visit Cardinal O'Brien said he made sure that this small Christian community knows it is not forgotten,

From an interview with Rome Reports - 7/19/12

Situation of the Christians in the Holy Land

Father Firas Aridah is pastor of Saint Joseph Parish in Jifna, Palestine. This speech was given in Germany, September 4, 2012. Fr. Firas (second from left) in the Parish of Aboud

I want to thank you for the honor of being able to speak with you this morning at this vibrant gathering here in Duderstadt about the situation of the Christian community in the Holy Land. My name is Father Firas Aridah from Jordan. I am a Roman Catholic priest of the Latin Patriarchate of Jerusalem, which serves the Christian community in Israel, Jordan, the Palestinian Territories and Cyprus.

It is a land sacred to Christians, Jews and Muslims; all three faith communities have existed there for centuries. Historically it was home to many nations, and now, in the modern context, it is a home to Israelis and Palestinians. One land, two peoples, three faiths; each rooted in conviction and vigor for Jerusalem, each who need to be reminded that there can be no exclusive claim which will be accepted.

What I had in mind when I came to serve in Jerusalem, was to focus all my energy in performing the 'normal duties' of a parish priest— tending to the needs of the Christian faithful and the community at large while being able to attract the youth as you are doing here. It was there, in the midst of my 'normal duties', where I became unwillingly drawn into this on-going conflict. It was never my intention to get involved in politics – and I am still resolute to leave the politics to the politicians – but my focus is the people. And in my service to the people, I dealt with the occupation. With the occupation came the confiscation of lands and the demolition of homes. With the confiscation of lands and demolition of homes came the building of walls of separation in the name of security inside the west bank, losing 8 % from our land not the borders of 1967. With the building of walls of separation came the destruction of olive orchards and stealing our own water. These 'normal duties' of a parish priest have been particularly painful in Palestine.

Olive trees are a main source of livelihood for Palestinians. They are used to derive products such as: olive oil, soap and wood crafts. These trees and this livelihood are thousands of years old, handed down from one generation to the next. The groves are a lifeline with great significance and value in our culture. In the aftermath of the 26 foot high wall that now surrounds most of the West Bank and with new border enforcement, people can no longer get to their farms. Families have been divided; many have lost their jobs or have become deprived of advanced medical care at hospitals which are no longer accessible. As a priest, a pastor of souls, my conscience and my calling drive me to be "a voice for those who have no voice and to defend the weak and the oppressed." (Patr. Sabbah. Seek Peace and Pursue it. 1998) How then can I say nothing as this tragedy befalls the people who I am serving? How can I remain silent when the Christian community I am serving is disappearing because of this occupation.

The current situation we face is this: Today, we have fewer Christians in the Holy Land than we had in 1947 going from 8% to 1.6% in 2000. When at one point we numbered 27,000 Christians in Jerusalem, now we are only 9,000 Christians. Our people are emigrating, our presence is threatened and if the trend continues, our future is moving towards extinction. This is impacted by the fact that there are over 550,000 Israeli settlers living in the West Bank and East Jerusalem. Many of our villages are under military control, with restrictions on movement from one village to the next, meaning that we have immediate family who have become separated from each other. Our lands are still being confiscated all around us to build more Israeli settlements or to expand settlements that already exist. Recently Israel has confiscated around three thousand acres from 59 Christian families in Beit Jala to continue expansion of the Gilo settlement and the separation wall where we lost more than 9 % from the land of West Bank.

The recent development of clashes between settlers and Israeli civil authorities is proof that settlements are a phenomenon which has grown far beyond Israel's grasp. They violate the laws which have been put in place to protect them and they unquestionably threaten peace and stability in the region. As the book of Proverbs says: "Where there is no hope, the people perish" – an entire generation of Israelis and Palestinians have grown up witnessing and experiencing violence, occupation, separation, and hatred. There continue to be fewer and fewer opportunities to interact. There is heightened suspicion and apprehension on both sides and so, our people deeply feel a sense of hopelessness and despair.

In the midst of this unfortunate reality it falls on us to speak out and remind everyone of the objective truth that is Jesus Christ. In the words of our Patriarch Fouad Twal: "ultimately, Israelis and Palestinians ... must work out their differences in a just and righteous manner, in ways that require painful compromises." No, we the Christian community of the Holy Land, the people of Calvary, will not allow our hope to die. We today live the Gospel – we live the hope it promises.

We are walking towards our Lord with conviction and with faith not allowing the huge obstacle of war, violence and occupation to hinder our path. Be assured friends we are walking towards Jesus Christ and nothing will keep us from him.

It is amazing to see that even in Gaza where our small Christian community not only suffers from the occupation and economic sanctions imposed by most of the free world – they also suffer from extremism and fanaticism caused by a lack of education. And with all this they are determined to stay, determined to live where Christianity has existed for two thousand years – no friends nothing will stand between us and the Lord. We will not allow others to use our voice. We will not stand for a fundamentalist interpretation of the Bible which seeks to legitimize the infringement of Palestinian rights, nor will we stand for Islamic extremism.

We have a unified Christian message which we are able and willing to give to the world. This message can be found in the Kairos Palestine document. "We are thinkers, we are theologians, we are philosophers, we are teachers, we are believers in the Bible and in Jesus Christ who "interpreted to the disciples of Emmaus the things about himself in all the scriptures" (Lk. 24:27) and we are rolling up our sleeves and are making a difference by shedding light in a bleak situation because nothing will stand between us and the Lord.

The Church in fact has found ways to give people hope and an opportunity for a better future. As an example, the Catholic Church is the largest private educator in the area which we serve, with some 70,000 children in the over 100 schools run by various institutions of the church.

We run 14 hospitals in the area with 3 Universities. We serve the poorest of the poor through our orphanages, nursing homes, centres for children with special needs and centres for the pastoral needs of families and young adults.

We run youth groups, scouts and we provide a safe place for children to come and play. We are doing our part in providing educational opportunities for our youth who are the future, we believe that if Christian, Muslim and Jewish children play together, they will become friends – then and only then will we have a prospect for lasting peace.

Sadly, in the midst of this conflict, few are looking to serve humanity; few are seeing the human faces of children, mothers, fathers and the elderly which are violated by oppression and violence. But we are in need of your help, we are in need of your support, we are in need for you to walk with us towards the empty tomb so that one day we can hear together the good news and reap the good reward: 'Well done, good and faithful servant! You have been faithful with little; I will put you in charge of much. Come and share your master's happiness!' (Matthew 25:23)

So you will say, what can we here in Germany do for you in the Holy Land? Let me tell you. Local governments and international intervention has failed for too long to do what is necessary. It is vital that administrations realize that time is no longer on our side and that actions to secure peace which is one sided (or in one's own vested interests) will bring us nowhere. Prolonging the conflict between Palestinians and Israelis will serve only the extremists on both sides and will weaken the supporters of peace on both sides. If you intervene you can save the prospect of peace, before it is extinguished by extremism and violence.

In our schools children learn and experience humanity, after all that is what Jesus taught: to love our enemies, to forgive those who do us harm, to be peacemakers, and promote dialogue and foster reconciliation.

The Christians in Palestine are small in number, but we are doing our part to work for a better future for both Palestinians and Israelis. Time and time again we have seen the youth who graduate from our schools and universities or those who benefit from the work of our institutions – they leave with a changed mindset. Despite the despair and the violence in society, they still believe in the ability to change the world and so they become leaders for justice, peace and tolerance instead of pupils of death and destruction.

I, like those who are hopeful, truly believe Israelis and Palestinians can live together, but in order for it to be a reality, each side must recognize the dignity of the other and be willing to unconditionally accept each other, for the sake of humanity. With great fervour and courage, we must make a renewed and genuine effort to promote peace and extend our hand to all faiths and peoples who share in the pursuit of peace, justice and liberty.

The occupation must end because it is a sin against God Himself. Violence and terrorism must stop. There must be no more settlements built on Palestinian land. Our Christian presence must be supported and nurtured. You must support the efforts of institutions who are working to serve humanity. Use your voice and your influence to bring the prospect of peace back. If you don't who will? Give us the chance to one day stand with you and say: Two Nations under God with Peace, Liberty and Justice for all!

I promise you when we walk towards Jesus we will never lose. I invite you to come to the Holy Land as pilgrims, to be present in our lives and to pray for us and with us, and to support our projects, so that we can arrive together one day to the goal in which we are all interested – Peace. May God bless you all, and bless every step you take to support the dignity of human life in this world.

A Background: Israel, Palestine and Christian Communities

"As Christians, we are a Church whose Via Crucis is not yet complete..."

Latin Patriarch Twal, Lenten Message, 2014

Country Report - Israel/Palestine

CNEWA(Catholic Near East Welfare Association) 2010

Sociopolitical Situation

Israel's closure of Gaza's borders has exacerbated the humanitarian crisis there. Reports indicate that 61% of Gaza's households are now "food insecure" and a further 16% are "vulnerable to food insecurity." Israel's ban on most construction materials entering the Gaza Strip continues to hinder severely all efforts to rehabilitate homes and buildings that have been left in rubble since the war. Thousands of families are still living in houses with shattered windows. U.N. agencies have begun building mud brick homes in response to the hundreds of families still living in makeshift tents. Lack of proper water and sanitation infrastructure in addition to electricity outages has also increased health concerns for the general population. Gaza's Ministry of Health warns that due to the border closure, there is a lack of medical equipment at Gaza hospitals and a shortage of at least 140 types of medication used to treat cancer patients and others suffering from blood-related diseases. Although a large majority of goods are still being smuggled through tunnels, the Egyptian government has intensified its counter-smuggling effort, dispatching more border patrols and constructing a 9-10 kilometer iron wall with depths of 20-30 meters along the Rafah border.

Area C of the West Bank (which is under the jurisdiction of the Israeli government and constitutes 61% of the West Bank) remains a high risk area. Israel's High Court of Justice recently ordered the state to issue demolition orders and has already demolished 180

Palestinian structures this year, displacing 319 Palestinians, including 167 children.

House demolitions and displacement of East Jerusalem Palestinians continues. In 2009, 64 structures were demolished, displacing 300 people, including 149 children. Israeli settlers and settler organizations are increasing efforts to take over Palestinian homes, particularly in Sheikh Jarrah and Silwan. The U.N. reports at least 475 Palestinians are at risk for forced eviction, dispossession and displacement due to settler plans in Sheikh Jarrah alone.

Israel's access restrictions continue to fragment the West Bank and impede upon the livelihoods of West Bank Palestinians. There are some 578 closure obstacles in place in addition to the Separation Wall and permit and gate regimes. In the closed area or "Seam Zone" in the northern West Bank, Palestinians (especially farmers) are severely restricted from agricultural land, health and education services, and social networks. The Israeli government has extended this closed area strategy to the central and southern West Bank. In the Bethlehem Governate, the planned construction of the Separation Wall will reduce access to land and water resources for some 21,000 Palestinians. Israeli daily water consumption per capita is four times higher than that in the West Bank and is affecting approximately 350,000 Palestinians, most of whom live in the southern West Bank. Water is so scarce that in some Palestinian communities, residents only have access to 20 liters of water per day.

Religious Situation

Israeli authorities assured Christian leaders in early December that Gaza's Christians would be issued permits to exit Gaza and visit Bethlehem for 24 hours. According to a human rights group investigation, Gaza Christians between the ages of 15 and 35 from both sexes were denied a permit for no apparent reason, resulting in a total of at least 550 Christians being denied travel permits to Bethlehem. Of the 450 permits that were actually issued, 70% were children under the age of 15. Many of those under 15 who were granted travel permits could not in fact travel because their parents were denied a permit. The issuance of visas for Christian clergy is still problematic as many are unable to receive a visa for an extended period. The problem is being shoved under the table as many Christian groups have stopped applying for visas, knowing that such requests will be denied. This has given the impression that the problem has eased.

There are difficulties within the Palestinian Greek Orthodox community. The day before the Christmas celebrations in Bethlehem there was a fight in Manger Square between groups opposing and supporting the patriarch. The Palestinian authority had to intervene and agreed to minimize public participation in the Christmas celebrations. The criticism of the Patriarch Theophilos III stems from his not delivering on his promises made over disputed Greek Orthodox property and other issues when elected patriarch.

Jewish extremist settlers in the Old City attacked young Armenian seminarians in the Armenian Quarter in early September, deliberately insulting the seminarians and their faith.

The Jerusalem municipality has undisclosed plans—dubbed Plan 2020—that will eventually make the Old City of Jerusalem a "tourist museum." This plan initially calls for the reduction of Christian and Muslim residents as much as possible by 2020. It is reported that over 250 Palestinian-owned shops have already closed, either to seek work elsewhere or to avoid high taxes. House demolition orders were issued against four Christian families in the Old City of Jerusalem in late June. Churches are also facing difficulty obtaining the necessary renovation permits and expansion rights for properties in the Old City.

Country Report - Palestine

CNEWA - Sept. 2010

The Vatican and Palestine flags side by side at Bethlehem University.

Palestine is among the oldest continuously inhabited regions in the world and has been coveted or dominated by almost every civilization of the eastern Mediterranean.

Modern Palestine now denotes the Palestinian territories of Gaza and the West Bank. According to the original terms of the 1947 U.N. partition plan of Mandate Palestine, the territories were to constitute a unified, independent Arab state. But neighboring Arab countries fiercely opposed the terms of the partition plan and attacked the nascent Jewish State of Israel. Over the years, some positive initiatives have advanced, but little real progress toward peace with justice has been made.

Demographics.

Generally, accurate population statistics throughout most of the Middle East are difficult to ascertain due to the lack of census data. In Palestine, the movement of peoples — despite security efforts to the contrary — makes it more difficult. Here are some reasonable estimates gleaned from a variety of sources: Palestine's total population is around four million people. Gaza's 1.5 million people are almost entirely Arab Sunni Muslims, but around 4,000 Christians remain. The West Bank is more diverse. Three-quarters of its 2.5 million inhabitants are Arab Sunni Muslims. Jewish settlers, who dominate strategic areas of the West Bank, account for 17 percent of the population. At most, 50,000 Arab Christians — less than 2 percent — live there, principally in and around Bethlehem and Ramallah.

Sociopolitical situation.

The Palestinian territories do not enjoy statehood, though there are some elements of self-governance. The Palestine Liberation Organization is recognized as the representative authority of the Palestinian people and has observer status at the United Nations. The Oslo Accords in 1993 established the Palestinian Authority as the territories' governing body, vesting it with some degree of control over internal security and civilian-related matters. Currently, the Palestinian Authority "controls" only the West Bank.

Israeli-imposed restrictions on right of entry and exit, as well as movement within the West Bank, have isolated and fragmented Palestinian society. Israeli authorities exercise full civil and military control of 61 percent of the West Bank and the 150,000 Palestinians who live in that area. Classified as a high-risk area by international humanitarian organizations, it lacks safe drinking water and basic sanitation facilities and is afflicted by high poverty and unemployment rates. According to the United Nations Office for the Coordination of Humanitarian Affairs, 10 percent of the West Bank will fall on the Israeli side of the separation barrier once it is complete.

After winning the parliamentary elections in January 2006, Hamas assumed complete control of Gaza. Conflict between Hamas and the Fatah-led Palestinian Authority in June 2007 effectively severed ties between the two Palestinian territories.

Much of Gaza's infrastructure was destroyed in January 2009 during the conflict between Hamas and Israel. The territory continues to lack a functioning sewage system (open sewage is commonplace) and basic necessities, such as food, medical supplies, construction materials and fuel. At present, Gaza's sole power plant does not operate at full capacity, shutting down between 8 and 12 hours a day.

Egypt has lifted its side of the blockade to allow humanitarian aid into Gaza. (Israel has not.) Still, residents depend on goods smuggled from Egypt via tunnels. Hamas authorities tax small businesses on the smuggled goods they purchase and charge tunnel operators an administrative fee.

Notwithstanding the current situation, education institutions in Gaza and the West Bank continue to operate. Public education is universal from grades one through 12. By regional and global standards, the territories' enrollment and literacy rates are high.

Many Palestinians do not have access to affordable, quality health care. In Gaza, clinics and hospitals lack basic supplies, medications and equipment. Most health care facilities in both territories depend heavily on international assistance, such as aid and church organizations, to help cover operating costs.

Economic situation.

Israel's blockade of Gaza, which began in 2007, has devastated its economy. Two out of every three banks have closed. Half of Gaza's residents are unemployed. More than three-quarters of the population live at or below the poverty line and more than half rely on international aid for survival.

Since the outbreak of the second intifada in 2000, the West Bank's economy has struggled. Real GDP growth dropped substantially between 2000 and 2002, making modest recoveries in 2003 and 2004. It then contracted in 2005 and 2006. Unemployment rose in that period, exceeding a staggering 30 percent.

Since 2007, the West Bank's economy has shown signs of recovery. The tourism industry, in particular, has experienced a relative boom.

Religious situation.

Christian emigration is most dramatic in Palestine — despite the Palestinian Authority's efforts to discourage it. Since 1967, Gaza and the West Bank combined have lost more than 35 percent of their Christian population to emigration. The most affected are the Christian communities of Bethlehem, Beit Jala, Beit Sahour and Ramallah, where they once dominated the population.

Church leaders worry that, if the last remaining Christians emigrate, the Palestinian church — which is an integral part of the church of Jerusalem — will be reduced to empty shrines and charitable works of mercy alone.

Jerusalem remains the center of religious life for Palestinian Christians, who for more than 1,600 years entered its gates to venerate the sites associated with Jesus. Yet in the last two years, Israeli authorities in Jerusalem have tightened security measures during the Easter liturgies, allowing far fewer Palestinian Christians access to the Old City's holy sites, particularly the Church of the Holy Sepulchre. This year, no more than a few hundred Palestinian Christians participated in the Holy Fire celebration, which once attracted thousands. This has fueled tensions between the Greek Orthodox patriarchate and the local Orthodox community, who perceive the patriarchate as endorsing Israeli security.

Gaza's beleaguered Christians continue their social service outreach to the community. Christians provide health care, education and rehabilitative and social services.

Christian History in the Holy Land

And when the day of Pentecost was fully come, they were all with one accord in one place. And suddenly there came a sound from heaven as of a rushing mighty wind, and it filled all the house where they were sitting. And they were all amazed and marveled, saying one to another, Behold, are not all these which speak Galileans?, and strangers of Rome, Jews and proselytes, Cretes and Arabians, we do hear them speak in our tongues the wonderful works of God."   Acts 2:1-11

"We are thinkers, we are theologians, we are philosophers, we are teachers, we are believers in the Bible and in Jesus Christ and we are rolling up our sleeves and are making a difference by shedding light in a bleak situation because nothing will stand between us and the Lord".

Fr. Firas Arideh

The history of Holy Land Christians goes back to the first century A.D. For over two thousand years, Christian families have lived and worshipped in the land where Jesus lived, died, and was resurrected. These Christians are not immigrants or converts. They are the descendents of those who first believed in Jesus Christ (*Acts 2:11*).

Ethnically, whether they live in Israel, the West Bank or Gaza, they are overwhelmingly Palestinian. Denominationally, they are Orthodox, Catholic, and Protestant. Together, they remain the first

Church - the "Mother Church". Many Christians are unaware that there even is an indigenous Palestinian Christian population in the Holy Land. Even fewer know the severity of the conditions they endure.

The Christians of the Holy Land give witness to their faith and speak of their hopes. They should learn of the practical ways this local Church lives the Gospel, and they should encourage their fellow believers to remain faithful to their commitment to Christ."

According to a recent Diyar Consortium study *(1)* entitled; *"The Presence of Christians in the West Bank and Their Attitudes Towards Church Related Organizations"*, most members of the Christian communities choosing to emigrate cite as the primary reason; the lack of freedom and security. Because of the hardships of the military occupation, Christians are continuing to leave the Holy Land and the Christian community is endangered in the land of its birth. Refugees fled in 1948 and 1967 as a result of the wars and Christians continue to leave because of the harsh military occupation and the second class treatment of even those who hold Israeli citizenship.

The second main concern and motivation cited for emigration is the deteriorating economic situation in Palestine. In relation to emigration trends amongst the Christian denominations, and according to a small select sample, Palestine had lost, thus far, about 61 percent of its Armenian Orthodox, 50 percent Assyrian Orthodox, 32 percent Arab Greek Orthodox, 28 percent Roman Catholic, 15 percent Greek Catholic, and 8 percent Protestant Christian populations *(Rishmawi, 2007)*.

Christians in the Holy Land now live in a predominantly Judeo-Muslim world. In Israel, they make up less than 2% of the population. Economic hardship, political uncertainty and discrimination have caused Christians to emigrate, from the Holy Land overall and especially from the Palestinian Territories.

The closure of the border between Palestinian territories (East Jerusalem, Gaza and the West Bank) and Israel has caused a desperate economic situation. Land confiscation, multi-day curfews and closures, house demolitions, the confiscation of identity cards, the building of a Separation Wall, the closing of schools, and denial of medical treatment have caused Christians, as well as, Muslims to leave the area. They want better conditions for themselves and their children and leave to join family and friends in Europe, the Americas and Australia. At least 25,000 Palestinian Christians live in the Diaspora. This creates a very real concern that Christianity in the Holy Land could become a dead religion without the presence of living communities.

After two thousand years, Christian families are still living and worshiping in the land where Jesus was born, died, and resurrected. These Christians are not immigrants. They are not converts from Judaism or Islam. They are the descendants of those who first believed in Jesus Christ. They live in Jerusalem, Bethlehem, Nazareth, and other places in Palestine and Israel. These Christians, whether they live in Israel, the West Bank or Gaza, are ethnically Palestinian. They are the Arab Palestinian Christians – Orthodox, Catholic, and Protestant. They have maintained a continual living witness in the land of our Saviors' birth and have helped preserve the Holy Sites sacred to all of Christianity. **Together, they comprise the Mother Church.** There are many practical ways this local Church lives the Gospel. These living witnesses of Christ's historic presence in the Holy

A Christian boy offering an olive branch to a soldier.

Land can help us understand the Bible by giving us a deeper understanding of its' cultural context. Palestinian Christians are also ideally placed as bridge builders in a land associated with conflict. They share the Old Testament with Jewish people. They share the culture, language and national aspirations with the Islamic peoples of the Holy Land. They also act as a conduit between the Churches and culture of the East and West. They provide a buffer between the growth of both Jewish and Islamic fundamentalism in the region. **They are the "Living Stones".** They are the living Church giving both breath and hands as evidence of the faith that the physical stones of the Holy Sites give witness to.

Yet, many Christians are even unaware there is an indigenous Palestinian Christian population in the Holy Land. Even fewer know the severity of the conditions they endure. It is easy to see how the Palestinian Christians have come to feel as though they suffer in solitude, without the solidarity of the rest of the Body of Christ. It is also easy to see why Christians are leaving the Holy Land in vast numbers. In 1948, the Christian population of the Holy Land was over 18%.

Today, it is less than 2%. In Jerusalem, in 1944, Christians numbered 30,000. Today, that number has dwindled to 9,000. The estimated number of Christians in the West Bank, Gaza and Jerusalem is 1.37% of the population (1). The percentage of Arab Christians in Israel, including Israeli controlled parts of Jerusalem is 1.66%. The Bethlehem Governorate is home to the highest percentage of Christians in Palestine (43.4%). Almost 6% of the Palestinian Christian population lives in the Gaza Strip. The village of Taybeh, Palestine, known ironically for their beer, is 100% Christian.

The Christian population continues to shrink as Christians emigrate for safer conditions. The Holy Land Christians are the living church in the land where Jesus was born, died, and was resurrected. They do not want to leave the land that their families have lived on for centuries. If they continue to leave at their current rate, there may soon be no living church left in the Holy Land. There will always be holy sites to visit, but there will be no living stones, no living Body of Christ. This creates a very real concern that Christianity in the Holy Land could become a dead religion without the presence of vibrant living communities.

The History: Yesterday's Roots and Today's Issues

"Here God entered into history and stayed with us forever."

Saint John Paul II, Bethlehem, 2000

Catholic Teaching on the Holy Land

❖ **State for Palestinians** — U.S. Bishops
"the establishment of an internationally recognized Palestinian state" [2000]; "a viable state for Palestinians"; "as supporters of the state of Israel and a state for Palestinians"; "the Palestinian people have a right to a free and sovereign homeland" (Archbishop Silvano Tomasi, permanent observer of the Holy See to the U.N. office in Geneva [August 11, 2006] and Pope Benedict XVI [July 24, 2006])

❖ **Israel's Right to Exist** — U.S. Bishops
It is also necessary for all to recognize that Israelis rightly see the failure of Palestinians to demonstrate full respect for Israel's right to exist and flourish within secure borders as a fundamental cause of the conflict. [2001]

❖ **Mutually Just Claims** — U.S. Bishops
"The just claims of both peoples should also enjoy the active support of Christians throughout the world." [2001]

❖ **A Just & Comprehensive Solution** — U.S. Bishops
A negotiated peace in the Holy Land should be part of a comprehensive and lasting negotiated settlement for peace in the Middle East. [2001] For example, the 2002 Saudi Peace Plan proposes that all Arab countries will recognize Israel if it withdraws to the 1967 Green Line.

❖ **Supports Key U.N. Resolutions** — Vatican
Respect for the U.N. Resolutions by all sides. (ibid.)
Resolution 194 states, among other things, that the Palestinian refugees created by the Arab conflict with the nascent State of Israel are allowed to return to their homes. Resolution 242 emphasizes, among other things, that acquisition by Israel of territory by the 1967 War must be relinquished.

❖ **End Israel's Military Occupation** — U.S. Bishops
"It is necessary for all to recognize that Palestinians rightly insist on an end to Israel's three-decade-long occupation of the West Bank and Gaza and [stop settlements] to the continued establishment and expansion of settlements." [2001]

❖ **Preserve Israel's Right to Security** — U.S. Bishops
Israel has a fundamental right to security, but security will not be won by ongoing annexation of Palestinian land, blockades, air strikes on cities, destruction of crops and homes, and other excessive uses of force. [2001]

❖ **Negotiations, not Unilateral Actions** — U.S. Bishops
"Does not acquiesce in unilateral actions which undermine negotiations" [2001]; "President Bush's recent announcement of support for the unilateral Israeli policy toward Gaza and the West Bank is deeply troubling. The President's acquiescence in Prime Minister Ariel Sharon's unilateral approach risks undermining the Road Map for Peace and prospects for a negotiated settlement of this conflict. U.S. leadership is put at risk if it accepts the view of Prime Minister Sharon that unilateral actions will delay negotiating an Israeli-Palestinian peace for a generation. A just peace cannot be imposed by one side. We urge the Bush administration to return to the traditional U.S. role of 'honest broker' ... in accord with international law and existing U.N. Resolutions." [April 26, 2004]

❖ **Condemns Any Terrorism** — Vatican
Unequivocal condemnation of terrorism, from whatever side it may come" be it movement terrorism (Palestinian) or state-sponsored (Israeli).

❖ **Condemns Injustice and Disregard for Human Rights** — U.S. Bishops
Disapproval of the conditions of injustice and humiliation imposed on the Palestinian people as well as reprisals and retaliation, which only make the sense of frustration and hatred grow. There should be a "scrupulous respect for human rights and humanitarian law." (ibid.) "Israel said ... it was shocked and distressed by a senior Vatican cardinal's likening of Gaza under Israel's military offensive to a concentration camp."

❖ **Proportionate Response for Self-Defense** — Vatican
Nine Israeli human rights groups accused the army of endangering Gazan civilians and called for a war crimes investigation. The groups wrote to Israeli leaders that the Gaza campaign has left civilians nowhere to flee." "The level of harm to the civilian population is unprecedented" while "military forces are making wanton use of lethal force."

❖ **Protect Holy Places** — Vatican
The duty for the parties in conflict to protect the holy places, which are of the greatest importance to the three monotheistic religions and a patrimony of all humanity. (ibid.) By the end of the 1945-1949 conflict, Vatican priorities shifted from shrines to the believers: "I would prefer that all of the shrines be destroyed rather than the Christian population be eliminated."

❖ **Duty of Solidarity of Mother Church** — U.S. Bishops
"Mindful of our historic debt to the Church in the Holy Land and our duties of solidarity to a sister church in severe need, we ask Catholics in the United States to join in strengthening the church there during the present crisis. [2001]

❖ **Opposes Jewish and Islamic Extremist Ideologies** — Vatican
"Zionism is not the embodiment of Israel as it is described in the Bible. Zionism is a contemporary phenomenon which undergirds the modern state [of Israel], which is philosophically and politically secular." Political Zionism is a secular Jewish movement intended to grant the Jewish people sovereignty over what was once Palestine.

[1] NCCB, "Resolution on the Israeli-Palestinian Crisis," Origins, July 5, 2001, vol. 31, 141-142.
[2] Msgr. Boccardi, "Five-Point Vatican Position on the Holy Land Conflict," Origins, April 25, 2002, vol. 31, 752.
[3] Detroit Free Press, January 13, 2009, 6A.
[4] Jewish Voice for Peace, January 16, 2009.
[5] L'Osservatore Romano, May 28, 1948.

IN MULTIPLICIBUS CURIS

ENCYCLICAL OF POPE PIUS XII

Given at Castel Gandolfo, on the 24th day of October, in the year 1948, the tenth of Our Pontificate.

Among the multiple preoccupations which beset us in this period of time, so full of decisive consequences for the life of the great human family, and which make Us feel so seriously the burden of the Supreme Pontificate, Palestine occupies a particular place on account of the war which harasses it. In all truth We can tell you, Venerable Brethren, that neither joyous nor sad events diminish the sorrow which is kept alive in Our soul by the thought that, in the land in which our Lord Jesus Christ shed His blood to bring redemption and salvation to all mankind, the blood of man continues to flow; and that beneath the skies which echoed on that fateful night with the Gospel tidings of peace, men continue to fight and to increase the distress of the unfortunate and the fear of the terrorized, while thousands of refugees, homeless and driven, wander from their fatherland in search of shelter and food.

2. To make Our sorrow more grievous, there is not only the news which continually reaches Us of the destruction and damage of sacred buildings and charitable places built around the Holy Places, but there is also the fear that this inspires in Us for the fate of the Holy Places themselves scattered throughout Palestine, and more especially within the Holy City.

3. We must assure you, Venerable Brethren, that confronted with the spectacle of many evils and the forecast of worse to come, We have not withdrawn into Our sorrow, but have done all in Our power to provide a remedy. Even before the armed conflict began, speaking to a delegation of Arab dignitaries who came to pay homage to us, We manifested our lifelong solicitude for peace in Palestine, and, condemning any recourse to violence, We declared

that peace could only be realized in truth and justice; that is to say by respecting the rights of acquired traditions, especially in the religious field, as well as by the strict fulfillment of the duties and obligations of each group of inhabitants.

4. When war was declared, without abandoning the attitude of impartiality which was imposed by Our apostolic duty, which places Us above the conflicts which agitate human society, We did not fail to do Our utmost, in the measure which depended upon Us, and according to the possibilities offered to Us, for the triumph of justice and peace in Palestine and for the respect and protection of the Holy Places.

5. At the same time, although numerous and urgent appeals are received daily by the Holy See, We have sought as much as possible to come to the aid of the unhappy victims of the war, sending the means at Our disposal to Our representatives in Palestine, the Lebanon, and Egypt for this purpose, and encouraging the formation among Catholics in various countries of undertakings organized for the same purpose.

6. Convinced, however, of the insufficiency of human means for the adequate solution of a question the complexity of which no one can fail to see, We have, above all, had constant recourse to prayer, and in Our recent Encyclical Letter, Auspicia Quaedam, We invited you, Venerable Brethren, to pray, and to have the faithful entrusted to your pastoral care pray, in order that, under the auspices of the Blessed Virgin, matters may be settled in justice and peace, and concord may be happily restored in Palestine. **As We said on June 2nd to members of the Sacred College of Cardinals, informing them of Our anxieties for Palestine, We do not believe that the Christian world could contemplate indifferently, or in sterile indignation, the spectacle of the sacred land (which everyone approached with the deepest respect to kiss with most ardent love) trampled over again by troops and stricken by aerial bombardments. We do not believe that it could permit the devastation of the Holy Places, the destruction of the great sepulcher of Christ.**

7. We are full of faith that the fervent prayers raised to Almighty

and Merciful God by the Christians throughout the world who, together with the aspirations of so many noble hearts, are ardently inspired by truth and good, will render less arduous to the men who hold the destinies of peoples the task of making justice and peace in Palestine a beneficial reality and of creating, with the efficient co-operation of all those interested, an order that may guarantee security of existence and, at the same time, the moral and physical conditions of life conducive to spiritual and material well-being, to each of the parties at present in conflict.

8. We are full of faith that these prayers and these hopes, an indication of the value that the Holy Places have for so great a part of the human family, will strengthen the conviction in the high quarters in which the problems of peace are discussed that it would be opportune to give Jerusalem and its outskirts, where are found so many and such precious memories of the life and death of the Savior, an international character which, in the present circumstances, seems to offer a better guarantee for the protection of the sanctuaries. It would also be necessary to assure, with international guarantees, both free access to Holy Places scattered throughout Palestine, and the freedom of worship and the respect of customs and religious traditions.

9. And God grant that the day may soon dawn when Christians may resume their pilgrimages to the Holy Places, there to see more clearly revealed, as they contemplate the evidence of the love of Jesus Christ, Who gave His life for His brethren, how men and nations may live harmoniously together, at peace with their world and themselves.

10. With reliance, then, on this hope, as a pledge of heavenly favors and in token of our affection, gladly in the Lord do we impart to you, Venerable Brethren, and to your flocks, as to all who will take this appeal of Ours to heart, Our Apostolic Benediction.

The History: Yesterday's Roots and Today's Issues

Honor in Israel

Originally printed in America Magazine March 26, 1949, then reprinted again by America Magazine in 2011. This is an article prophetic in what it says. Used here with permission of America Press, Inc., 2011. All rights reserved. Subscription information, call 1-800-627-9533 or visit www.americamagazine.org.

Edward Duff | Archived Article

In the spring of 1947 the statesmen of the world were feverishly seeking a solution to the tormenting Palestine problem. Pan-Arabism and Zionism were locked in menacing debate over their conflicting claims to what Hilaire Belloc called "The Battle Ground" of history. While the statesmen and lawyers and propagandists toiled at Lake Success, the Catholic Near East Welfare Association reminded the Secretary General of the United Nations on May 8 of an almost forgotten factor in any just settlement of the problem. Disputing the claims of neither side, prescinding wholly from all political considerations, its statement, "The Christian Factor in the Palestine Equation," outlined the Christian stake in the Holy Land and indicated certain guarantees regarded as indispensable for the protection of Christian interests.

Events seem to have obscured memory of "The Christian Factor in the Palestine Equation." Partition was voted; a bitter war followed; shells desecrated the Holy City; the Zionists triumphed in a determined and resourceful display of arms; Israel was established as a sovereign state, fulfilling the ancient aspirations of the Jewish people. Today an armistice is being discussed and the provisions of the UN settlement are being reviewed.

It is time to assert once again that there are factors that transcend political considerations, issues that must be respected.

There is the matter of justice for the Palestinian refugees. There is the matter of honoring the commitments of the UN settlement that provided, among other things, for the internationalization of Jerusalem and the Holy Places and the freedom of religious organization.

Both Israel and the Arab States must accept the verdict of world opinion. If these reminders fall particularly on Israel, it is because victory imposes its own restraints. The public policy of the State of Israel must be subject to scrutiny without the easy retort of "Anti-Semitism!"—a slogan which stultifies discussion and betrays either an utter irresponsibility or an obtuseness to the expectations of the world community.

The Jewish attitude on the refugees was stated, in what can scarcely be less than an official answer, in a letter in the New York Times of March 15 from Mr. Harry Zinder, Press Adviser of the State of Israel Mission. "The tide of history cannot be turned back," is Mr. Zinder's ultimate verdict on the situation. Palestine, he explains, is a different country since the refugees fled over the borders. What's done, can't be undone. Let them, therefore, migrate to some other country.

The voice of the world's conscience replies to such a casual and even callous solution of the fate of nearly a million persons in other tones and in accents of growing impatience. Whatever the alleged reasons for the hurried exodus of the refugees, they have claims that cry for recognition. They have claims, first of all, to sheer preservation. At present they are dying at the rate of a thousand a day. The UN's Disaster and

Relief Committee, appointed last November, began operations February 1 with a fund of $32 million, half of which the American Government is committed to contribute. Even if efficiently administered, the money would underwrite merely the cost of food for the refugees for less than eight months. Voluntary agencies must be employed to supplement official UN relief. On March 9, Lessing Rosenwald, president of the American Council for Judaism, wrote the leaders of all religious faiths in the United States:

To avert a major human catastrophe, elementary justice requires that in addition to adequate relief there must be early repatriation, resettlement and social rehabilitation of 750,000 refugees from the recent hostilities. It is unfortunate that the UN Committee did not see fit to utilize adequately the voluntary agencies composing the American Appeal for Holy Land Refugees. It is particularly unfortunate that UN Reports obscured the contribution of the Catholic effort in aiding the refugees. For the Catholic effort in this humanitarian endeavor illustrates the fact that the Palestine problem is not bipartite but tripartite. There is a Christian stake in the Holy Land.

True, only 150,000 of the war sufferers are Christian, and of these only 55,000 are Catholics. On hand, however, to expend their energies in an all-encompassing charity are 2,000 priests and nuns. They came to Palestine many years ago from all parts of the Christian world. Long before governments began to assist in the present emergency, our Catholic parishes were feeding and sheltering many thousands of refugees in their parish halls, in their church yards and schools. The Catholic Church has been associated with all the problems of the Near East since the birth of Christ. The purposes of our Catholic personnel, native and missionary, are nonpolitical. That Catholic missionaries remained through the fighting, that Catholic institutions continued to care for the homeless and helpless, is proof of their nonpolitical purpose. It is proof, too, that they expect their rights to be protected and, where infringed, restored.

There is scarcely a religious house in Palestine that is not sheltering refugees. The officials at Tel Aviv know this. Someone in the office of Moshe Sharrett, Israel's Foreign Minister, might well send word to Mr. Zinder in Washington that Jewish officials are well posted on the job the missionaries are doing. They know of the tireless work of the Sisters of Charity, for example, who care for hundreds of feeble-minded children in an overcrowded home in Jerusalem.

At every Mass on Laetare Sunday, March 27, American Catholics will contribute to the Bishops' Emergency Relief Fund. The whole world's anguish calls upon America for alms. Though irresistible pleas for aid were coming from the needy in Europe and Asia, the bishops last year set aside a portion of that collection for relief in Palestine. Other subsidies sent the missionaries there by generous Catholics throughout the world are being ungrudgingly siphoned off to care for 200,000 homeless and the hungry. The week after Cardinal Spellman blessed a shipment of supplies on February 8, valued at $200,000, the National Council of Catholic Women announced that they had collected 150,000 children's garments for distribution to Holy Land sufferers without reference to race or creed. Monsignor Thomas J. Mc• Mahon, national secretary of the Catholic Near East Welfare Association, has just returned from four months on the scene, supervising operations. His findings are striking evidence of the Third Factor, the Christian Stake in Palestine.

What is the future of these victims of the Palestinian struggle? With the guns muted in the land of the Prince of Peace, can Israel afford to affront the conscience of the world by sticking to a convenient official assumption that these people do not want to be repatriated? Can Israel win confidence in its political maturity if it suggests that the refugees don't want their preferences discovered in a democratic plebiscite, that the homeless would spurn payment for their land? Whatever the political claims of Jew and Arab, there are requirements of "elementary justice" involved—to use the language of Mr. Rosenwald.

There remains—as UN was reminded on May 8, 1947—a Christian factor in the Palestine Problem. Jesus Christ must not be exiled by political maneuver or military coup from the land that bears the indelible mark of His sacred footsteps, from the scenes filled with sanctuaries of His precious life and life-giving death. The Christian world had no partisan position in the partition solution voted by the General Assembly on May 29, 1947. The internationalization of Jerusalem was included in the UN settlement as a dispassionate recognition of the nonpolitical factors in the problem, as evidence of equally historical claims of Christians. While Arab and Jew haggle over the division of the Holy City across the armistice table, the Christian world repeats anew its insistent demand that the decision of the world community, working through the United Nations, be respected. There is, of course, reparation to be made for the destruction and desecration of Christian property. Essential, however, is the guarantee of the freedom of religious organization and the internationalization of the Holy City and of the Holy Places- Nazareth (in Jewish territory), for instance, and Bethlehem (in Arab hands).

America reported the disappointment the Christian world felt at the proroguing of the United Nations session at Paris last December without coming to a definite conclusion on the future of the holy places in Palestine (AM. 12/25/48, p.306). The United Nations' Special Committee on Palestine in its final report to the General Assembly recommended that an impartial system for preserving the special character of the holy places should be devised. Similar recommendations were made by the General Assembly's partition resolution of November 29, 1947, as AMERICA reminded its .readers last Fall (AM. 11/13/48, p.145). The encyclical letter of Pope Pius XI issued on October 23 evoked America's editorial judgment that the internationalization of Jerusalem is the only "feasible escape from this intolerable situation" (AM. 11/6/48, p.120).

The Christian conscience, nonpolitical in its aims, today renders with larger evidence the identical judgment on the Palestine problem expressed in the Statement of the Catholic Near East Welfare Association to UN's Secretary General: We demand adequate, factual, implemented guarantees to the effect 1) that all our sanctuaries will be respected and continuously and unconditionally accessible and 2) that the Christian majority will actually enjoy not merely the vague, frequently distorted and facetiously neutralized right of freedom of religion but also freedom of religious assemblage; freedom of religious organization in conducting schools, hospitals, orphanages and other institutions of welfare and mercy; and freedom from civil, social and economic discrimination. Anything less will cost Israel and the Arab respect of the Christian world.

The Papal Voice

"The Holy See and the Pope have never failed to speak out ... for the destiny of so many brothers and sisters, whose rights are too often not recognized, indeed, are often trampled upon."

Saint John Paul II, Bethlehem, 2000

Five Key Points of the Holy See

INTERVENTION BY MSGR. LEO BOCCARDI AT THE 387th SESSION OF THE PERMANENT COUNCIL OF THE ORGANIZATION FOR SECURITY AND COOPERATION IN EUROPE (OSCE) - Thursday, 11 April 2002

Mr. Chairman,
My Delegation wishes to stress, in this important forum, the Holy See's recently reconfirmed position, regarding the continuing conflict in the Holy Land. This position is articulated in the five following points:

1. Unequivocal condemnation of terrorism, from whatever side it may come.
2. Disapproval of the conditions of injustice and humiliation imposed on the Palestinian people, as well as reprisals and retaliation, which only make the sense of frustration and hatred grow.
3. Respect for the United Nations Resolutions by all sides.
4. Proportionality in the use of legitimate means of defense.
5. The duty for the parties in conflict to protect the Holy places, which are of the greatest importance to the three monotheistic religions and a patrimony of all of humanity.

The Holy See is in close contact, among others, with the Latin Patriarch of Jerusalem and the religious communities of Bethlehem, and has conveyed to them the Holy Father's complete solidarity in this sorrowful moment. Acts of solidarity will bring the return to negotiation After recalling that nothing can be resolved by conflict and that it only brings greater suffering and death, Pope John Paul II stressed that no political or religious leader can remain silent and inactive. Denunciation must be followed by practical acts of solidarity that will help everyone to rediscover mutual respect and return to frank negotiation. In this spirit and convinced that, when the merciless logic of arms prevails, only God can bring hearts to peaceful thoughts, Pope John Paul II asked the Catholic Church to pray more intensely on Sunday, April 7 last, for the people suffering from this terrible violence. Commitment to peace initiatives.

Mr. Chairman,
The protection and the promotion of peace has always been high in the Agenda of our Organisation. Many Religions proclaim that peace is a gift from God. This was also the experience of the recent meeting of Assisi. At that time, my Delegation informed the Permanent Council of the meaning of that event and the purpose of the "Commitment for peace" signed by the Religious leaders present at Assisi and subsequently sent to the Head of States and Governments. The Holy See hopes that the aforementioned initiatives will effectively encourage those who have the responsibility and the possibility to take the necessary action, however difficult it might be, to demand scrupulous respect for human rights and humanitarian law and to urge the parties in conflict towards agreements which are fair and honorable for everyone.

Thank you, Mr. Chairman.

Stand by Those Crosses where Jesus Continues to be Crucified

Pope Francis speaks on the Mount of Olives to Priests, Religious and Seminarians.

Vatican City, 26 May 2014 (VIS) – At 11.45 a.m., after a five-kilometer journey by car, the Holy Father arrived at the Notre Dame of Jerusalem Centre where he received in audience the prime minister of Israel, Benjamin Netanyahu. An hour and a half later, the Pontiff was scheduled to lunch with the papal entourage, but instead he changed his plans and decided to eat in the refectory of the Convent of San Salvador with the Franciscans. At 2.15 p.m., after blessing the Tabernacle of the chapel in the centre built by the Legionaries of Christ in Galilee, he left the centre for the small Greek Orthodox "Viri – Galilaei" church on the Mount of Olives. From there he paid a brief private visit to the Ecumenical Patriarch of Constantinople, after which they both blessed a group of faithful gathered outside the church. The Pope departed for the Gethsemane church, located on the slopes of the Mount of Olives and entrusted to the Custodian of the Holy Land. Upon entry, he venerated the rock upon which Jesus prayed before his arrest, situated at the foot of the altar. He then entered, where he was awaited by priests, consecrated persons and seminarians.

"At the hour which God had appointed to save humanity from its enslavement to sin, Jesus came here, to Gethsemane, to the foot of the Mount of Olives", said the Pope. "We now find ourselves in this holy place, a place sanctified by the prayer of Jesus, by his agony, by his sweating of blood, and above all by his 'yes' to the loving will of the Father. We dread in some sense to approach what Jesus went through at that hour; we tread softly as we enter that inner space where the destiny of the world was decided. In that hour, Jesus felt the need to pray and to have with him his disciples, his friends, those who had followed him and shared most closely in his mission. But here, at Gethsemane, following him became difficult and uncertain; they were overcome by doubt, weariness and fright. As the events of Jesus' passion rapidly unfolded, the disciples would adopt different attitudes before the Master: attitudes of closeness, distance, hesitation.

"Here, in this place, each of us – bishops, priests, consecrated persons, and seminarians – might do well to ask: Who am I, before the sufferings of my Lord? Am I among those who, when Jesus asks them to keep watch with him, fall asleep instead, and rather than praying, seek to escape, refusing to face reality? Or do I see myself in those who fled out of fear, who abandoned the Master at the most tragic hour in his earthly life? Is there perhaps duplicity in me, like that of the one who sold our Lord for thirty pieces of silver, who was once called Jesus' 'friend', and yet ended up by betraying him? Do I see myself in those who drew back and denied him, like Peter? Shortly before, he had promised Jesus that he would follow him even unto death; but then, put to the test and assailed by fear, he swore he did not know him. Am I like those who began planning to go about their lives without him, like the two disciples on the road to Emmaus, foolish and slow of heart to believe the words of the prophets?

"Or, thanks be to God, do I find myself among those who remained faithful to the end, like the Virgin Mary and the Apostle John?" he continued. "On Golgotha, when everything seemed bleak and all hope seemed pointless, only love proved stronger than death. The love of the Mother and the beloved disciple made them stay at the foot of the Cross, sharing in the pain of Jesus, to the very end. Do I recognise myself in those who imitated their Master to the point of martyrdom, testifying that he was everything to them, the incomparable strength sustaining their mission and the ultimate horizon of their lives? Jesus' friendship with us, his faithfulness and his mercy, are a priceless gift which encourages us to follow him trustingly, notwithstanding our failures, our mistakes, also our betrayals." Pope Francis emphasised that "the Lord's goodness does not dispense us from the need for vigilance before the Tempter, before sin, before the evil and the betrayal which can enter even into the religious and priestly life. We are all exposed to sin, to evil, to betrayal. We are fully conscious of the disproportion between the grandeur of God's call and of own littleness, between the sublimity of the mission and the reality of our human weakness. Yet the Lord in his great goodness and his infinite mercy always takes us by the hand lest we drown in the sea of our fears and anxieties. He is ever at our side, he never abandons us. And so, let us not be overwhelmed by fear or disheartened, but with courage and confidence let us press forward in our journey and in our mission".

He reminded those present that they were called to follow the Lord with joy in this holy land. "It is a gift and also a responsibility. Your presence here is extremely important", and added that the whole Church was grateful for their work and sustains them with her prayers. He also offered his greetings to all Christians in Jerusalem: "I would like to assure them that I remember them affectionately and that I pray for them, being well aware of the difficulties they experience in this city. I urge them to be courageous witnesses of the passion of the Lord but also of his resurrection, with joy and hope". He concluded, "let us imitate the Virgin Mary and Saint John, and stand by all those crosses where Jesus continues to be crucified. This is how the Lord calls us to follow him: this is the path, there is no other! 'Whoever serves me must follow me, and where I am, there will my servant be also'".

Who will have Lunch with Pope Francis?

JERUSALEM – An interview with Bishop William Shomali, Auxiliary Bishop of Jerusalem, about the families who will have lunch with Pope Francis in Bethlehem after Mass in Manger Square.

1 – Why did the Pope choose to lunch with Christian families? What is his reason for doing so?

Pope Francis wants to spend a little time with the poor families in the Bethlehem and their children to listen to them, permitting them to feel his closeness and tenderness. He did not want to have lunch with the cardinals, bishops and politicians, but with poor families. It took time to understand the reasons for this gesture. It really makes the Pope admired: how Jesus wants to stay close to the poor.

2 – How were the families chosen who will share the meal?

The Assembly of Catholic Ordinaries of the Holy Land, which oversaw the organization of the entire trip of the Holy Father appointed a committee for the task of choosing. The Committee established criteria for identifying "categories" of poverty. Each family was then selected to represent a certain category of need. The poor who have no daily bread or living on the street have not been selected. Our poor are those who suffer for humanitarian reasons, political and social. We contacted the parishes and consulted many people. Many lay people offered us names. We discussed together and finally arrived at a final list. Many would have liked to be selected, but it was not possible to please everyone. It was a tough choice!

3 – Can you give us some examples of families that you have chosen?
A family from Ikrit, a village in northern Galilee that was evacuated and razed in 1948 by the Israeli Army. Only the church was spared. Although there have been court decisions, Christian Arab inhabitants were never able to return to their village.

Another family from the group of 58 families who have land in Cremisan area of Beit Jala. According to the planned route of the separation wall built by Israel, the land will be on the other side of the wall and therefore inaccessible for the owners. There are ongoing negotiations with the legal authorities that we hope will have a positive outcome.

Also a family that represents those who struggle for a family reunion. One spouse living in Jerusalem, the other in the territories. Under Israeli law, it is difficult for the Palestinian spouse to obtain a permit for permanent residence in Jerusalem.

Another family has a son sentenced to life imprisonment, another a son exiled to Gaza for political reasons. Another one comes from the Gaza Strip, which is a big prison. These are the families selected for this occasion.

4 – Then, it will be a diverse group, both from the point of view of age, but also of origin and various daily sufferings ...
Yes, there will be families with father, mother and children. If a spouse is missing, the replacement will be a close relative. There will be young and middle-aged families. Several will be elderly. There will be 20 people in total, just according to the number requested. After Mass, they will meet at the Casanova of Bethlehem, managed by the Franciscan friars. Lunch will last about an hour. Having taken their place at table with the Pope Francis, they will discuss with him their situation and receive from him words of comfort. Some families speak Italian and some Spanish. There will be an Argentine friar who speaks Arabic to help with translation.

5 – Pope Francis, where he visits, always wants to share a meal with simple people, the poor and marginalized. What are the lessons for the Church in Jerusalem?

This is a lesson for us bishops and priests. We need to get closer to the suffering people of God, and not live isolated in our homes. The Pope says we are always to go out, to go to the others, to go in search of the sheep and not wait until the sheep seeks the shepherd. This is a great example for us. The Pope will not see all the misery of the Holy Land. He only meets five families, and giving us a good boost, it inspires us to continue our mission.

Interview by Andres Bergamini

Pope Francis makes a stop along the Separation Wall encircling Bethlehem

AFP PHOTO/ OSSERVATORE ROMANO /RESTRICTED TO EDITORIAL USE - MANDATORY CREDIT "AFP PHOTO / OSSERVATORE ROMANO"

VISIT TO AIDA REFUGEE CAMP ADDRESS OF HIS HOLINESS BENEDICT XVI

Bethlehem - Wednesday, 13 May 2009

Pope Benedict XVI greets worshippers as he arrives at the Nativity Church in the West Bank city of Bethlehem, 13 May. (Mustafa Abu Dayeh/MaanImages)

Mr. President,
Dear Friends,

My visit to the Aida Refugee Camp this afternoon gives me a welcome opportunity to express my solidarity with all the homeless Palestinians who long to be able to return to their birthplace, or to live permanently in a homeland of their own. Thank you, Mr President, for your kind greeting. And thank you also, Mrs Abu Zayd, and our other speakers. To all the officials of the United Nations Relief and Works Agency who care for the refugees, I express the appreciation felt by countless men and women all over the world for the work that is done here and in other camps throughout the region.

I extend a particular greeting to the pupils and teachers in the school. By your commitment to education you are expressing hope in the future. To all the young people here, I say: renew your efforts to prepare for the time when you will be responsible for the affairs of the Palestinian people in years to come. Parents have a most important role here, and to all the families present in this camp I say: be sure to support your children in their studies and to nurture their gifts, so that there will be no shortage of well-qualified personnel to occupy leadership positions in the Palestinian community in the future. I know that many of your families are divided — through imprisonment of family members, or restrictions on freedom of movement — and many of you have experienced bereavement in the course of the hostilities. My heart goes out to all who suffer in this way. Please be assured that all Palestinian refugees across the world, especially those who lost homes and loved ones during the recent conflict in Gaza, are constantly remembered in my prayers.

I wish to acknowledge the good work carried out by many Church agencies in caring for refugees here and in other parts of the Palestinian Territories. The Pontifical Mission for Palestine, founded some sixty years ago to coordinate Catholic humanitarian assistance for refugees, continues its much-needed work alongside other such organizations. In this camp, the presence of Franciscan Missionary Sisters of the Immaculate Heart of Mary calls to mind the charismatic figure of Saint Francis, that great apostle of peace and reconciliation. Indeed, I want to express my particular appreciation for the enormous contribution made by different members of the Franciscan family in caring for the people of these lands, making themselves "instruments of peace", in the time-honored phrase attributed to the Saint of Assisi.

Instruments of peace. How much the people of this camp, these Territories, and this entire region long for peace! In these days, that longing takes on a particular poignancy as you recall the events of May 1948 and the years of conflict, as yet unresolved, that followed from those events. You are now living in precarious and difficult conditions, with limited opportunities for employment. It is understandable that you often feel frustrated. Your legitimate aspirations for permanent homes, for an independent Palestinian State, remain unfulfilled. Instead you find yourselves trapped, as so many in this region and throughout the world are trapped, in a spiral of violence, of attack and counter-attack, retaliation, and continual destruction. The whole world is longing for this spiral to be broken, for peace to put an end to the constant fighting.

On both sides of the wall, great courage is needed if fear and mistrust is to be overcome, if the urge to retaliate for loss or injury is to be resisted. It takes magnanimity to seek reconciliation after years of fighting. Yet history has shown that peace can only come when the parties to a conflict are willing to move beyond their grievances and work together towards common goals, each taking seriously the concerns and fears of the other, striving to build an atmosphere of trust. There has to be a willingness to take bold and imaginative initiatives towards reconciliation: if each insists on prior concessions from the other, the result can only be stalemate.

Humanitarian aid, of the kind provided in this camp, has an essential role to play, but the long-term solution to a conflict such as this can only be political. No one expects the Palestinian and Israeli peoples to arrive at it on their own. The support of the international community is vital, and hence I make a renewed appeal to all concerned to bring their influence to bear in favor of a just and lasting solution, respecting the legitimate demands of all parties and recognizing their right to live in peace and dignity, in accordance with international law. Yet at the same time, diplomatic efforts can only succeed if Palestinians and Israelis themselves are willing to break free from the cycle of aggression. I am reminded of those other beautiful words attributed to Saint Francis: "where there is hatred, let me sow love, where there is injury, pardon ... where there is darkness, light, where there is sadness, joy."

To all of you I renew my plea for a profound commitment to cultivate peace and non-violence, following the example of Saint Francis and other great peacemakers. Peace has to begin in the home, in the family, in the heart. I continue to pray that all parties to the conflict in these lands will have the courage and imagination to pursue the challenging but indispensable path of reconciliation. May peace flourish once more in these lands! May God bless his people with peace!

Pope urges Israel to ease Palestinian Suffering

21-May-08 - Zenit.org

Benedict XVI says Israel will be a "shining example of conflict resolution" on the day when the peoples of the Holy Land live in peace in two independent, side-by-side states.

The Pope affirmed his hopes for Mideast harmony when he received in audience today Israel's new ambassador to the Holy See, Mordechay Lewy. The Holy Father expressed his "cordial good wishes on the occasion of Israel's celebration of 60 years of statehood." He also affirmed that Israel and the Holy See share numerous areas of mutual interest. "The holy cities of Rome and Jerusalem represent a source of faith and wisdom of central importance for Western civilization, and in consequence, the links between Israel and the Holy See have deeper resonances than those which arise formally from the juridical dimension of our relations," the Pontiff said.

Christians' status

Benedict XVI expressed his concern at "the alarming decline in the Christian population of the Middle East, including Israel, through emigration."

"Of course, Christians are not alone in suffering the effects of insecurity and violence as a result of the various conflicts in the region, but in many respects they are particularly vulnerable at the present time," he said.

"Christians in the Holy Land have long enjoyed good relations with both Muslims and Jews," the Pope continued. "Their presence in your country, and the free exercise of the Church's life and mission there, have the potential to contribute significantly to healing the divisions between the two communities."

With Palestine

Turning his attention to the Israeli-Palestinian conflict, Benedict XVI affirmed: "The Holy See recognizes Israel's legitimate need for security and self-defense and strongly condemns all forms of anti-Semitism. It also maintains that all peoples have a right to be given equal opportunities to flourish.

"Accordingly, I would urge your government to make every effort to alleviate the hardship suffered by the Palestinian community, allowing them the freedom necessary to go about their legitimate business, including travel to places of worship, so that they too can enjoy greater peace and security. Clearly, these matters can only be addressed within the wider context of the Middle East peace process."

Quoting from the Book of Isaiah, the Holy Father said that "when all the people of the Holy Land live in peace and harmony, in two independent sovereign states side by side, the benefit for world peace will be inestimable, and Israel will truly serve as 'light to the nations,' a shining example of conflict resolution for the rest of the world to follow."

Holy See relations

The Pontiff also spoke about relations between the Holy See and Israel.

"Much work has gone into formulating the agreements which have been signed thus far between Israel and the Holy See, and it is greatly hoped that the negotiations regarding economic and fiscal affairs may soon be brought to a satisfactory conclusion," he said. "I know that I speak on behalf of many when I express the hope that these agreements may soon be integrated into the Israeli internal legal system and so provide a lasting basis for fruitful cooperation.

"Given the personal interest taken by Your Excellency in the situation of Christians in the Holy Land, which is greatly appreciated, I know you understand the difficulties caused by continuing uncertainties over their legal rights and status, especially with regard to the question of visas for church personnel. [...] Only when these difficulties are overcome, will the Church be able to carry out freely her religious, moral, educational and charitable works in the land where she came to birth."

Pope *John Paul II address to delegation of Palestinian Christians*

VATICAN CITY, NOV. 10, 2003

Distinguished Guests,

I am pleased to welcome your delegation and I ask you kindly to convey my greetings and good wishes to President Arafat and to all the Palestinian people. I am confident that this visit of prominent Palestinian Christians to the Holy See will lead to a better understanding of the situation of Christians in the Palestinian territories and the significant role which they can play in promoting the legitimate aspirations of the Palestinian people.

Despite the recent setbacks on the road to peace and fresh outbreaks of violence and injustice, we must continue to affirm that peace is possible and that the resolution of differences can only come about through the patient dialogue and persevering commitment of people of good will on both sides. Terrorism must be condemned in all its forms, for it is not only a betrayal of our common humanity, but is absolutely incapable of laying the necessary political, moral and spiritual foundations for a people's freedom and authentic self determination.

I once again call upon all parties to respectfully the resolutions of the United Nations and the commitments made in the acceptance of the peace process, with engagement in a common quest for reconciliation, justice and the building of a secure and harmonious coexistence in the Holy Land. I likewise voice my hope that the national Constitution presently being drafted will give expression to the highest aspirations and the most cherished values of all the Palestinian people, with due recognition of all religious communities and adequate legal protection of their freedom of worship and expression.

Dear friends, through you I send warm greetings to the Christians of the Holy Land, who have an altogether special place in my heart. Upon you and all the Palestinian people I invoke God's blessings of wisdom, strength and peace.

Pope John Paul II Address to Refugees

Dheisheh Refugee Camp (Bethlehem)

22 March, 2000 - Dheisheh Refugee Camp is one of many camps administered by UNRWA, the UN Relief and Works Agency for the estimated three to four million Palestinian refugees and displaced persons in the Middle East.

Dear Friends,

1. It is important to me that my pilgrimage to the birthplace of Jesus Christ, on this the two thousandth anniversary of that extraordinary event includes this visit to Dheisheh. It is deeply significant that here, close to Bethlehem, I am meeting you, refugees and displaced persons, and representatives of the organizations and agencies involved in a true mission of mercy. Throughout my pontificate I have felt close to the Palestinian people in their sufferings.

I greet each one of you, and I hope and pray that my visit will bring some comfort in your difficult situation. Please God it will help to draw attention to your continuing plight. You have been deprived of many things which represent basic needs of the human person: proper housing, health care, education and work. Above all you bear the sad memory of what you were forced to leave behind, not just material possessions, but your freedom, the closeness of relatives, and the familial surroundings and cultural traditions which nourished your personal and family life. It is true that much is being done here in Dheisheh and in other camps to respond to your needs, especially through the United Nations Relief and Works Agency. I am particularly pleased at the effectiveness of the presence of the Pontifical Mission for Palestine and many other

Catholic organizations. But there is still much to be done.

2. The degrading conditions in which refugees often have to live; the continuation over long periods of situations that are barely tolerable in emergencies or for a brief time of transit; the fact that displaced persons are obliged to remain for years in settlement camps: these are the measure of the urgent need for a just solution to the underlying causes of the problem. Only a resolute effort on the part of leaders in the Middle East and in the international community as a whole—inspired by a higher vision of politics as service of the common good—can remove the causes of your present situation. My appeal is for greater international solidarity and the political will to meet this challenge. I plead with all who are sincerely working for justice and peace not to lose heart. I appeal to political leaders to implement agreements already arrived at, and to go forward towards the peace for which all reasonable men and women yearn, to the justice to which they have an inalienable right.

3. Dear young people, continue to strive through education to take your rightful place in society, despite the difficulties and handicaps that you have to face because of your refugee status. The Catholic Church is particularly happy to serve the noble cause of education through the extremely valuable work of Bethlehem University, founded as a sequel to the visit of my predecessor Pope Paul VI in 1964.

Dear refugees, do not think that your present condition makes you any less important in God's eyes! Never forget your dignity as his children! Here at Bethlehem the Divine Child was laid in a manger in a stable; shepherds from the nearby fields were the first to receive the heavenly message of peace and hope for the world. God's design was fulfilled in the midst of humility and poverty.

Dear aid workers and volunteers, believe in the task that you are fulfilling! Genuine and practical solidarity with those in need is not a favour conceded, it is a demand of our shared humanity and a recognition of the dignity of every human being.

Let us all turn with confidence to the Lord, asking him to inspire those in a position of responsibility to promote justice, security and peace, without delay and in an eminently practical way.

The Church, through her social and charitable organizations, will continue to be at your side and to plead your cause before the world.

Taken from: L'Osservatore Romano Weekly Edition in English 29 March 2000, page 4

Peace is possible in Middle East, Pope says at Synod's closing Mass

Cindy Wooden - *Catholic News Service - Vatican City*

Closing the Synod of Bishops for the Middle East, Pope Benedict XVI said, "We must never resign ourselves to the absence of peace." "Peace is possible. Peace is urgent," the Pope said Oct. 24 during his homily at the Mass closing the two-week synod.

Peace is what will stop Christians from emigrating, he said. Pope Benedict also urged Christians to promote respect for freedom of religion and conscience, "one of the fundamental human rights that each state should always respect."

Synod members released a message Oct. 23 to their own faithful, their government leaders, Catholics around the world, the international community and to all people of goodwill. The Vatican also released the 44 propositions adopted by synod members as recommendations for Pope Benedict to consider in writing his post-synodal apostolic exhortation.

Although the bishops said the main point of the synod was to find pastoral responses to the challenges facing their people, they said the biggest challenges are caused by political and social injustice and war and conflict.

"We have taken account of the impact of the Israeli-Palestinian conflict on the whole region, especially on the Palestinians who are suffering the consequences of the Israeli occupation: the lack of freedom of movement, the wall of separation and the military checkpoints, the political prisoners, the demolition of homes, the disturbance of socio-economic life and the thousands of refugees," they said in one of the strongest sentences in the message.

They called for continued Catholic-Jewish dialogue, condemned anti-Semitism and anti-Judaism and affirmed Israel's right to live at peace within its "internationally recognized borders."

Although relations between Christians and Jews in the region often are colored by Israeli-Palestinian tensions, the bishops said the Catholic Church affirms the Old Testament -- the Hebrew Scriptures -- is the word of God and that God's promises to the Jewish people, beginning with Abraham, are still valid.

However, they said, "recourse to theological and biblical positions which use the word of God to wrongly justify injustices is not acceptable. On the contrary, recourse to religion must lead every person to see the face of God in others."

Addressing the synod's final news conference Oct. 23, Melkite Bishop Cyrille S. Bustros of Newton, Mass., said, "For us Christians, you can no longer speak of a land promised to the Jewish people," because Christ's coming into the world demonstrated that God's chosen people are all men and women and that their promised land would be the kingdom of God established throughout the world.

The bishops' point in criticizing some people's use of Scripture was intended to say "one cannot use the theme of the Promised Land to justify the return of Jews to Israel and the expatriation of Palestinians," Bishop Bustros said.

In their message, the bishops expressed particular concern over the future of Jerusalem, particularly given Israeli "unilateral initiatives" that threaten the composition and demographic profile of the city.

Much of the synod's discussion focused on the fact that many Christians are emigrating because of ongoing conflicts, a lack of security and equality and a lack of economic opportunities at home. They praised those who have remained despite hardship and thanked them for their contributions to church and society.

Copyright © 2011 Catholic News Service. www.catholicnews.com - Reprinted with permission of CNS

Living as a Christian in the Holy Land

"Don't be satisfied with what you read in the newspapers. Dig deeper. There you will find the truth."

        Latin (Catholic) Patriarch Twal, CNEWA interview, 2014

Conference to Address Pressures Facing Holy Land Christians

Lambeth Place, London, 18-19 July 2011

Your Eminence, Excellencies, dear friends of the Holy Land, dear lovers of peace,

I express my gratitude to Archbishop Williams and Archbishop Nichols for jointly hosting this two-day conference and for organizing this forum that will focus on the situation of our Christians in the Holy Land. I thank all of you for your presence here today. I recognize and appreciate your concern for our 'living stones' and your solidarity with the Churches in the Holy Land; for taking to heart our dream and desire for lasting peace; for your prayers and hopes that someday a peaceful situation can be attained; that all the people of the Holy Land can co-exist and live a normal life without fear.

The Current Reality

We live in an ancient and historic land, a holy place for the followers of the world's three great monotheistic faiths. As Christians, it is a powerful and moving experience to be where Jesus was born and grew to manhood, where he lived and taught. It is the land of his passion, agony and resurrection. We stand just steps away from the site of his crucifixion and burial and from where he rose from the dead. But it is also heart-wrenching and painful, because we are still in the midst of an ongoing modern geopolitical conflict in this very same land.

The buzz and familiar words of this land are occupation, terrorism, settlements, rocket attacks, home demolitions and security walls. All these are powerfully resonant, alarming, hotly debated, and politically-charged.

But beyond the buzz words, are the people and their lives in this Land called Holy. Two national narratives, three great religions are well-represented in this gathering. For too long, the people of this land have been mired in conflict. Many innocent people especially the youth have suffered and continue to suffer.

Sadly, the conflict seems more entrenched than ever, and more complicated. Most of the trend lines are in the wrong direction:

- more than 550.000 Israelis living in East Jerusalem and the West Bank.
- the demography of Jerusalem is changing rapidly, and a judicious and sensible balance of sacred space is being threatened,
- some groups of Israelis and Palestinians refuse to mutually recognize the right of the other to exist, and
- let us never forget the human tragedy taking place in Gaza.

And perhaps, the most complicating and alarming of all, is the fact that hope is being shattered. "Where there is no hope, the people perish." (Proverbs 29:18) An entire generation of Israelis and Palestinians grew up witnessing and experiencing violence, occupation, separation, and hatred. There have been fewer and less opportunities to interact, and a heightened suspicion and apprehension on both sides persist.

- it is more and more difficult to envision a future of coexistence,
- it is easier to demonize the other,
- It is harder to forgive, and strenuous to start a constructive dialogue.

<u>Why is this conflict not resolved?</u>
There are many reasons, and the past is replete with missed opportunities and a lack of good political determination. And of course, much of the blame must rest with the political leadership and authorities. Yet you, dear friends, are external influential forces who bear a responsibility as well.

Ultimately, the Israelis and Palestinians who live in the Holy Land must work out their differences in a just and righteous manner, and in ways that may require painful compromises. I would point out

that both sides must abandon maximalist claims to a life in the land without the other, and reconcile themselves to the belief, that we live in a world, where proximate justice is the best we can hope for. While we can agree that it is up to Israelis and Palestinians to find a solution, we must also realize that they are not able to do this without external intervention for a number of reasons:

- it is an asymmetrical power relationship,
- the lack of trust in the political alliances existing on both sides
- the vested nature of the conflict, in which interests exist within the political power structures to continue the conflict , and
- the fusion of political, historical and religious dimensions.

The International Community does not simply have a role to play but a responsibility and self-interest, based on:

- the way in which this conflict is used and perpetuated by a variety of outside powers and interests,
- the universal nature of Jerusalem as a sacred city to billions of Jews, Christians and Muslims from around the world, and
- the way in which this conflict reverberates throughout the region and beyond.

The Israeli-Palestinian conflict is rather unique in Europe and America. It is a foreign policy issue, with crucial foreign policy and national security implications, but it functions more like a domestic political issue.

We understand that the only solution to the conflict is the recognition of the inherent and fundamental right to live in dignity for all people in the Holy Land –Israelis and Palestinians, Jews, Christians and Muslims, which supposes a two State solution. Our desire is to help faith-based people of the world to understand that the only authentic pro-Israel position, is one that is also pro-Palestine and pro-peace. And this is as well, the only authentically pro-American and pro-European stance.

Two important issues are often absent from discussions of the Israeli-Palestinian conflict: the human face of the conflict (the mothers, the children, the young and elderly longing just for a normal life), and the international and the whole Middle East interest in resolving it.

This is a crucial time because:

- the possibilities for a just resolution are rapidly decreasing,
- the forces of extremism are growing and gaining followers and supporters,
- there is a regional context conducive to peace. The Arab Peace initiative remains on the table, and there is a recognition by many Arab governments that regional threats to their security come from somewhere other than Israel.
- the U.S. Administration, along with the European Union and the United Nations, all agree on the urgency to bring about an end to the conflict,
- the recent uprising Arab Spring of the young generations in the region is spreading across sooner or later, with violence or peacefully. It is coming, and no regime is immune from these events, not even Israel.

If now is an important time to act, what can we do?

1. Connect, and be in communion with the Christians living in the Holy Land, share in their joys and suffering, bear their burdens with them, reflect and consider your responsibility towards your Mother Church.

- Talk about your observations, and your reactions, your admiration your surprises, good and bad, what you have seen, the people you have met during your pilgrimages and support the Christian institutions in the Holy Land. After all, these are the institutions that provide decent employment opportunities for our Christian youth, and these are the institutions that provide quality services in education, health and social services to the whole population, mostly a non-Christian population. This solidifies the presence of the living stones

2. Inform your communities that:
- There are historic Christian communities in the Holy Land, with antecedents in the time of Christ.
- The Christian presence is threatened by virtual extinction, and the land of Jesus cannot become an equivalent of a spiritual Disneyland with beautiful buildings, historic sites and museums on display.
- All people - Jews, Christians and Muslims suffer the consequences of the conflict. Occupation is a terrible image for any democratic

State, as it is horrible for the people of the occupied areas, where hatred and aversion are fostered and nurtured. We are aware of the persecution and suffering of our Christians in some Muslim countries in the region, but this is not an excuse to forget the dire reality of our situation in the Holy Land.

- The silent majority of both Israelis and Palestinians want peace and support a two-state solution.
- Encourage and persuade people to "come and see." There is no substitute for a real and tangible experience of encountering the people, to speak with them, to eat with them and to affirm their dignity, and make them feel that they are never forgotten. Visit the Christian institutions and see the Christian witness at its best.
- The Jews of this land have a narrative that is authentic and should be respected, but so do the Muslims, and the Christians too. There is an Israeli story that must be respected, and there is also a Palestinian story to be told and respected as well.
- To remind our people that every man, woman and child who lives in the Holy Land today is created in the image of God, is endowed with inherent dignity, and is worthy of respect and esteem.
- To ignore the dignity of the other - whether the other be Christian, Muslim or Jew, is to live in violation of God's will for us.

Once again, I express my gratitude to Archbishop Rowan for launching a "Holy Land Appeal" for funds to help alleviate suffering Christians in the Holy Land, and support development and job creation initiatives, especially in the West Bank's community. Our heartfelt gratitude for your most noble collaboration as we all work together to uphold the dignity of every human being in the land of Jesus Christ, our Savior.

+Fouad Twal, Latin Patriarch of Jerusalem

Living Stones of the Holy Land

Drew Christiansen, S.J., an associate editor of America, conducted this interview during Patriarch Michel Sabbah's visit to the Washington, D.C., area in October. Gaudium et Spes

"Beatitude, the al-Aqsa intifada has gone on now for more than two years. In September you declared it has been "a catastrophe" for the Palestinian people. What did you mean?

The conditions of life imposed by the Israeli military are simply inhuman. The whole population, more than three million people, is under siege. There is no movement between cities or from village to village. Normal routine is impossible. Ordinary economic activity has come to a stop. Unemployment is rampant. Worse still, curfews keep people in their homes for days on end. It is forbidden to go to work, to school, even to the hospital. How can you describe the suppression of an entire people except as inhuman?

The confrontation has pushed the Palestinian people to despair. The Israelis take any expression of resistance, violent or not, as a pretext to kill and destroy as much as they can. Neither side deals with the other as if they were human beings. Each side kills and humiliates the other.

The 40-day siege of the Church of the Nativity in Bethlehem last April seems to have been a great blow to Palestinian Christians and particularly to Christian-Muslim relations. How did it affect the morale of Christians in Palestine?

In one word, we felt abandoned. Though various people interceded, no one was able to intercede effectively for us. Today there are no Christian powers to protect us as in the 19th and 20th centuries. There are Christian people in the West, of course, but no Christian nations. People waited for an effective intervention. When it did not come, they felt abandoned.

The siege actually strengthened Christian-Muslim relations, because Muslims found refuge in a Christian shrine. We share everything, as we share the sufferings of daily life. Life is terrible for everyone. Until last month, there was a complete curfew. [Ed. A siege remains in place around the whole West Bank. A curfew was re-imposed on Bethlehem on Nov. 21.] Some people have found the situation too much to bear and have emigrated. Most remain, living in harsh conditions and feeling abandoned by the world.

Does the experience of abandonment extend to the churches as well?

No. There is strong solidarity between the churches of Jerusalem and those abroad, especially in the United States. They give great attention to what is happening in the Holy Land. Their statements and actions regarding U.S. and Israeli policy are most welcome. There is much solidarity and friendship with the church in the United States, especially the U.S. Catholic Conference of Catholic Bishops. This type of advocacy is not often repeated elsewhere, though the Bishops' Conference of England and Wales has become very active in the last few years too. Some parishes and dioceses have even begun to twin with ours. There are even efforts at direct action to conciliate the two peoples, Israelis and Palestinians. This is a special contribution to peace of the American church.

This support has been ecumenical with help from the Holy See, the World Council of Churches and direct contacts on the part of the world church with the churches in the Holy Land. U.S. Protestant groups, especially World Vision and the Presbyterian Church, have been notable in their support of the Latin Patriarchate along with the Holy Land Christian Ecumenical Foundation, a group founded to assist the churches in the Holy Land.

How do you assess the prospects for peace between Israel and the Palestinian Authority?

It is not pessimistic to say the prospects for peace are poor. The situation is very difficult. The fundamental facts are demographic. Those resisting occupation are young, unmarried, without fear and with conviction in their souls. They are committed to struggle for the freedom of their people and their land. Half the population is young. They are ready to go on resisting for years and years. The resistance of the young is the basic dynamic Israel must understand.

Israel's survival depends on being surrounded by friends, not enemies. Israeli repression of the Palestinian people creates hostility in the whole neighborhood of the Middle East. All Muslims and Arabs are hostile to Israel because of its occupation. One day all Israel's strength will not be enough to resist their anger. It will crumble from fatigue. Making peace with the Palestinians is Israel's only hope of lasting security. When relations with Palestine become normal, then the hostility of other Arab neighbors will vanish. When there is friendship with the Palestinians, there will be friendship in the region.

As you visit the United States, there is a great deal of talk about impending war with Iraq. What effect would war with Iraq have on the situation in Palestine and Israel?

We fear an eventual war with Iraq. It will inevitably have a direct, negative influence on the situation on the West Bank and in Gaza. Israel's security measures will doubtless be increased with the result that repression of the Palestinian people will worsen. There is real risk of "transfer," that is, the mass deportation of Palestinians and Arab Israelis into exile. The fear is palpable.

So far, the talk of war has deepened Palestinians' sense of abandonment. Europeans offer economic help, when the Israelis permit them to, but they cannot offer political support. Without strong U.S. involvement, Israeli Prime Minister Ariel Sharon has a free hand.

More and more, events move toward an East-West clash. Opposition to the West will grow in the streets, if not with the regimes. The regimes are committed to the West. The people are not. They also think of things Western as "Christian," and for that reason local Christians in Arab countries are less accepted. In the Middle East, feelings of resentment are beginning to affect daily relations between Christians and Muslims.

People on the Arab street do not understand that there are no longer any Christian states in the West. Christians as such no longer control the levers of power. There are secular states with Christian populations. It is for those Christian populations to dissuade their governments from taking the path to war. It is for them to curb the extremists who favor war.

The Holy Land is a place of pilgrimage. How have these last two years of conflict affected the visits of pilgrims there?

There are a few hardy pilgrims who continue to come, especially from Europe, and we are pleased to receive them. They are people of conviction. People think of the situation as dangerous, but there is little actual danger for pilgrims if they restrict themselves to Galilee, Jerusalem and, when it is possible, Bethlehem. With a little advance planning, they can avoid hot spots.

Pilgrims are an essential feature of the Holy Land. Before the 20th century, pilgrims endured a great deal of hardship on the road and in crossing the sea. They frequently had to pass through hostile territory and to move through armies at war. Today's pilgrims, who come in this time of trouble, are more like their predecessors in times past. We need a new type of pilgrim, less like a tourist, one who comes out of conviction, who is fearless, who supports the churches in the land, whose presence is a sign of hope for the three religions.

We urge your readers to join the ranks of these new pilgrims and live out their solidarity with us, the living stones of the Holy Land. It would be wonderful for them to join us in Bethlehem this Christmas to experience our commemoration of the Nativity under occupation. It would add to our hope for peace and freedom.

Editor's note: *Born in 1933 near Nazareth, in Galilee, Michel Sabbah is the first Palestinian to serve as Latin (Roman Catholic) patriarch of Jerusalem. (Patriarchates are churches founded by Apostles. James, the brother of the Lord, is reckoned the founder of the Church of Jerusalem.) Patriarch Sabbah is president of Pax Christi International.*

Reprinted from America, December 23, 2002 with permission of America Press, Inc., 2002. All rights reserved.

A Life Under Occupation

ONE magazine's interview with Maher Turjman, Regional Director for the Pontifical Mission for Palestine

Maher Turjman, Pontifical Mission's regional director for Palestine and Israel, has spent his entire life under occupation. A Palestinian Christian, Mr. Turjman's childhood unfolded against the 1967 and 1973 Arab-Israeli wars and he came into adulthood during the first intifada. Now, as he and his wife, Selina, rear two young children in Jerusalem, the possibility of living free of oppression and violence seems bleak. Here, Mr. Turjman shares his story of life as a Palestinian under Israeli military occupation.

Where did you grow up?

I was born in 1966 in the Old City of Jerusalem, which the Hashemite Kingdom of Jordan controlled until 1967. My mother was born into a Greek Orthodox family from Ramleh, a town just south of modern Tel Aviv. She and her family fled to Amman, Jordan's capital, during the first Arab-Israeli war in 1948. My father, who is Coptic Orthodox, fled West Jerusalem when in 1948 it became a part of the new state of Israel. He and his family settled in the Old City. He worked with delinquent children for the Social Welfare Department, which the Jordanians administered until the Israelis took over after the 1967 war. Now it is in the hands of the Palestinian Authority.

Can you remember any of the 1967 war?

I was young, just over a year old. My family sought refuge in a shelter in a flower shop in Ramallah during the fighting. Later, my mother told me she was expecting another child, my younger brother, Nabil. I can better recall the 1973 war. We had painted the windows of our house black, so light from the house couldn't be spotted by bombers. Still, I was young then. I remember not knowing at all who the enemy was.

What was it like growing up in this atmosphere?

The Israeli Defense Forces were a constant presence; the soldiers were like boogiemen: 'If you don't finish your meal,' our parents would say, 'the Israeli army will get you.' Growing up like this, too young to know about the history of anti-Semitism, World War II and the Holocaust, you thought of Jews as the bad guys. And we were too young to make a distinction between Jews and Israelis.

Was it different being a Christian, a minority?

At the time, Bethlehem, Jerusalem and Ramallah had significant numbers of Christians, but religion wasn't that big of an issue. Politics then was largely secular; you had a lot of secular leftist groups, including Fatah. There were many Christians who held important posts in the various Palestinian political parties. So, while you generally knew who was a Christian and who was a Muslim, it wasn't that important.

Did you know any Israelis?

No, I only had contact with Israeli soldiers, who patrolled the streets. There weren't checkpoints at the time — they didn't appear until after the first Gulf War in 1991.

We were foolish. As children, we would throw stones at the soldiers and then run. It was a cat-and-mouse game, but we didn't realize how dangerous it was, because sometimes they'd shoot back in response.

Though just a boy, I was arrested several times for throwing stones at Israeli military vehicles, and each time I was quite scared.

Why were you throwing stones?

Part of it was just being a kid and impressing your friends. It was a game. But we also came to know the political aspect of it. Though Yasser Arafat and other Palestinian resistance leaders were in exile, many of us felt that something should be done at home.

But our resistance to the occupation was not only about throwing stones. It included also "throwing" revolutionary songs. Though we had the same feelings that most teenagers would have, it was not customary for Palestinian teenagers to sing love songs. We could not see the beauty of life; we faced injustices and hardships daily. These early experiences helped us to mature early, but they deprived us from growing up normally.

Where did you go to college?

In 1985 I entered Bethlehem University to study business administration. It was a relatively quiet time. Arafat's Palestine Liberation Organization (P.L.O.) had been kicked out of Lebanon a few years earlier. That was when I first got involved in following the politics of our situation. During the latter half of Lebanon's civil war (1975-1990), I was glued to Radio Monte Carlo, a French radio station that broadcast uncensored news in Arabic.

Though the university was a Catholic institution administered by the De La Salle Brothers of the Christian Schools, religious identity was not the issue it is today — it was still a nonsectarian environment. Occasionally, you'd see a few Muslim women on campus wearing the *hijab*, but that was rare.

My first few years at university were not unlike those of any student in any university. I played the guitar in a band called Al Baraem. We became quite popular, performing at Palestinian weddings and parties all over the occupied West Bank. Reportedly, we were even popular with Israelis.

Some friends told me they heard our songs playing from Israeli military jeeps.

Did the campus atmosphere change?

Yes. Even before the intifada, which in Arabic means uprising, Israeli soldiers shot and killed a student at a demonstration on campus. Two months later, the intifada broke out and everything changed. The Israeli Defense Forces shut down the university. But to continue our education we had to gather in secret in houses, monasteries and hotels. In a way, it really made you appreciate your education, because you were literally risking your life to study.

It was much the same during the first Gulf War [during which Arafat declared his support for Iraq], when we were put under curfew for 40 days. We spent much of this time in our rooms, which were completely sealed. We were equipped with gas masks, in case Iraq attacked Israel with chemical weapons, but they were only given to us after a long legal struggle with the Israeli Defense Forces.

Do you recall how you felt about the Oslo Accords that ended the intifada?

The Oslo Accords, signed in 1993, brought a lot of hope. Finally, we thought, the nightmare of occupation is going to be over. When Egyptian President Anwar Sadat came to Jerusalem in 1977, we thought he was a traitor. But now, most Palestinians are ready for peace. With Oslo, our economy started booming and Palestinian émigres were returning to invest here. The Palestinian Authority received significant international financial support and started building.

My band participated in the first anniversary celebrations of the accords, held in Norway's capital city of Oslo, performing in front of 20,000 people, including Arafat and Shimon Peres. It was our first opportunity to play alongside Israeli musicians. One of the more touching moments was seeing Israeli, Palestinian and Norwegian children sing together for peace.

Is this when you joined CNEWA?

Yes, in 1993 I was hired as projects coordinator for CNEWA's operating agency in the Middle East, the Pontifical Mission. My job, based in the Old City of Jerusalem, allowed me to see more broadly just what the needs of the Palestinian community were. And, for the first time of my life, I was challenged to contribute to long-term development and relief work.

How has the situation changed since?

Well, a lot has changed. In 2000, you had Camp David and the beginning of the second intifada. For Palestinians, there was frustration at the failure of the peace process to secure rights, such as Palestine's borders, the status of Jerusalem, settlements and the right of return for refugees. We had the Palestinian Authority, but our lives weren't improving.

What is the situation for Palestinians like you?

It's getting worse. The frustrations continue to grow daily. It's difficult to move around even in Palestinian areas. The West Bank has been separated from Jerusalem by the separation wall, and Jerusalem is where many Palestinian services are located. Why should I, whose family has lived in the area for generations, be checked by Israeli soldiers who have just arrived from Ethiopia or Russia? Last Christmas, I had to argue for one hour with a young Israeli soldier to allow my wife and me to go to Bethlehem to visit the Church of the Nativity. We cannot drive more than 30 minutes without hitting one of the hundreds of checkpoints, which paralyze traffic.

Traveling internationally is also humiliating. We are singled out and routinely checked. Once I had to remove my underclothes. My children are also searched thoroughly.

But aren't such measures useful in preventing acts of terrorism?

It's a good excuse to punish the larger Palestinian population for the misdeeds of the few. There will always be ways for people to carry out attacks, as long as the motive remains. Of course, Israel has a right to protect itself, but if you live here as a Palestinian you know firsthand that what you are being subjected to is not intended solely for protecting Israel. These measures not only humiliate ordinary Palestinians, they dehumanize us.

As the situation deteriorates, can Christians play a special role?

Well, let's face it: This conflict is evolving into an interfaith clash, pitting Muslims against Jews. Of course Christian Palestinians are Palestinians — we also seek a Palestinian state — but if there's some special role it would be as mediators, to help Muslims and Jews come together, to dialogue and to listen. Last year, I visited a synagogue for the first time. I was invited by some Jewish friends and it was an eye-opening experience. Until then, I never had understood how Judaism is a major source of our Christian faith. Conflict makes people blind to the good things in others.

Were you, as a child, better off than your children are now?

My wife, Selina, and I often discuss this. Thank God, we live relatively well compared to the rest of the population, who are poorer, generally, than they were just 10 years ago. Unemployment or underemployment affects most of the population. And for those who are lucky enough to earn an income, they lack the freedom to enjoy it.

When I was a child, the West Bank, East Jerusalem and Gaza were not divided, literally and figuratively. Of course this is not the case today. Because of walls, checkpoints and political divorce, we are a divided lot. We used to have access to Israel, where many Palestinians worked. As Christians, we once knew where we stood. But now, those of us who are left feel confused and isolated, as if we have been excluded from the game.

Why do you stay?

Selina and our boys, 4-year-old Fouad and 2-year-old Faris, are citizens of the United States. So we could settle there. But this is our country. Palestine is home. Our families live here. Many of our friends live here. Yet, we are very concerned about this growing climate of violence. What will happen when they are old enough to get involved?

If we emigrate, we may rear our children in a better place, but it will never be their home. We will also risk our right to return, even as tourists. In a way, our departure from Jerusalem — our home — would be final. Honestly, I do not blame my friends for leaving and settling elsewhere, for looking for a better life. Making that decision is painful and it consumes a lot of people a lot of the time.

Are you optimistic?

No, I'm sad to say. As a people, we are in a state of shock. There's no vision for our future. My sons are the third generation of my family to live under occupation. Every time we see a light in this dark tunnel, we discover that it was only a mirage.

And if this is how I feel, remember that I have a good job and a relatively good life. Imagine how some unemployed Palestinian living in a refugee camp feels. For now, there doesn't seem to be any hope.

The Work of the Papal Relief Agency in the Holy Land

Appointed by the Pope, Monsignor Robert L. Stern, archimandrite of the Greek-Catholic Patriarchy of Jerusalem, has presided since 1987 over this special agency of the Holy See which has its headquarters in New York, and offices in the Vatican, Jerusalem, Beirut, Amman, and currently performs charitable and pastoral activity in Palestine, Israel, Lebanon, Syria, Jordan and Iraq. He tells us about his work, and about the Pope's charity for the Palestinians. Interview with Msgr. Robert L. Stern by Giovanni Cubeddu. Extract from No. 5 - 2006

More than a million Palestinians live in conditions of absolute misery in refugee camps. It is one of the principal destabilizing elements in the Middle East. We talked about it with Msgr. Robert L. Stern, who presides over the Pontifical Mission for Palestine (The Papal Relief Agency in the Holy Land)

"The entreaties of many, many refugees still reach us, of every age and condition, forced by the recent war to live in exile, scattered through concentration camps, exposed to hunger, epidemics and dangers of all kinds". In his encyclical letter Redemptoris Nostri of Good Friday of 1949 Pope Pius XII thus described the situation of the Palestinians after the first Arab-Israeli conflict following on the birth of the State of Israel, on 14 May 1948. The Pontifical Mission for Palestine was thus instituted on the 18 June 1949, in the aim of directing and coordinating all the Catholic associations and organizations involved in aid to the Holy Land. In 1974, to mark the twenty five years of activity of the Pontifical Mission, Pope Paul VI spoke of it as «one of the clearest signs of the concern of the Holy See for the fate of the Palestinians, particularly dear to us because they are a people of the Holy Land, they number faithful followers of Christ and they have been and are even now so tragically tried".

Which Palestine does the Pontifical Mission help?

ROBERT L. STERN: Since 1967, when Israel took over political control of Palestine, there has been an entire population living under military occupation by another country. And the Palestine National Authority is not a real government. The Pontifical Mission is offering help in a situation where the governing institutions to which people usually turn are inadequate. And where public institutions, even if they exist, don't function as they normally should. So, necessarily, other than the support of the Churches and the Christian Communities present in the Holy Land, we try to do something good for the people.

Can you give us recent examples of your help?
STERN: Our Mission has operated in the areas of Bethlehem, Beit Jala, Beit Sahour, and also north of Jerusalem, in Ramallah, where there was a Christian presence. But our service is not only for the Christians. For example, whereas the local church encourages the construction of new housing the Pontifical Mission has for years been repairing ruined houses, especially in the area of the old city of Jerusalem where a section of indigenous Palestinian population survives. The tension between Israelis and Palestinians has brought about much poverty and so today we back initiatives apt to create jobs, especially funding works that require many workers and therefore feed more families...

Doesn't repairing houses go beyond the original activity of your Mission in a certain sense?
STERN: But it's absolutely necessary to help these poor people. When our Mission was founded, the primary purpose was the mobilization of aid in the international Catholic world for the Holy Land, and the coordination in the Holy Land of all the sectors of the Church – the patriarchs, the bishops, the male and female religious, the lay associations... In 1949, nobody took care of this coordination, today we are many more.

Who are the principal beneficiaries of your activity?
STERN: All those who find themselves in need. Statistically they are not Jews, for whom a very numerous series of aid bodies exist. Whereas the overwhelming majority of Muslims – given that the Christians are few in

number – are hit by poverty, even if a great many Muslim charitable institutions do exist. So... the criterion adopted by our Mission is to bring help to the areas where there are still Christians, but without ever excluding others, such as the Muslims, from aid. The pertinent example is the University of Bethlehem – founded by an agreement between the Congregation for the Eastern Churches and the Brothers of the Christian Schools – known here as the Vatican University. About 35% of the students are Christian, the others are all Muslim. We say that "not belief but need guides the charity we exercise in the name of the Pope in the Holy Land".

How would you describe the poverty in Palestine?
STERN: In Gaza a large part of the population still lives in refugee camps, administered by the United Nations. The camps are like a completely disorganized old village. The people live in cramped houses made of blocks of cement, there are no proper streets, but pathways more or less uneven, and they all live crammed together. Up to twelve people even may live in one room, because the children are numerous. Freedom of movement is limited. They live off the contributions of the United Nations. There is no work. When one of these numerous children becomes an adult and wants to marry, he must first have a place to go, and a wage. But there is neither the one nor the other for those who live in the camps. Only one extra room, brick-built can be added on to the original house. A room that will again look out on to the usual dirty streets, and the camps that have no easy access to drinkable water and where there is never order. It is sad to live like that.

Two years ago we built a small play park for the children of Gaza. You should have seen their curiosity, their looks. It was the first time in their lives that someone had given them something to play with. They who are used to receiving the minimum for survival, used to living in the worst conditions. Words fail me to explain the difficulty of life in Gaza. And allow me to add something else that matters to me. Please.

There are people who ask the rhetorical question as to why young Palestinian boys and girls accept blowing themselves up as martyrs. They can't study, they can't travel, they can't work, they can't have a family, theylive in the absurd, they have no other hope except to annihilate themselves in a moment of glory for their religion.

I am neither a politician nor an economist, but I can at least imagine that the day when we can offer work to these young Muslim, we will have disrupted the plans of the terrorists: with an honest weekly wage and the possibility of going out with one's girlfriend.

I'm convinced, despite their very negative rhetoric, that the Hamas leaders understand this situation perfectly. They want a future for their people, as do all of those who run politics. And the positive aspect of their politics is the amount of social services and of well-being that they have tried to give their people. This remains true, despite the words they use and the slogans that, according to Arab rhetoric, they yell.

Do you consider it a mistake to interrupt the flow of international economic aid to Palestine as a form of pressure on the Hamas government?
STERN: I repeat that I don't intend to formulate a political judgment. My impression is that precisely by doing this the people – and the youth – are presented with yet another form of despair that can be exploited by the terrorists. The proclaimed objective of those who want the aid embargo is, in the short term, to force the current government to a change of political direction, leaving as a long term goal that of achieving peace... it's a total mistake. First, the blocking of funds is a punishment for the people, never for the leadership, and the people are already suffering too much. Second, for the Arab mentality, we are offending their honor, their sense of dignity, with all the consequences that derive from that. The embargo is a hundred per cent counter-productive. I am convinced, and certainly hope, that through mutual collaboration the result of gaining Hamas consent can be achieved.

You have also brought help to the refugee camps in Lebanon. What is the situation?
STERN: It is different but equally painful. The Palestinian refugees in Lebanon all live in camps run by the United Nations. The difficulties also come from the traditional and by now deteriorating balance of constitutional powers in Lebanon between Maronite Christians, Sunni Muslims and Shiite Muslims, based on the respective numbers of the population. Now, none of these three groups wants a numerous Palestinian component to enter the picture, and all are agreed in saying that the only prospect for these refugees is that of returning to their own countries. But this is now practically impossible. Thus the refugee camp is the only thing left for these poor people, to live in prison that is. I dream of the day when there is a universally recognized Palestinian State, and

perhaps all of these poor people can have a Palestinian passport, so as to obtain a residence visa to work in Lebanon. Because, things being as they are, Lebanon will never accept these people as proper citizens. Today more than two hundred thousand Palestine Muslims are refugees in the camps, armed, in complete isolation, prevented from going to Palestine. It is an unbearable way of life, that has made them nasty, with reason. The Palestinians are also now leaving Iraq. The Palestinians leaving Iraq are not however as numerous as the Iraqis who currently migrate toward Jordan, Syria and Lebanon in ever increasing numbers. And, in proportion, it is constantly more Christians who flee. The director of our office in Amman, which deals with Jordan and Iraq, told me that there is the concrete possibility, even though official data are still lacking, that Iraqi refugees in Jordan will reach millions, on top of a Jordanian population of about five million. Our Pontifical Mission attempts to do everything possible to support the local church and give a hand to these refugees. Normally we help whoever wants to leave Iraq and go to Europe, North or South America, or Australia...

In the charitable work in Palestine you represent the Pope. Is there something in particular that you recall?
STERN: Pope John Paul II came to the Holy Land in 2000. And in cases such as these small privileges also are due to the President of the Pontifical Mission, such as participating from close up in what is taking place. I remember in particular the open air mass that Pope Wojtyla celebrated in Bethlehem, in front of the Basilica standing where Jesus was born. At a certain point, as happens every day, the voice of the muezzin who calls people to prayer could be heard from the nearby mosque. The voice was strong, broadcast by loudspeakers. The Pope, at that moment stopped, he didn't raise his voice to counter the loudspeakers, but waited. Until the end of the Muslim prayer. Then he resumed the liturgy. It was as if the Pope himself had told us, in that way, that the Palestinian Christian community must understand and respect the Muslims, who are brothers, and hope and pray that understanding will also come from their side.

The respectful silence of the Pope was the image of the coexistence between Christians and Muslims in Palestine.

© *30Days in the Church and the World. All rights reserved*

Separated by a Wall at Christmas

Fr. Firas Arideh, Parish Priest, December 2005

The Chapel at Bethlehem University

As a parish priest in the West Bank village of Aboud, my Christmas preparations include recording the identity card numbers of my parishioners to request permits from the Israeli authorities to allow us travel to Bethlehem. Some may be denied permits and prevented from worshipping there. While decorating our church for the joyous birth of Our Lord, we also prepare banners for the next protest against the wall that Israel began to build on our village's land one month ago.

Aboud is nestled among terraced olive groves in the West Bank west of the city of Ramallah. The village has 2,200 residents. Nine hundred of them are Christian. Within the village are seven ancient churches. The oldest dates to the third century. We believe that Jesus passed through Aboud on the Roman road from the Galilee to Jerusalem.

The wall that Israel is building through Aboud is not for the security of Israel. It is for the security of illegal Israeli settlements.

The Israeli government continues to falsely claim that it is building the wall on Israeli land, but Aboud lies 3.75 miles inside the Green Line, the pre-1967 border between Israel and the West Bank. The wall will cut off 1,100 acres of our land for two illegal Israeli settlements.

Sometimes the Israelis give special treatment to Christians. Sometimes they give Christians permits to go through checkpoints while they stop

Muslims. They do this to try to separate us, but in reality we Muslims and Christians are brothers.

Our church organist Yousef told me, "Some foreigners believe that Islam is the greatest danger for Palestinian Christians rather than Israel's occupation. This is Israeli propaganda. Israel wants to tell the world that it protects us from the Muslims, but it is not true. In Aboud, we Muslims and Christians live a normal, peaceful life together.

"Last week our village celebrated the Feast of Saint Barbara for our patron saint whose shrine outside our village was damaged by the Israeli military in 2002. We invited the Muslims to share the traditional feast of Saint Barbara. They also invite us to share their traditional Ramadan evening meal. We have good relations. Muslims are peaceful people."

With signs, songs and prayers, our village has been protesting against Israel's apartheid wall every week. Through peaceful demonstrations and the planting of olive trees, we want to tell the Israelis and the international community that we are against Israel taking our lands. We are working for peace here, but still the Israeli soldiers have attacked our peaceful protests with clubs, sound bombs, tear gas and rubber-coated steel bullets.

On Dec. 11, we were honored with a visit to Aboud by the highest Roman Catholic official in the Holy Land, the Latin Patriarch of Jerusalem, Michel Sabbah. Patriarch Sabbah, a Palestinian, planted an olive tree on the planned route of the wall, and told 1,000 peaceful protesters, "The wall doesn't benefit the security of either Israel or anybody else. Our prayers are for the removal of this physical wall currently under construction and the return of our lands."

"Our hearts are filled with love, and no hatred for anybody. With our faith and love, we demand the removal of this wall. We affirm that it is a mistake and an attack against our lands and our properties, and an attack against friendly relationships between the two people."

"In your faith and your love you shall find a guide for your political action and your resistance against every oppression. You may say that love is an unknown language to politics, but love is possible in spite of all the evil we experience. We shall make it possible!"

Just after Patriarch Sabbah left, an Israeli protesting with us was arrested by Israeli soldiers as he planted an olive tree. We have good Israeli friends.

We do not say that every Israeli soldier is bad, because they are just soldiers following orders.

Yes, there are Palestinian Christians here in Aboud, Bethlehem, Jerusalem, Ramallah and Gaza. We are the Salt of the Earth.

My religion tells me that I have to love everybody and accept everybody without conditions. We have here good Jewish people, good Muslims and good Christians. We can live together. This is the Holy Land. If we in Aboud can send a message to the world this Christmas, it is that Jews, Christians and Muslims have to live together in peace.

Aridah is a Jordanian priest serving the Roman Catholic Holy Mary Mother of Sorrows Church in the village of Aboud in the Occupied Palestinian West Bank.

Writing on the Wall

Israel's security barrier foreshadows further misery for Palestinians caught on the wrong side.

text by Marilyn Raschka - Photographs added: Jeff Abood

Inside the Wall around Bethlehem

As hard as the trip from Nazareth to Bethlehem was some 2,000 years ago, if Mary and Joseph were to do it today, the journey might be impossible.

In June 2002, the Israeli government decided to erect a barrier to separate Israel, where Nazareth is located, from the West Bank, where Bethlehem lies.

The barrier, now partially constructed, is a combination of electronic and barbed wire fencing, military roads and concrete walls, stretches of which reach 26 feet in height.

The barrier does not run along the pre-1967 boundary between Israel and the West Bank. It is being built, for the most part, on West Bank land taken without compensation. Israel has occupied the West Bank since the conclusion of the Six Day War in 1967.

The barrier, which the Israeli government says is necessary to prevent terror attacks within Israel, snakes through the West Bank, separating farm from farmer, student from school, grandchildren from grandparents, one side of town from the other. By making movement difficult, it is keeping people from living their lives and earning their livelihoods with dignity.

Lamia is a nurse at Muslim Muqassad Hospital on the Mount of Olives. She is a resident of Bethany, the hometown of Lazarus, whom Jesus raised from the dead.

The Israelis had annexed Bethany, an Arab village, to Jerusalem, which means Lamia has an Israeli-issued Jerusalem permit allowing her to travel freely. But her status is about to change.

The barrier will put Bethany outside Jerusalem and make Lamia and her family West Bankers. Israeli law forbids West Bank residents to work in or travel to Jerusalem without a special permit. Lamia is about to be handed a pink slip.

But the hospital counts on Lamia. Duty and financial need have now forced her to do what many Palestinians do, use a route that skirts the not yet completed wall and the Israeli border guards. Backyards, convent gardens and even cemeteries are commonly used alternate routes.

The Sisters of Our Lady of Sorrows live and work next door to Bethany in Abu Dis. The sisters run a home for the elderly, which has received CNEWA assistance for years and provides seniors with a clean environment, good meals and companionship.

The neighborhood was a haven of peace and quiet. Then the wall came.

The wall was routed right outside the home's front gate. The space between the gate and the wall is just big enough for a car or ambulance to pass. The sisters and their elderly charges now live in a construction zone.

Buildings shake as the bulldozers roll by. The home's walls have cracked from the pounding. Dust covers the gardens and filters into the buildings. At the beginning of the construction work, the sisters and their residents were without water and electricity.

It took a demonstration by foreign volunteers to draw attention to the home's predicament and get the responsible authorities to make repairs.

The long-term effect of the wall has the sisters worried. Although the home will remain on the Jerusalem side, many of their workers come from the West Bank. So do a number of the families of the residents.

The sisters may have to fire loyal staff because the workers will not be able to get to work. As for the elderly, their children's visits are the best medicine – and "medicine" should be taken on a regular basis.

And when a death occurs, how will the family come for the body?

Even pilgrims feel the pinch of the barrier. The traditional Palm Sunday procession from Bethany to the Mount of Olives will have to change its course.

The present crossing point in the Bethany section of the wall is a crowded, noisy, dusty and generally unpleasant place, wide enough for an Israeli border guard and one pedestrian.

Pilgrims and tourists constitute a small percentage of the people using the crossing. Most are students, housewives, merchants, office workers and delivery boys with coffee cups on trays.

Cars cannot pass. Instead of taking one bus or taxi from Bethany to Jerusalem, the commuter or shopper or student or sister must get out on one side of the wall, line up, pass the scrutiny of the border guards and then take another car from the other side.

Making life easy or difficult for the Palestinians trying to cross the wall falls to the discretion of the guards.

A French friend in Bethany called with the warning: "If you come to visit today, you will have to dirty your clothes."

At the crossing point it was clear what she meant. The guards had obstructed the crossing with huge cement blocks.

No one could say why.

The guards stood on top of the blocks and watched as young males scampered their way up. The women struggled, hoisting themselves and their children, waving their identification cards in their hands, then swinging their legs over and descending to the other side. Everyone got their clothes dirty. The next day the blocks were gone, as were the guards. People moved freely back and forth as if there were no wall at all.

El Ram, another Arab town near Jerusalem, will become part of the West Bank once the wall is built. El Ram's wall story is full of questions, mostly rhetorical ones. How will the children get to their schools in Jerusalem? How will workers get to their jobs?

For town officials, two more issues will have to be solved: El Ram has no landfill and no cemetery. El Ram's agreements on these two services with other Jerusalem- area towns will soon be obsolete.

Ironically, the town's new status will affect Jewish wholesalers who have done business for years with El Ram shopkeepers. Jewish and Palestinian shoppers find El Ram a great place to shop on Saturdays when Jewish-owned shops are closed for Shabbat.

Life is not easier outside Jerusalem.

The Emmanuel Sisters in Bethlehem are a contemplative order. Their simple lives became complicated when the road leading to their convent became part of the barrier project.

To compensate, the Israeli government took land from their neighbor's front yard and built the sisters a new road. The neighbor now has a road and a 26-foot-high wall outside his home where a view across the valley once greeted him and his family each day.

Military law does not allow him to plant or landscape the remaining land. It is too close to the wall. He also had to reconfigure his driveway.

The family is prohibited from using the roof of their house, where his wife would hang the laundry and where summer breezes would cool the family on hot nights.

Wherever the wall is in place, there is also graffiti. Popular are political slogans criticizing the Israeli and U.S. governments, as well as colorful pleas for peace and calls to halt the wall's construction.

Construction of the barrier has left the land scarred by bulldozers busy uprooting the natural environment to make room for concrete and metal. The stone retaining walls of some convents and monasteries on the Mount of Olives have been so damaged by the construction that one good rain may spell collapse.

Whatever biblical image pilgrims have of the Mount of Olives is erased by the most incongruous combination of dusty olive trees and concrete wall segments awaiting assembly.

Everywhere in the West Bank, sections of the wall stand in the distance, but with each day they move closer along their projected path.

And then the day comes when the homeowner, the farmer or the mother superior of a convent is notified that their land is being taken for the barrier.

In Bethlehem, one landowner found a notice nailed to one of his olive trees. Three or four strikes with a hammer and the land was no longer his.

After the bulldozers have finished uprooting the olive trees, farmers sneak back onto the property and haul away any survivors for replanting.

Aware that mature olive trees fetch good money inside Israel, construction crews often illegally take the trees away for resale.

The specter of the wall also features prominently in meetings of humanitarian groups, health care facilities and other nongovernmental organizations. Their staff spends hours planning for the barrier's impact on their work.

The mobility problem – employees living on the "wrong side" of the wall – is the greatest.

The Jerusalem-area family home of Maher Turjman, CNEWA's Regional Director for Palestine and Israel, will be surrounded by two walls by the end of the year, making his daily trip to the office in the Old City a near impossibility.

The main exit for those living in Bethlehem

Rather than lose valuable hours navigating a circuitous route to work, Mr. Turjman and his young family have taken an apartment at St. Joseph Hospital.

"The wall will do little to serve peace," he said. "Anything that breaks up families, makes work more difficult and threatens the free flow of people will only harden divisions that have already cost both Israelis and Palestinians so much suffering."

The Changing Face of the Holy Land:
Eager for Security and Stability, Christians Move on.

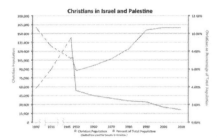

Dr. Bernard Sabella is professor emeritus of sociology at Bethlehem University in Bethlehem, Palestine. This interview is reprinted from ONE magazine, a publication of CNEWA and has been edited for length.

The city of David was once a Christian town. But, its churches are emptying as families pick up and move to Chile or Honduras or Florida. Since the second Palestinian uprising against Israeli occupation, or intifada (2000-2003), up to 4,000 Palestinian Christians, especially from the Bethlehem area, have left their homeland. The violence of the intifada and Israel's retaliatory actions are over. But the stalemate between Israel and Palestine and the impact of the Israeli separation barrier and other measures impeding the freedom of movement have crippled the Palestinian Christian community. Pope Benedict XVI, while on his pilgrimage to Bethlehem in 2009, reflected on this stating: "A stark reminder of the stalemate that relations between Israelis and Palestinians seem to have reached — the wall. In a world where more and more borders are being opened up — to trade, to travel, to movement of peoples, to cultural exchanges — it is tragic to see walls still being erected. How we long to see the fruits of the much more difficult task of building peace! How earnestly we pray for an end to the hostilities that have caused this wall to be built!"

Who are Palestinian Christians?

The expression "Palestinian Christian" or "Arab Christian" often

confuses Westerners. How can one be Arab or Palestinian and Christian? Are not all Arabs and Palestinians Muslims? Arabs make up the Arab Nation, a term that refers to the cultural, ethnic and linguistic identity of the Arab people. Palestinian is a national identity while religion is a particular form of identification. Hence, one can be an Arab Palestinian Christian much like an Irish American Catholic. Arab Palestinian Christians are an "integral part of their societies," and claim that in their homeland, which we call the Holy Land, "the continuing presence of a living Christian community is inseparable from the historical sites. Through the 'living stones' the holy archaeological sites take on life." These "living stones" belong to a number of churches, but all follow Jesus. Some of these churches are rooted in the early church and were embraced by the original Arab tribes while others were imported during the Crusader and Colonial periods. The Aramaic, Arabic, Armenian and European family names of these Christians of the Holy Land reflect the kaleidoscopic nature of the community. Intermarriage among the Christian faithful is common. Almost 50 percent of current marriages are mixed, which makes for Christian unity at the grassroots.

Christian Numbers Since the June 1967 War

If 1947 is taken as the base year, when the Christian population was at 143,000, population experts would expect the figure to have doubled naturally by 1980 and to have reached the mark of 400,000 or more by 2010, assuming a growth rate of 2 percent per year. To the contrary, the present figures indicate the disappearance of six out of every ten Christians since 1948. Some would argue this is strictly due to trends of demographic nature. But in reality, these matters alone do not explain the steadily declining numbers, particularly in the occupied Palestinian Territories.

The first Israeli-run census of the population of the Palestinian Territories in 1967 placed the number of Palestinian Christians at 42,494, of whom 2,478 were in Gaza. By a standard growth equation, this number should have been more than 100,000 by 2012.

Some would argue that the Christian population in Israel has tripled since 1948. But this argument does not tell the whole story; recent surveys point to a desire among 26 percent of respondents to emigrate from Israel — the same percentage as those in the Palestinian Territories. Christians in Israel are not fully integrated in Israel's society and economy. Feeling marginalized, the younger generation in particular seriously contemplates emigration.

A positive side of the argument, however, is that when there is some political and economic stability, people are less likely to think of emigrating. Respondents in one survey said they would not think of leaving if there were peace in the region. But in a number of surveys undertaken since the 1990's, more than 60 percent of Christian respondents in both the Palestinian Territories and Israel consistently cited political and economic factors as reasons to emigrate. Religious fanaticism was not cited as a cause until a survey in 2006, which found that 8 percent of respondents thought the rise in religious fundamentalism *(both Jewish and Muslim- Ed.)* was making them think about emigrating.

The role of the churches has been crucial in sustaining the Palestinian Christian community, whether in education, housing or providing medical and other social services. But the work is not restricted to Christians as witnessed by the Pontifical Mission and its mandate by the Holy See to serve all those in need irrespective of religion. The churches reinforce the commitment of local Christians to be an integral part of their society.

In the end, however, it is the "much more difficult task of building peace" as His Holiness has insisted that will ensure that walls will fall and hopefully enable the Holy Land's Christians — and all Israelis and Palestinians — to remain in the Holy Land and allow it blossom in the love and hope of us all being created in the image of God.

Adapted with permission from the original article published in ONE magazine.

Obstacles to Peace

"We recite the seemingly endless list of difficulties separating Israelis and Palestinians, which makes it all the more urgent to address the problem of the fundamental injustice at the heart of this question. To make a litany of symptoms without addressing the root cause is hardly helpful to either party".

Pope Benedict XVI, 2006

The Assembly
of Catholic Ordinaries
of the Holy Land

Latins, Melkites, Maronites, Syrians, Armenians, Chaldeans, Custody of the Holy Land

Statement Regarding the Separation Wall from The Patriarchs and Head of Churches in Jerusalem

We the head of Churches in Jerusalem affirm our determination to do all in our power to work for Peace in the Holy Land - a Peace that is concerned with the well-being of every resident of this Land, be they Israeli or Palestinian, to give them security , justice, freedom, independence and personal dignity.

Let no-one doubt our abhorrence of violence, whoever the perpetrator. Peace will only be established when all violence is eradicated from both sides. If the present Road Map for Peace is to bring positive results, we believe the Separation Wall constitutes a grave obstacle. For both nations the Wall will result in a feeling of isolation. Moreover from many Palestinians it means the deprivation of land, (some 10% more than that of the Occupation in 1967) livelihood, statehood and family life. **Occupation remains the root cause of the conflict and of the continuing suffering in the Holy Land.** *

Take for example the proposed Separation Wall around Bethlehem, for us Christians, the birthplace of Jesus Christ, the Prince of Peace. The consequences will be devastating to the Christian Community; not least the psychological impact on daily life. The community will be isolated following the deprivation of access to land and freedom of movement. Visits of pilgrims will be further discouraged.

We appeal to both Authorities - Israeli and Palestinian - and to all Peace-loving peoples around the world, (who should make urgent contact with their leaders, both Political and Religious), in an effort to remove this impediment to a comprehensive and lasting Peace.

Jerusalem 26th August 2003

+Patriarch Michel Sabbah
Latin Patriarch of Jerusalem

+Patriarch Torkom II
Armenian Apostolic Orthodox
Patriarch of Jerusalem

Fr. Giovanni Battistelli, O.F.M.
Custos of the Holy Land

+Anba Abraham
Coptic Orthodox Archbishop of
Jerusalem

+Swerios Malki Murad
Syrian Orthodox Archbishop of
Jerusalem

+Abba Cuostos
Ethiopian Orthodox Archbishop of
Jerusalem

+Riah Abu El-Assal
Anglican Bishop in Jerusalem

+Munib A. Younan
Lutheran Evangelical Bishop of
Jerusalem

Archmindrite Mtanious Haddad
Greek Catholic Patriarchal Exarch.
Jerusalem

*+Butros Malki
*Syrian Catholic Bishop in
Jerusalem

*emphasis added

Bethlehem Nuns in West Bank Barrier Battle

By Yolande Knell BBC News, Jerusalem (from BBC News at bbc.co.uk/new)

Cremisan convent and school

The barrier Israel has been building in and around the West Bank is set to deprive a Christian community of its land, and appears to have caused an unholy row between some monks and nuns - who could now end up on opposite sides.

In the green Cremisan valley, west of Bethlehem, a goatherd leans against a rock while his flocks graze under the olive and fig trees.

Nearby, a narrow road winds along the hillside to a 19th Century convent and a secluded monastery where monks run the only Palestinian winery.

For the mainly Christian town of Beit Jala, this is the local beauty spot. Residents come here to take a stroll or for a weekend barbecue. Many own small plots of agricultural land. They also send their children to the convent school and visit the monastery to sell grapes or buy its wine.

That is why an Israeli government plan to build a wall through the valley, cutting off their access to most of it, is causing great alarm.

Red line is the proposed path of the Wall. Yellow is the Convent / School and the Monastery (Google)

In an unusual move, priests like Father Ibrahim Shomali are speaking out.

"When people suffer the Church must be near them. This is not politics. This is human rights and this is Christians who must be defended," he says. "Here, 57 Christian families will lose their land. Losing the land means losing their hope."

Every week, Father Ibrahim invites members of the community to join an outdoor mass as a form of peaceful protest.

Large parts of Israel's West Bank barrier have already been built. From the Cremisan valley, the high concrete wall separating Palestinian Bethlehem from Jerusalem is clearly visible in the distance. When it is extended here, the purpose will be to divide Beit Jala from two Jewish settlements - Har Gilo and Gilo - which sit on opposite hilltops.

While both are considered illegal under international law, Israel disputes this.

Palestinians see the barrier as a land grab and believe this valley is wanted for settlement expansion. Israeli officials argue that security is their main concern.

"The route of the security barrier is based on the specific security considerations of the area. In the Beit Jala region, it is there solely to keep terror out of Jerusalem," says Israeli Defence Ministry spokesman, Joshua Hantman.

West Bank barrier

Total length is 708 km (440 miles), more than twice the length of the 1949 Armistice Line (Green Line) between Israel and West Bank

About 61.8% of the barrier is complete; a further 8.2% is under construction and 30% is planned but not yet constructed

When completed, only about 15% of the barrier will be constructed on the Green Line or in Israel, isolating 9.4% of the West Bank

Source: UN 2011

He adds that 10 years ago, during the second Palestinian uprising or intifada, there were regular attempts to shoot at Gilo from Beit Jala. Local Palestinians have launched legal action to prevent them from being blocked off from the Cremisan land. This is one of dozens of cases that have ensured that work on the barrier, begun in 2002, remains only two-thirds complete. What makes this case different is the presence of the convent and monastery. Two years ago, the

Salesian Sisters of Cremisan joined the challenge to the route in an Israeli court. "We want to build bridges, not walls," their director, Sister Fides says through lawyers, emphasising the importance to the convent of its primary school for West Bank children.

The Salesian Sisters worry that the barrier could close down their school for Palestinian children.

"We are committed towards education for justice, peaceful living and peace between all people without distinction."

Schoolchildren at the Cremisan

The latest proposals for the barrier would see it looping round the convent, keeping it on the Palestinian side, but splitting it from the neighbouring monastery.

Children would still be allowed to attend the school, though they would have to pass by soldiers at an Israeli checkpoint to do so. Landowners would be given limited access via an agricultural gate, at the time of the olive harvest, for example.

For now, the barrier stops half-way up a hill behind the monastery. For a long time the monks remained silent about the developments, earning criticism from others in the Christian community.

"It is of vital importance to have all the interested parties together against this wall because together we are strong," says Samia Khalilieh, who is involved in the court case. "The monastery being with us is an important factor. It is part of our heritage."

In December, the monks published a carefully worded condemnation of the barrier route. It said they never asked to "pass on the Israeli side" and that "the entire route of the wall was established independently by the Israeli authorities".

The monastery also tried to join the legal appeal but the court would not allow it. Nuns and residents are due in court again in September.

Ministering to the Elderly

Marie, an elderly resident of the Home of Our Lady of Sorrows in East Jerusalem.
Photo: Georgi Lazarevski

Our Lady of Sorrows is a Catholic-run nursing home primarily serving elderly Palestinians of various faiths, many who are poor and disabled. The facility is run by a small group of nuns and a staff of 18, whose work provides the residents with the bare necessities. The majority of residents — and staff — come from the West Bank, and most of their families continue to live there. The state of Israel first put up a security barrier across from Our Lady of Sorrows in 2002. The wall has made daily life more difficult for the staff and residents of the home, as anyone coming from the West Bank must obtain permits and go through a series of checkpoints. The access issues have also made the delivery of supplies and transportation of the home's residents to medical facilities more complicated. Below is a letter from the Homes' Directress.

I would like to inform you about what is happening in our neighborhood and around our house concerning the construction of the new wall of separation, 9 meters high (30 feet), which began on January 11, 2004. It replaces a much lower wall that allowed people to climb over it once they were no longer permitted to go from Bethany and Abu Dis to Jerusalem. This first so-called security wall was built in August 2002. It disorganized and deeply affected the life of the population as well as our own.

Separating Jerusalem from the West Bank and running along the road leading to our house, it passes in front of the main entrance to our property. Thousands of people have climbed over this first wall: children, students, mothers with their babies, elderly people, etc. Many people have fallen; some have even died from their fall. Two months ago, we had to call the ambulance for a man about 65 years old who fell on his head and lost consciousness. It took the ambulance more than a half-hour to get here. As it reached the Bethany intersection on its way to the hospital, the army searched the ambulance and forced the wife of the injured person to get out, thereby further delaying arrival at the hospital. The things that happen in front of this wall have become intolerable!

Hundreds of persons have passed through our property on a daily basis over a period of many months, climbing over our fences in order to escape military control, because many of them work in Jerusalem but do not have the required permits.

The people around us live in fear: fear of being arrested, fear of being tear-gassed, and fear of being mistreated, as so often happens. Tension is constant for the entire population whose living conditions have become more and more miserable. It's a daily struggle for these people who are constantly humiliated and assaulted. We really feel alone and helpless in the face of generalized inertia. We want to be spokespersons for these voiceless people who, each day for more than two years, have had to fight their way to reach their workplaces, schools, etc., to say nothing of all the sick who die for want of medical treatment.

In trying to accomplish our own mission, we too meet up with many difficulties when it comes to hospitalizing elderly people from the West Bank because Palestinian ambulances do not have the right to enter Israel. We must therefore find a way of getting these people to the other side of the wall without crossing any checkpoints so that their families can then bring them to the hospital. The same problem arises when someone dies. The families must shift for themselves to bring the bodies back to the other side. Life has become very complicated these last two years, and things are about to get worse with the construction of this new wall.

Elderly people who are still able to get around have not been able to run their errands for the last several months because all the shops are on the other side of the wall. Very often, they have been obliged to call merchants to the front of the wall and place their orders through an opening between two cement blocks.

Many of our elderly patients from the West Bank are very lonely because their families can no longer come to visit them.

Since the construction of the wall, we have had to be more vigilant than ever about the security of our elderly people. We have had to change suppliers. This represents an increase in the cost of our overhead because life is more expensive in Jerusalem. Today, we do not really know what will happen if the construction of this wall is completed because the majority of our elderly people and of our personnel come from the West Bank. Of our 18 employees, only three have a Jerusalem ID card. For two years, they have had to climb over the wall and constantly change their route in order to avoid the checkpoints because, even with a laissez-passer, the soldiers do not always let them come to our house.

This wall of 9 meters (30 feet) will oblige us to:

1. Hire new personnel from Jerusalem and, at the same time, fire the majority of our present personnel.

2. Stop receiving elderly people from the West Bank, i.e. to say, the poorest among them.

We are worried. Also, thousands of people are anguished as they see the wall being built without anyone resisting or protesting on the construction site itself. We were not apprised of the government's plans, and our house is now more isolated than ever because of the condition of the road. Everyday we must pick up our personnel at various places because the neighbourhood has become a military zone. Purchasing supplies has become extremely complicated, and we spend our time trying to manage the unforeseen. Given the terrible condition of the road giving access to our property, we hope that we won't have to hospitalize any of our elderly persons during the current rainy season.

This week many journalists and photographers have visited the neighborhood to see this land of desolation and humiliation. We all hope that the interviews they've conducted for the various newspapers, radio stations and TV networks will alert public opinion and stir the consciences of politicians.

We hope that you in turn will become our spokesperson and call for the destruction of this wall of shame. We count on your prayers so that a dialogue can resume between the responsible parties involved on both sides. Also, we count on your taking action, thanking you in advance for diffusing this information.

Sr. Marie Dominique Croyal

Bishops call for support of the Cremisan Valley

Committee on International Justice and Peace

Dear Secretary Kerry:

As Chair of the Committee on International Justice and Peace of the United States Conference of Catholic Bishops, I write to protest in the strongest terms a recent decision of the Israeli Special Appeals Committee for land seizure under emergency law in the Cremisan Valley. I had written to your predecessor late last year regarding this case.

The Cremisan Valley lies in the West Bank on the Palestinian side of the Green Line adjacent to Beit Jala and Bethlehem. The State of Israel plans to re-route the separation barrier through the Cremisan Valley. The route will separate a Salesian monastery from a Salesian convent, and will separate both from their lands. The Salesian Convent and Primary School will be surrounded on three sides by the barrier that will confiscate most of the convent's lands.

At the same time the route will harm 58 Christian families whose livelihoods depend on these lands .Proceeding with this plan will cut families off from agricultural and recreational lands, other family members, water sources and schools – including depriving Christian Palestinian youth of fellowship with their peers.

In solidarity with our brother bishops in the Holy Land, we oppose re-routing the separation wall in the Cremisan Valley and ask the State Department to raise the concerns expressed by the bishops of the Holy Land in the enclosed statement with the government of Israel.

In the wake of the Appeals Committee decision, the Latin Patriarch of Jerusalem, speaking for the bishops of the Holy Land, reminded

"Israeli decision-makers that the expropriation of lands does not serve the cause of peace and does not strengthen the position of the moderates."

The Cremisan Valley is a microcosm of a protracted pattern that has serious implications for the ongoing Israeli-Palestinian conflict. As the wall moves and constricts more communities in the West Bank, the possibility of a future two-state resolution becomes less likely. Moving the wall and disassociating Palestinian families from their lands and livelihoods will incite more resentment against the State of Israel among residents of the West Bank, not less, increasing the frustrations that can lead to violence. Such policies put Israeli citizens at risk and weaken initiatives for reconciliation and peace.

Sharing the overwhelming sentiment of the world's nations, USCCB supports a two-state solution to the Israeli-Palestinian conflict, and a reversal of Israeli policies, like those proposed in the Cremisan Valley, that undermine a just resolution of the conflict.

Sincerely yours,

Most Reverend Richard E. Pates
Chairman, Committee on International Justice and Peace - United States Conference of Catholic Bishops

SOCIETY OF ST. YVES – Catholic Center for Human Rights

The Society of St. Yves, Catholic Center for Human Rights, is working under the patronage of the Latin Patriarchate of Jerusalem. St. Yves provides gratis legal assistance and counsel to members of the community.

The Separation Barrier in Cremisan
Summary of the case and legal proceedings

The Salesian Convent and School
Around 450 children – girls and boys, Muslims and Christians alike - from the surrounding towns and villages (e.g. Bethlehem, Beit Jala, Beit Sahour, Al Walajeh) enjoy the services provided by the Salesian Sisters Convent and School in Cremisan. As the convent wants to serve the needy, they charge just minimal fees. Following the educational method of the Don Bosco school systems, the convent is one of 1,500 educational facilities around the world teaching value s of truth, just peace and co-existence between different people and religions.The convent lies at the outskirts of Beit Jala, next to it are a few houses belonging to Beit Jala and the Salesians Monks Convent of Cremisan which are affected by the planned wall as well. Cremisan itself is situated between two illegal Israeli settlements: Har Gilo and Gilo.The nuns' convent has been pre sent since 1960 and includes a developing primary school (today until 5th grade, expanding each year), a kindergarten, a school for children with learning disabilities, as well as extracurricular activities and three summer camps for children.

The legal case
In 2006 the Israeli commander of the West Bank issued a military order[1]

seizing land for the purposes of building a fragment of the separation wall around the Beit Jala area and Har Gilo settlement. According to the order as well as to the maps and detailed plans annexed to it – the separation wall is to be built in a route which highly affects the Convent and the agricultural land surrounding it.

Since 2006 the Salesian nuns have been in contact with Israeli army officials to make their position clear that they reject the wall in total, and the wall in its suggested route in particular. In 2010, after they realized that their position was wrongly presented in court by the army, the nuns requested to join their neighbors' court appeal against the route of the wall, the court agreed. Beside the nuns, also the Monks monastery and 5 4 mainly Christian families are affected by the planned course of the wall. In 2011, during the procedures in court, the army issued new orders seizing m ore land to present a suggested second route, where the wall will run along the first terrace of the olive grove surrounding the convent and encircling it from three sides.

The suggested routes

1. The wall will pass in front of the convent, leaving the educational compound and the lands on the Israeli side of the wall, while the community it serves is left on the Palestinian side. The wall would have a guarded gate at the entrance of the compound, to be opened at specific times to allow the passage of children, teachers and convent staff, who will also have to apply for permits in order to be able to cross the wall into their school and work place. Many of the parents of the children have already made clear, that they will not send their children to the school anymore if they have to pass a military guarded gate (**dotted yellow line on the map**).

2. The wall is to be built on the convent land and leaves convent and school on the Palestinian side of the wall. As a consequence the convent is cut off from its land and will have access to it through an agricultural gate, guarded by the military. This will be opened only during certain periods of the year, and twice a day for the monks to pass. Also, as a consequence any possibility for

expanding the school and using the land for educational activities is blocked for years to come, as 75% of the land will remain behind the wall, on the Israeli side (**blue line on the map**).

Map of the Cremisan valley (Google)

Implications

The main arguments in court – beside an expert opinion given by the Council for Peace and Security, the association of retired experts of national security in Israel, which offered an alternative route adjacent to Gilo – were mainly based on International Humanitarian and **Human Rights Law:**

A   According to the advisory opinion of the International Court of Justice, the separation barrier is contrary to international law, as long as it passes in occupied territory. Cremisan lies behind the green line of 1967 and is mainly privately owned Palestinian Christian land. According to experts from the Council for Peace and Security, the now planned route is neither necessary nor logical for serving the Israeli security needs. The main purpose of the wall in Cremisan seems to be the annexation of land to give the settlements Gilo and Har Gilo the possibility to expand and have territorial continuity.

B   Building a separation barrier around the school, guarded by military presence will increase the friction around the school and endanger the children's well being an d at times endanger their lives.

C   The Right to Education is a basic human right, and is directly linked to the protected Right to Human Dignity. Right to Education is guaranteed in Human Rights conventions which Israel is part to. This Right to Education has to be respected, especially in case of children in elementary school, and especially in case of needy children. But the planned route of the wall will set an end to the educational compound of the Salesian sisters in Cremisan. The school will be surrounded by heavy military presence, turning the school – which is serving under the motto "bridges, not walls" – into a prison. 450 Palestinian children – girls and boys, Muslims and Christians alike, mainly from needy families – will either be endangered by this military presence or will have to leave their school.

D   Disconnecting the convent and monastery from each other and from the community its serves infringes on the Right to Freedom of Religion, as it is enshrined in the Human Rights Law covenants, which specifically call on states to protect the religious cultural life of minorities and especially focus on allowing them to manifest their religion in community and not only in the individual freedom of thought.

E   Seizing mainly Christian land is an attack on a religious minority which is specifically forbidden by international law. States should protect the existence of minorities and not confiscate their land and source of living as this forces them into migration, exile and displacement. Although emigration is a normal process among all nations, Christian emigration from the Holy Land is a unique one. Emigration from such a small community represents one of the major constraints, affecting population growth and threatening the future existence of Christians in the Holy Land.

F   According to a landscape and environmental expert opinion, Cremisan is one of the last remaining agricultural areas for the Bethlehem area. The local landowners grow olives, fruit trees and grapes for the local Cremisan wine in the valley, the land is cultivated well and the old terraces are carefully kept. Further the valley is used by people from the whole surrounding area for their family outings - on the weekends children play in the olive groves and families meet to sp end time in the nature. Beside all practical arguments, the valley is a unique living cultural and historical landscape. After the construction of the Israeli separation wall the valley will be damaged irreparably and cut off from the community.

G The seizure of the Salesian land in Cremisan is violating the "Agreement between the State of Israel and the Vatican" which was signed in 1993

The state attorney on behalf of the Ministry of Defense claimed that the wall is necessary for the security of the State of Israel and does not create permanent borders. He stated further that the situation of the status quo in the valley will be preserved by offering several solutions. These solutions would include building an agricultural gate which will guarantee access for the farmers to their lands, compensating the land owners for their losses and relocating any affected trees according to the wishes of their owners to reduce the damages. A written ruling will be issued in due time according to the courts agenda and priorities, till then a standing injunction preventing the construction of the wall remains.

The Cremisan Monastery

*The Assembly
of Catholic Ordinaries
of the Holy Land*

مجلس رؤساء الكنائس الكاثوليكية
في الأرض المقدسة

Latins, Melkites, Maronites, Syrians, Armenians, Chaldeans, Custody of the Holy Land

Why are Christians again the Target?

Declaration of the Assembly of Catholic Ordinaries of the Holy Land-Jerusalem, 2012

A recent graffiti and arson attack on the Latrun Monastery

The Christian community awoke this morning, Tuesday, September 4, 2012, to discover with horror that once again it is the target of forces of hatred within Israeli society. In the early hours of the morning, the door of the Cistercian (Trappist) monastery in Latroun was burned and anti-Christian graffiti was sprayed on the walls. The monks of Latroun have dedicated their lives to prayer and hard work. The monastery is visited by hundreds of Jewish Israelis each week and they are received with love and warmth by the monks. A number of the monks have learned Hebrew and promote mutual understanding and reconciliation between Jews and Christians, according to the teachings of the Catholic Church.

Sadly, what happened in Latroun is only another in a long series of attacks against Christians and their places of worship. What is going on in Israeli society today that permits Christians to be scapegoat and targeted by these acts of violence? Those who sprayed their hateful slogans, expressed their anger at the dismantlement of the illegal Jewish settlements in the West Bank. But why do they vent this anger against Christians and Christian places of worship?

What kind of "teaching of contempt" for Christians is being communicated in their schools and in their homes? And why are the culprits not found and brought to justice? This morning, the Christians in Israel are asking many questions as they grieve and seek consolation and assurances. The time has come for the authorities to act to put an end to this senseless violence and to ensure a "teaching of respect" in schools for all those who call this land home.

"Which of you desires life, and covets many days to enjoy good? Keep your tongue from evil, and your lips from speaking deceit. Depart from evil, and do good; seek peace, and pursue it."

Signatures

+ **Fouad TWAL** Patriarch of Jerusalem for Latins President, A.C.O.H.L.

+ **Giorgio LINGUA** Apostolic Nuncio for Jordan

Rt **Rev. Waldemar S. SOMMERTAG** Chargé d'Affaires of the Apostolic Nunciature for Israel

+ **Michel SABBAH** Latin Patriarch of Jerusalem Emeritus

+ **Elias CHACOUR** Melkite Catholic Archbishop of Akka Vice president, A.C.O.H.L.

+ **Yaser Al-AYYASH** Melkite Catholic Archbishop of Petra and Philadelphia

+ **Mussa El-HAGE** Maronite Archbishop of Haifa and the Holy Land Maronite Patriarchal Vicar for Jerusalem

+ **Joseph SOUEIF** Maronite Archbishop of Cyprus

+ **Boutros MOUALLEM** Melkite Catholic Archbishop of Akka Emeritus

+ **Gregoire Pierre MELKI** Syrian Catholic Exarch of Jerusalem

+ **Joseph Jules ZEREY** Melkite Patriarchal Vicar of Jerusalem

+ **Maroun LAHHAM** Latin Patriarchal Vicar for Jordan

+ **Giacinto-Boulos MARCUZZO** Latin Patriarchal Vicar for Israel

+ **William SHOMALI** Latin Patriarchal Vicar for Jerusalem and Palestine

+ **Kamal-Hanna BATHISH** Latin Auxiliary Bishop Emeritus

+ **Selim SAYEGH** Latin Auxiliary Bishop Emeritus

Msgr. **Joseph KELEKIAN** Armenian Catholic Exarch of Jerusalem Very Rev. **Pierbattista PIZZABALLA**, O.F.M. Custos of the Holy Land

Rev. **David NEUHAUS**, S.J. Patriarchal Vicar for Hebrew speaking Vicariate

Rev. **Evencio HERRERA DIAZ**, O.F.M. Latin Patriarchal Vicar for Cyprus

Rev. **Raymond MOUSSALLI** Patriarchal Vicar in Jordan for Chaldeans

Rev. **Pietro FELET**, scj Secretary general

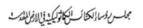

אסיפת ההגמונים הקתולי"ם
של ארץ הקודש

THE ASSEMBLY OF CATHOLIC ORDINARIES OF THE HOLY LAND
Latins, Melkites, Maronites, Syrians, Armenians, Chaldeans, Custody of the Holy Land

ACOHL publicly condemns "Price Tag" attacks

May 12, 2014

PRESS RELEASE - Good day to you! On behalf of the Assembly of the Catholic Ordinaries, I thank you for being present for this press conference. I thank the Mass Media for their collaboration. I commend your courage in speaking and writing the truth. I commend your investigative tenacity to get to the root of issues and problems. Keep up the good work!

All of you are well aware of the recent acts of vandalism against Christians, Muslims and Druze. There has been a marked increase of "price tag" provocations within Israel. This wave of extremist actions of terror, are surely of grave concern to all reasonable persons. The government of Israel must be concerned, because it is very bad for the State of Israel's image abroad. It is also a blight on the democracy that Israel ascribes to itself.

The actions are only drawing condemnation by Israeli leaders but few arrests. "All that is necessary for the triumph of evil is, that good men do nothing", to use an often quoted line.

At this point, the unrestrained acts of vandalism poison the atmosphere; the atmosphere of co-existence and the atmosphere of collaboration, especially in these two weeks prior to the visit of Pope Francis.

At the same time, we are encouraged by the fact that the Justice Minister, Tzipi Livni, held an emergency meeting to combat this senseless vandalism. We are aware that, in 2011, "the Israeli general in charge of the West Bank, Nitsan Alon, described the violence by radical settlers as 'terrorism' and urged the IDF to 'do much more to stop it"; and in 2014, Israeli Defence Minister, Moshe Yaalon, branded settler attacks as "outright terrorism" and that he would show "zero tolerance". Hopefully, the issue does not remain solely a matter of sound bites and round table discussion. Until these words become acts, we remain skeptical.

Nevertheless, there are many questions arising from the situation.

> 1. Who is behind the violence? Are the attacks solely the work of isolated individuals? Who instructs them in this bad education? How could it be that they don't catch the perpetrators?"

Carmi Gillon, the former head of Israel's Shin Bet security agency says, its current head, Yoram Cohen, "does not take seriously recent vandalism by ultranationalist Jews on Palestinian and Arab Israeli property." And that he "does not invest enough resources to stop the vandalism and that he belittles the danger of these activities. He apparently does not prioritize this matter." If this is so, we ask: Why?

> 1. It is known that Israeli police had set up special units to pursue such cases and the government had designated groups responsible as "illegal associations," giving authorities broader powers to act against them. Given that the vandals are largely unprosecuted, one must question the priority of the government to get to the bottom of the problem?

> 2. Treatment of this sad affair cannot be restricted only to issues of "law and order". There is a question of how are we educating our children? What do they learn about those who are different from them with regard to religion, nationality or ethnic identity? What is learned in those circles, that are producing the young people who commit these acts of hatred? What is the pedagogical effect of an official discourse, that

insists that the State is only for one group of people?

3. Today, we are holding the procession in honor of the Blessed Virgin in Haifa. Outside of the Palm Sunday procession, it is certainly the largest gathering of Christians in the Holy Land. We implore Mary's intercession as we all pray together for strength of Faith in the many challenges we face as Christians. We also pray for the perpetrators of vandalism and their families. We pray, too, that the government will do what is right.

+ Fouad Twal, Patriarch

Residency Laws Separate Families

15 Mar 2012 – text by Judith Sudilovsky

Palestinian Joseph Hazboun, 46, poses at the piano with his daughters, Layal, 16, Yazan, 14, and son, Lene, 12, in their apartment in East Jerusalem 28 Feb. For 17 years Hazboun, who is from Bethlehem, West Bank, has been living with his family in Jerusalem without a permanent Israeli residency permit. (photo: CNS/Bob Roller)

JERUSALEM - Joseph Hazboun remembers when he could hop into his car in Jerusalem and drive the few miles to the nearby West Bank city of Bethlehem to see his family. It was easy enough, even passing through mandatory checkpoints, that he and his Jerusalem-born wife and children would make the trip at least twice a month.

It has been years, though, since the Hazbouns, who are Catholic, could make the 25-minute drive on their own. Now the family must take light rail, two taxis and walk across a checkpoint to get from their home in East Jerusalem to Bethlehem. The venture takes at least 90 minutes. The result: The Hazbouns have curtailed their visits to once every several months.

Israeli laws on the book since 2003 strictly limit who can obtain permanent residency status and thus enjoy the related benefits, including driving privileges. The Supreme Court recently upheld the law.

Although he is the spouse of a Palestinian resident of East Jerusalem who holds an Israeli permanent resident ID, Hazboun is prohibited from becoming a permanent resident of Israel because he is from Bethlehem. Only those with permanent residency can enjoy benefits of Israeli society, including coverage under the health care system and social security benefits.

Every year the couples keep close track of their rent receipts, utility bills, school tuition payments and vaccination records. They trek to the Ministry of Interior and then to the Civil Administration in the West Bank to get the piece of paper that allows them to live together legally as a family.

They are among thousands of Palestinian couples who continue living in a state of limbo and uncertainty because they must apply for a temporary residence permit annually.

"That puts us at their mercy as, at any given moment, they can rebuke our residency permit and tell us to go away somewhere. But I have nowhere else to go. Here is where my work is, here is where we have our home," said Hazboun, 46, who has worked in the Jerusalem office of the Pontifical Mission for Palestine for 18 years. He has lived in the city since he married his Jerusalem-born wife, Rima, 17 years ago.

"I can't understand what the security threat is to Israel if we drive," Hazboun said. "This is just another prohibition to make our life in Israel difficult. It is a demographic war. (They think) that if they make it difficult for us we will say, Why live such a life in Jerusalem when we can move about freely in the West Bank?"

Hazboun's wife is allowed to drive, but she has a driving phobia. She declined to be interviewed.

Hazboun said he is looking forward to next year when the couple's oldest daughter will be eligible for a driver's license. Under the law, their children have been registered under their Jerusalemite parents' Israeli identity card. The couple's hopes for the system to be eased were dashed because of the Supreme Court ruling.

Under the law, the residency application status of couples like the Habouns has been frozen, although couples who had applied for family reunification before the statute was passed in 2003 may still apply for a temporary residency permit every year. Couples who married after the law was passed may not even do that. The end result is that they live in fear that the spouse from the West Bank will be expelled from Israel.

Since the beginning of 2012, the Society of St. Yves, a Catholic human and civil rights legal aid center, has taken on 89 family reunification cases like that of the Hazbouns, said director Raffoul Rofa. In the past, he said, the agency sometimes has been successful in upgrading a spouse's status to resident status with full rights if the family reunification application was submitted in the 1990s.

Rofa estimated that more than 100 Christian couples are affected by the law, though no official statistics exist. The center's staff estimates that thousands of couples remain dependent on the Israeli Ministry of Interior for the renewal of their temporary residency permits each year.

Elias, 39, is from Jerusalem and has an Israeli-issued permanent residency card but his wife, Abeer, 34, is from Bethlehem and lives in Jerusalem with only a temporary resident permit. The Catholic couple asked that their real names not be used because they fear their public comments will lead to difficulties with Israeli authorities.

The driving prohibition cuts into even the most mundane details of family life during the winter months. When it rains, as it has often since November, Abeer must either hire a taxi to take her children to afternoon activities or she must walk with them herself, even though the family car sits unused in the apartment building parking lot.

"It is a small prison here," Abeer said, sitting in her neat two-bedroom apartment in a Palestinian neighborhood of East Jerusalem.

Israel's citizenship and entry laws also affects young couples who are dating, Rofa said. Before beginning a relationship, many young people first learn where their prospective partner is from in an effort to avoid getting caught in the web of family reunification, he explained. None of these complications figured into the plans of Elias and Abeer when they fell in love and married almost a decade ago.

Abeer said that if she and Elias had thought about the ramifications of their marriage, they might not have married. For now, they see that only solution to their predicament is to move abroad but they do not want to leave their family, friends and the place where they grew up.

"It is part of our cross," Elias said. "The West thinks Israel is the only democratic state in the Middle East, but having to go through all this system is very humiliating. Every day you have to prove you are not a liar and that you don't forge documents. It makes me nervous to lose a bill or an invoice."

Hazboun expressed similar sentiments: "We would have still gotten married and lived in Jerusalem, but after what we have gone through, my wife tells our children not to even think about getting married to someone from the West Bank. It is difficult because we know what awaits them if they do."

Reprinted from CNEWA.org - Copyright © 2011 Catholic News Service www.catholicnews.com Reprinted with permission of CNS

10 years of Family Reunification Freeze in Jerusalem

The Society of St. Yves, Catholic Center for Human Rights, is working under the patronage of the Latin Patriarchate of Jerusalem. St. Yves provides gratis legal assistance and counsel to members of the community. Further, St. Yves raises awareness for the legal situation of the poor and marginalized in the Holy Land through national and international lobby and advocacy. Today St. Yves manages some 700 cases per year and assists about 2,000 people. December 2013 - Legal supervision by Adv. Haitham Al-Khateeb

SUMMARY AND RECOMMENDATIONS

During the last years, Israel has justified many of its actions in the Occupied Palestinian Territory on the grounds that they are necessary to preserve security for its citizens. Security became a "new religion" in Israel, and is used to justify almost any debated action which is taken by the State.

Israel used the same pretence also in order to freeze the possibility of family unification for Palestinian residents and citizens of the State of Israel. However, reality draws a different picture: The freeze of family unification has to be seen as one instrument in a whole series of measures used to displace Palestinians from Jerusalem.

For ten years, the only way for a Palestinian couple, who is going through the process of family unification, has been to apply and reapply for a yearly permit.

A permit which did not allow, until a few months ago, its holder to work.

A permit which does not allow its holder to drive a car.

A permit which does not give its holder any social benefits, not even health insurance.

A permit which puts the legal status of the couple's children at risk.

The situation has huge negative psychological, economical and social effects on the affected families. These effects and the requirements of the Ministry of Interior pertaining to family unification applications, combined with very intransparent legal procedures in front of the different committees and limited remedies against decisions of the Ministry of Interior, lead already to the displacement of numerous Palestinians from Jerusalem.

The "Citizenship and Entry Into Israel Law" of 2003 which froze all family unification procedures is discriminatory - to say the least - and violates basic human rights of thousands of Palestinians in East Jerusalem and beyond. It further infringes International Law as well as International Humanitarian Law.

The family is recognized as the most natural and fundamental unit of society and therefore the right to marry and establish a family is especially protected in Human Rights Law. Where spouses are from different nationalities, states are obliged by International Law to deal with their requests for unification in a humane and expeditious manner.

However, in the case of Palestinian Jerusalemites, this is - as it was shown in this report - not the case.

In Jerusalem both, the applicants and their spouses are Palestinians, both living under occupation. The root cause of their problem is the different legal status incurred on them by Israel after the occupation. The laws and regulations that were enacted by the Israeli Knesset and the Ministry of the Interior over the years are the reason that it became very difficult for these couples to be able to live legally together.

For more than fifteen years, St. Yves has been dealing with the issue of family unification – before and after the enactment of the

"Citizenship and Entry into Israel Law" of 2003. St. Yves assisted hundreds of families in the long and difficult process to finally live together. But the Israeli system is a discriminatory system. Because of the discriminatory Israeli laws, for hundreds and thousands of families there is no legal possibility to come together.

Bishop Desmond Tutu says: "You don't choose your family. They are God's gift to you, as you are to them." St. Yves would like to add: therefore a family must not be divided.

The Society of St. Yves calls upon the international community to put pressure on the Israeli government and insist on the:

• **Revocation of the discriminatory "Citizenship and Entry Into Israel Law" of 2003.**

• **Facilitation of family unification for all citizens and permanent residents without discrimination.**

• **Recognition of the right to family and ensuring the widest possible protection of, and assistance to, the family.**

His Beatitude on the Israeli Demolition of Patriarchate Property

Latin Patriarchate of Jerusalem

Bulldozers of the Jerusalem Municipality, accompanied by Israeli Security forces, demolished the property on the Jerusalem-Hebron road, near the northern checkpoint number 300. This was a residential property of about 140 square meters, on which lived a family of 14 people.

The Patriarch's statement came during his visit to inspect the demolished home, in the company of Bishop William Shomali, Patriarchal Vicar of Jerusalem, and Bishop Boulos Marcuzzo of Nazareth, Father Hammam Khzouz, General Director of the Patriarchate and Father George Ayoub, Chancellor, and a number of priests as well as the director of the Patriarchate Endowment, lawyers and engineers, and consuls of foreign countries, including Italy, and Belgium, representatives of churches and institutions, and a crowd of journalists from both domestic and foreign news agencies.

In a press conference held at the site of the demolished home, the Patriarchate said "looking upon a painful and upsetting scene raises discontent and anger. There is no justification for the demolition, but when the municipality and the Israeli government enact demolitions and displace people from their homes, these practices increase hatred and endanger the future of peace. This land has belonged to the Latin Patriarchate since long before 1967. The Patriarchate possesses the official deed, and all legal paperwork proving ownership. Even worse, the legal tenants of the property, Mr. Salameh Abu Tarbush and his family, were taken by surprise by the demolition."

The Patriarch added "We are the rightful owners, and you will hear our voice before all governments worldwide, and we will bring suit in appropriate courts to amend this injustice, to restore justice and reconstruct this home. We have willpower and a spirit of belonging to this land of our ancestors, this sacred land which is home of our past, present and future"

The home's residents spoke about the displacement, which was carried out in the early hours of the morning rendering them suddenly homeless. Their living situation is now tragic, in the open without shelter. The Red Cross is providing them with tents and assistance. The lawyer of the Latin Patriarchate, Mr. Mazen Copti, confirmed the illegality of the demolition of this home and land declaring "We will take all legal measures against the municipality of Jerusalem the Israeli Ministry of the Interior to rebuild the house as it was."

The U.S. Bishops: Respect the Property of the Church

06 December 2013

Jerusalem - *The U.S. bishops took the field to protest the demolition of a house owned by the Latin Patriarchate of Jerusalem which took place on 28 October.*

The intervention took the form of an official letter addressed on November 26 by Richard E. Pates - American Bishop of the Diocese of Des Moines and President of the Committee on International Justice and Peace of the Catholic Bishops' Conference of the United States (USCCB) – to newly appointed Ron Dermer, Israeli Ambassador to the U.S.. "It is unpleasant" deplores Bishop Pates "that our first contact takes place in the context of protests".

In the letter, released by the official bodies of the Latin Patriarchate and sent to Fides Agency, Bishop Pates asked the diplomat to convey to the Israeli government the "strong objections" expressed by him as president of the body connected to the U.S.A. Episcopate about the demolition of the house where a family of 14 people lived, and now "are forced to live in tents".

In early November, the Latin Patriarch of Jerusalem, Fouad Twal, had visited the site of the demolition, defined by him on that occasion "an act of vandalism that violates international law". During his visit, the Patriarch added that "when the municipality and the Israeli government validate the destruction and move people from their homes, these practices feed hatred and undermine chances of a peaceful future". In the letter signed by Bishop Pates, the U.S.

Episcopate echoed the protests carried out by Patriarch Twal: "these actions", reads the letter, "violate human rights and contribute to impair efforts to find a solution to the Israeli-Palestinian conflict".

Bishop Pates also announced that next year he will lead a "pilgrimage of Bishops in Holy Land, during which we have the intention to pray for peace with Jewish and Muslim leaders. But efforts in favor of peace", the U.S. Bishop says "will be compromised if these actions continue ". The final request addressed to ambassador Dermer is "to convey our serious concern to your government and demand that the rights of Church property are respected and that everything is returned to the Church and to the family that was evicted".

By: Agenzia Fides

"Destroy Our Churches" not People's Homes, Lenten Letter Says

Jerusalem Patriarch's Bold Appeal to Israeli Army

February 27, 2001

JERUSALEM (ZENIT.org-FIDES) - The Latin Patriarch of Jerusalem has made a bold appeal to the Israeli army: "Destroy our churches if you must, but leave the people their homes."

It is one of the most striking passages in His Beatitude Michel Sabbah's Lenten Letter for 2001. In the letter he writes: "If you need, at all costs, some sort of collective punishment or ransom, we offer you our churches to destroy, in order to restore tranquility to innocent children and families."

Before writing the letter, the 67-year-old Latin Patriarch visited Palestinian parishes, communities and civil authorities. The letter addresses Christians, but in many parts speaks openly to Muslims and Jews.

The Patriarch refers to fighting in Gilo and Beit Jala, Jewish and Palestinian (mostly Christian) villages, respectively, used by both the army and militants as a shield for attacking the opposite side.

Patriarch Sabbah addresses the Israelis, and pleads: "Look at the Palestinian, Christian or Muslim, not as a terrorist, or as someone who wants to hate and kill. ... Remember, [in the past] you also cried out for freedom, with the same cry of the oppressed. ... What you term security measures are no more than a call for more violence. Restore the land to its rightful owners, restore their freedom."

The Patriarch's pleas are also addressed to the Palestinian militants, requesting them to "spare the homes of innocent civilians," and not to turn "tranquil homes into gunfire lines." Moreover, he urges Palestinians to remember the "difficult commandment, love your enemy. ... Love is not weakness or running away. It is seeing the face of God in every man, whether Jew or Arab. The Jew who keeps us prisoners, still bears the image and likeness of God."

The Patriarch wrote the letter after witnessing the people's living conditions: "roads closed, towns and villages in a state of siege, no work, constant bombing." The desperate situation is causing many Christians to abandon the area. "Brothers and sisters, do not leave your land," the Patriarch says. "Have patience. God wants you to believe in him and witness to his Son Jesus Christ here, in this land. Remain here in these Holy Places ... why let others build your future?"

Referring to the conflict as a "war imposed on us," Patriarch Sabbah calls Christians to acts of friendship and charity, in view of the growing poverty in the Occupied Territories: "We invite you all ... to share your bread with those who have none, either by inviting them to sit at your table, or by giving to Caritas or some other similar organization, the same amount you would spend on food for a day."

© Innovative Media Inc.

Jerusalem Church Chiefs Protest Against New Israeli Tax Move

By Arthur Hagopian - 13 Apr 2011 http://www.ekklesia.co.uk

Good Shepherd Parish as it sits in front of the Mount of Temptation, Jericho, Palestine.

The heads of Christian Churches in Jerusalem have expressed grave concern over renewed moves by the Israeli authorities to tax church buildings and properties.

While previous such moves have ended in failure, the Israelis have not tried hard to mask their intention to persist in their efforts to impose an arnona (property tax) on properties owned by the various churches, including those which have been vacant for some time.

In a statement issued on 13 April 2011, the Heads of Churches of the Holy City of Jerusalem, a loose conglomeration of the 13 Christian churches officially recognised by the Israeli state, warned of dire consequences that would ensue should Israel carry out its plans.

"Such imposition would constitute a radical departure from the consistent practice of every previous State to have governed any part of the Holy Land, including the Ottoman empire, the British Mandate, the Hashemite Kingdom and the State of Israel itself," the church leaders said.

"It would represent a significant worsening of the conditions of the Churches in the Holy Land. It would also be in direct contradiction of the mandate of the United Nations Organisation in General Assembly resolution 181, of 29 November, 1947, as it applied not only to Jerusalem but also to the two national states that it authorises to be established in the Holy Land," they warned.

The churches argued the Israeli move would be in contravention of the so-called "status quo" agreements promulgated in the 19th Century, which have governed relations between the churches and governments since Ottoman times. Under the terms of the status quo, the Ottomans pledged to exempt church properties from taxation, recognised their rights and granted them special privileges, in documents termed 'firmans'.

One Ottoman ruler, Sultan Chakmak, even went so far as to damn any "accursed [person] or son of accursed" who dared impugn on the rights and privileges of the Armenian church, in an edict engraved in a marble plaque that hangs at the entrance to the Convent of St James, seat of the Armenian Patriarchate of Jerusalem.

Subsequent administrators of the Holy Land, like the Jordanians, expressed their support of the status quo and adhered to its tenets.

The churches warned that "any erosion of the understanding of the status quo agreements between the State of Israel and Christian churches threatens the well-being of the Christian churches and their ability to continue the various ministries of pastoral care, education and health care which they provide."

They also complained that an arnona on Church properties would "contradict the solemn promises given to the Churches by successive Israeli governments, most notably confirmed in the wake of the June 1967 war" that saw Israel overrun Jerusalem and most of the West Bank.

The church statement minced no words in describing the Israeli move as "aggressive," expressing astonishment at the timing, in a hint at the unpredictable political disturbances spreading across the region.

"The Heads of Churches cannot understand how it could be in the interest of the State to take such aggressive action with regard to the Churches, especially at this time," it said.

It urged official relations to remain on a correct and friendly basis, confident that "such will indeed turn out to be the continuing choice of the government of Israel."

"The Heads of Churches believe this respect is essential for the ongoing health of the relationship between the three Abrahamaic faiths which exist in Israel as well as the relationship each has with the government of Israel," the statement said.

The churches are particularly concerned that the "abrupt imposition of unprecedented new taxation on the Christian Churches could only come at the expense of their ability to maintain their presence in the Holy Land and to continue their ministries of pastoral care, education, welfare and health.

Archdiocese appeals to the Israeli High Court on Tax moves

http://www.asianews.it/files/img/1454_suora gerusalemme %28150 x 100%29.jpg

Jerusalem (AsiaNews 2004) – The Archdiocese of Cologne, owner of various religious and social operations in Israel, has asked the Israel High Court of Justice to order the Israeli Government to declare its position on the question of tax exemptions for religious activities, as foreseen by the accord between the Holy See and Israel. A representative of the Archdiocese in Jerusalem lodged its appeal several days ago, in which it asks the Court to order the Israeli Government to express itself on two points: a) if it considers itself bound by the Fundamental Agreement signed with the Holy See (30 December 1993); and, b) if it is true that, by these accord, fiscal authorities are forbidden to demand the payment of back taxes. The High Court accepted the appeal and ordered the Government to reply within 30 days of September 3rd.

This appeal is the first of its kind, and is the culmination of a series of attempts made by the German diocese to obtain an answer from government authorities. Up to now, when various tax collectors have pursued ecclesiastical entities, they have declared themselves to be unaware of Vatican-Israel accords. The Foreign Ministry and other government departments have been refusing to commit themselves on the question.

Since 1993, there has been only one occasion in which obligations undertaken by the Israeli Government toward the Catholic Church were officially acknowledged: this was in a letter released by a top official of the Finance Ministry. This unprecedented acknowledgement has never been repeated since, despite the avalanche of letters and protests addressed to the Government by both top officials of the Catholic Church and by small convents and institutes run by nuns.

This question is being tracked with the utmost attention and concern by the Church at all levels, including the so-called "French hospital" of Jerusalem where the Sisters of Charity of Saint Vincent de Paul care for terminal patients. This hospital is a singular and much acclaimed institution in Israel. Yet, in these very days, the sisters are being targeted by tax officials who are demanding the settlement of new and exorbitant taxes, contrary to the obligations undertaken by the state in signing the Fundamental Agreement with the Vatican.

The hope in Church circles is that the powerful and influential German Archdiocese can win its case: such a victory would be a boon to poorer and needier institutions such as the Sisters of Charity hospital.

A Right to Education

"Dear young people, continue to strive through education to take your rightful place in society, despite the difficulties and handicaps that you have to face because of your refugee status. The Catholic Church is particularly happy to serve the noble cause of education through the extremely valuable work of Bethlehem University"

Saint John Paul II, Dheisheh Refugee camp, 2000

"Challenges of a Christian University in the Holy Land"

"Religious Freedom & Human Rights: Path to Peace in the Holy Land
- That All May Be Free"
The Catholic University of America, 9 September 2013
Brother Peter Bray, FSC, EdD, Vice Chancellor, Bethlehem University, Palestine

I feel honoured to have the opportunity to speak with you today about the only Catholic/Christian University in the Holy Land. In the short time I have I want to touch on three things:

1. The wider context in which Bethlehem University exists.

2. The situation in Palestine within that context.

3. How Bethlehem University is responding to the challenges it faces.

1. **Bethlehem University is in Bethlehem in Occupied Palestine in the Middle East.** It is situated in the region where three continents come together, where for thousands of years there has been a great mix of peoples, of religions and cultures. It has been a place characterised by diversity. Down through the centuries there have been attempts to squash that diversity through such episodes as the Crusades and later by Muslims in order to have a single entity. They all failed. In the course of the time I have been a Bethlehem University I have become increasingly aware of the extraordinary history the region

has had. What is so evident is the complexity of the region and the vast range of influences that impact on people and institutions in this region. It is in this complex context that Bethlehem University exists and this context is something that influences what we do. There has been a great diversity in the region as a result of all that has been part of its history and Bethlehem University needs to reflect that in what it does.

2. The situation in which Bethlehem University exists is the small town of Bethlehem south of Jerusalem. It is a town made up of Christians and Muslims with three refugee camps imbedded in it. It is a diverse mix and it is important to remember it is not a secular society. Religion is at the heart of the identity of the people. It is also a tribal society where membership is key and loyalty and support are expected and given.

This makes for some difficulties for Westerners to sometimes understand what is happening. It is so easy to generalise and make judgments which are based on wrong assumptions. In some cases, for instance, actions are interpreted as being persecution of Christians whereas they emerge from the fact that Christians are the smallest tribe, just as in other circumstances the smallest tribe is another Muslim tribe and the smallest tribe gets the raw end of the stick! This does not take away the fact that there are some extremists who do persecute Christians, but we need to be careful about interpreting everything from that perspective.

Religion is to do with the community one belongs to and, therefore, freedom of religion is to do with, not so much freedom of conscience, which is a top priority in the West, as with freedom of worship and the ability to gather with others from that community to worship. Freedom of religion is something that is important to Palestinians. The implications of the occupation are that so many Palestinians are not able to worship where they want and with whom they want. Recently a visitor from Washington came to Bethlehem University and wanted to speak with a group of students.

A group of about forty were assembled and in the course of the discussion it became clear that about a third of these students had never set eyes on the sea. It then became obvious that the Christians among these had never been able to get into Jerusalem to worship at the Holy Sepulchre and the Muslims had not been able to get to Al-Aqsa Mosque to worship there. This is one example of the stark reality of how religious freedom is lacking in the experience of these young people and the situation in which they exist.

3. Bethlehem University is responding to the challenges. Forty years ago this year Bethlehem University began when 112 students walked through the gates to begin the first registered university on the Palestine. The students who began and the groups since have been diverse made up of men and women, Muslims and Christians, students from Jerusalem, from Bethlehem, from Hebron, from Ramallah, and from villages, sons and daughters of professional people, shop keepers, craftspeople, farmers, street sweepers, day labourers, a diverse group. It has been the policy of Bethlehem University to continue with a diverse population of students because of the way experience of diversity can enrich them.

However, the reality of the last ten years has meant restrictions of movement for many students. The Wall has made it virtually impossible for us to have students from Ramallah and north of Jerusalem because of the checkpoints they would have to go through to get to campus. This has meant over recent years the areas we draw students from have been restricted to East Jerusalem, Bethlehem and Hebron. This is unfortunate because it limits the diversity that so enriches the experience of students.

There are some 3000 students on campus and of these 75 % are women and 25% men, 70% are Muslims and 30% Christians. In a country where around 1% of Palestinians are Christians, Bethlehem University is reaching out in a significant way to support Christians by having a student body made up of 30% Christians. In the midst of this we need to ask what it is that Bethlehem University is trying to do. Bethlehem University is unashamedly a Catholic University to which Muslims feel comfortable in coming. At the very heart of what Bethlehem University is seeking to do is the mission of Jesus. We make no apology for that nor do we try to water that down. When we look at what Jesus proclaimed his mission to be it was clear: "I have come that they may have life, life in all its fullness." That is what we want! To have students, faculty and staff all living life as fully as they can. What we are seeking to do, therefore, is provide the opportunity where people can do that.

We have structures and programmes that attempt to do that, but it is not always clear what is the best thing to do. However, it is clear what things are preventing people from living life to the full, so our mission is to work against all those things that are preventing people at Bethlehem University from living life to the full.

Hence, as an educational institution, we work against ignorance, we work against prejudice, we work against fear, we work against injustice, we work against isolation, we work against anything we can see that is closing people off and preventing our students from living life to the full. We are very conscious of the need we have to link back to the context I mentioned earlier and to provide the opportunity for the diversity that has been so important in the area to be a source of enriching their lives. We provide, therefore, opportunities when students can be exposed to that diversity.

Some of these opportunities are planned, are organised and part of our structure, like specific classes. We have a Religious Studies course in which they explore the nature of Christianity, Islam and Judaism and do that together. This is a new experience for them. In secondary school during religious studies the Muslims went off and studied the Koran and the Christians went off and studied the Bible. We require a mixture of students to sit together and study each of these religious traditions. This is an attempt to address the ignorance so many of them have about what the other believes. I have had Muslims say to me that they were surprised at what they learned about Christianity and did not realise some of the things Christians believed. Christians have reflected on what they learned about Islam in the same way. These structured opportunities help to enrich the diverse experience of students, but other, more important opportunities, arise from the environment we seek to provide. One of our goals is to provide an oasis of peace for these students so that they know when they walk onto campus that they are safe, that there are people there who care about them and want what is best for them. In that environment it is possible for students in their diversity, to engage with one another in an enriching way. In merely being beside one another in class, or on campus, or in the cafeteria, there is opportunity for them to grow to know one another.

Thus what Bethlehem University is doing is providing the opportunity for that diversity to be evident and to become enriching. Thus to see a young veiled Muslim women walking around the campus arm and arm with a young Christian woman clearly wearing a cross, reveals the degree to which this diversity is evident. Last week I saw a young veiled Muslim woman and a Catholic Nun engaged in deep conversation and obviously enjoying the opportunity to engage with one another. Diversity is at the heart of the enriching programme we offer. I have, I hope not a too naive expectation, that as a result of being in those Religious Studies classes together and being around one another, that our students develop an appreciation of each other and go back into their respective communities to help undermine some of the prejudices that exist there. Given all that, we work against whatever is preventing that diversity from being present such as the restrictions on movement of students. These restrictions are evident, for example, in trying to organise for students to go on pilgrimages.

Several times we have tried to take a group of Christian students to Galilee to visit the holy sites there. However, we could not get permits for a number of them to go and so the pilgrimage had to be cancelled.

At Christmas and Easter some Christians can get permits to go to Jerusalem. However, many of the families have the experience of only some members of the family getting permission. This means that going to worship in Jerusalem for those who have permits means the family is split. These restrictions are evident also in the experience of students who come from East Jerusalem to Bethlehem University. I was speaking with one young woman just before she graduated last year. She lived in East Jerusalem and I asked her what it was like living in East Jerusalem and coming to Bethlehem University. She thought for a while and then said the worst part was coming in the bus up to the checkpoint and wondering "This time, what is it going to be? Is a soldier going to get on the bus and just glance at their IDs? Is a soldier going to get on and take all the IDs and have the students sit there for half an hour, an hour or an hour and a half while they check them? Are the students going to be herded off the bus and made to stand in the sun while their IDs are being checked? Are they are going to be strip searched? Are they going to be individually interrogated?"

All of those things had happened to her during her four years at Bethlehem University. So as she is coming in the bus up to the checkpoint, she is wondering "This time what will it be?" Despite having to face that experience she came back to Bethlehem University each day!

It is that resilience, that determination, that courage that I find so inspiring among so many of our students. The restrictions on movement discourages others from coming. We struggle to get qualified faculty and staff prepared to come through the Wall to work at Bethlehem University.

A few years ago we had a senior administrator who lived in the Old City in Jerusalem and travelled to Bethlehem University each day. His house in the old city is only about seven kilometers from Bethlehem University. I have walked there a number of times. However, sometimes it would take him two hours to get home and in going through the checkpoint he would be subjected to interrogation and abuse. After having spent over twenty years at

Bethlehem University, he decided he did not want to continue to waste that time and endure the abuse anymore and now he has a job in the Old City. This meant Bethlehem University lost a valuable employee. Attracting new members and retaining present faculty and staff can be a challenge given the restrictions those working at Bethlehem University have to face. Bethlehem University has tried to address this in some way by what we call "growing our own" programme whereby we take graduates and arrange scholarships for them to go and get a masters degree on the condition they come back to teach at Bethlehem University.

The same applies to faculty who have master's degrees and are open to study for a doctorate. This is helping in some way to bring qualified people to Bethlehem University, but still deprives us of the diversity that would enrich us so much. It would be wonderful to have international professors coming for a semester or a year. Indeed to have international students enrolled would provide that diversity. However, there are limits on bringing in international professors and students because of visa restrictions, and this is another way in which the diversity is being affected. Yet in spite of these challenges, Bethlehem University is thriving and is on the cusp of the biggest development since it opened 40 years ago.

This development will provide further opportunities for students' lives to be enriched and for Bethlehem University to be deeply involved in serving the Palestinian people through education. What the future holds for them is unpredictable. However, the longer I am in Palestine the less optimistic I am about the possibility of peace. There seems just too many obstacles, too many engrained positions, too many agendas to lead to a solution. However, while I am not optimistic, I am hopeful and I think keeping hope alive is one of the real challenges Bethlehem University faces.

So where do I stand? I go back over 30 years to 1981. I come from New Zealand and in 1981 the South African Springbok rugby team came to New Zealand. It was a watershed time for New Zealand because it forced people to take a stand either in favour of the tour or opposed to it. I was deeply opposed to it because, with many other people, we felt welcoming the tour supported the apartheid system in South Africa. However, none of us at that time could see how Apartheid could end and the very thought that a black man sitting in a jail in South Africa would be the president of South Africa never entered our thinking. Yet it happened! I have friends in the North of Ireland and I can remember discussions about the impossibility of peace coming there. Yet it did! I have other friends in Germany and we had discussions about how East and West Germany might be one again, but could not see how the communist regime could end. Yet it did! Closer to my home in East Timor, again it seemed impossible that a resolution could be reached with Indonesia. Yet it was!

In each of these cases the solution was beyond how I could see it coming. That is the hope I hold onto. That somehow, beyond how I can see or understand, peace will come. And when it does come what Palestine is going to need are educated, resourceful, creative Palestinians who are going to create that future! That is why Bethlehem University is so important because it is helping to create that pool of people who are seeking to live life to the full, with a respect for others, enriched by diversity, continually looking for better ways to do things. It is these people who are going to build that future.

Shukran, Thank you

Bethlehem University Alumna Elected First Female Mayor of Bethlehem

www.Bethlehem.edu 2013

"I found hope at the heart of where my educational journey had begun at Bethlehem University, the beginning of my career and what would become a great stepping stone for my future."

Every Christmas, international focus is on Bethlehem, the place of Jesus' birth. This winter, Bethlehem is again in the spotlight, this time for electing its first female mayor, Ms. Vera Baboun. A graduate of Bethlehem University (class of '85), Ms. Vera has invested deeply in Bethlehem University – not only as a graduate but also as faculty.

As a former English faculty member at Bethlehem University, Ms. Vera's lectures were inspiring and memorable for her former students. Until her recent mayoral election victory, she continued her work in education, serving as the principal at a Catholic High School in neighboring Beit Sahour. Though she is now assuming mayoral duties, she continues to work toward her PhD. Highly regarded by students and colleagues alike, Ms. Vera is a great triumph for all Palestinian women and is indeed a positive role model for future generations, though she is unpretentious and unassuming.

"An optimistic character radiates hope and promise for many others to follow," Ms. Vera said. However, her success did not come without challenge, and she encountered a bumpy road and many detours to her success. Through her strong will and resilience, she managed to overcome what would have been impossible for many.

"My husband was imprisoned by the Israeli Authorities," Ms. Vera said. "I was left with five kids to look after, having just graduated from Bethlehem University and in a desperate state to feed my family, Ms. Vera Babounl found hope at the heart of where my educational journey had begun at Bethlehem University, the beginning of my career and what would become a great stepping stone for my future."

It was here at Bethlehem University, in the summer of 1985, when a young, ambitious Ms. Vera marched with confidence across the auditorium to collect her hard-earned degree in English literature. At the time, Dr. Violet Fasheh was the Dean of the newly established Faculty of Education, while Br. Thomas Scanlon was the Vice Chancellor of Bethlehem University. Then, in the early '90s, Ms. Vera returned to Bethlehem University, this time as an English lecturer. In addition to teaching the standard course material for English, Ms. Vera recognized the importance of integrating relevant and related topics, such as gender equality and human rights.

"If you want to create change, you have to start with yourself from within in order to create the change in others," Ms. Vera said. No stranger to creating change in one of the world's oldest religious cities, Ms. Vera will certainly face challenges, particularly during a time of political instability and a weak economy in Palestine. It will be a tough challenge for the new Mayor, but Ms. Vera and her team at Bethlehem Municipality will work persistently as this Holy City continues to shine.

Gaza Student Completes Her Bachelors Degree from Bethlehem University

www.Bethlehem.edu

11 January 2010:Bethlehem, Palestine - Bethlehem University officials traveled to Gaza on Sunday, 10 January to mark the occasion of Ms. Berlanty Azzam completing her semester courses, to encourage other students from Gaza who seek to pursue their education at Bethlehem University or other Palestinian universities in the West Bank, and to recognize the more than 430 other graduates of Bethlehem University from Gaza.

Brother Peter Bray, Vice Chancellor, the Papal Nuncio H.E. Archbishop Antonio Franco, Chancellor, Brother Joe, Vice Chancellor Emeritus, and Trappist Abbott Thomas traveled to Gaza for the 10am Mass at the Holy Family Church where they met Ms. Berlanty Azzam and her family and friends among the parishioners, as well as some of the other Bethlehem University students who await permission from the Israeli military authorities to come to Bethlehem to pursue their education at the Vatican-sponsored Bethlehem University.

"I never imagined that my graduation ceremony would be held in a Church in Gaza with no one from my classmates attending," said the exuberant 22-year-old Berlanty Azzam, "but I am so happy and grateful to my teachers and all of the friends of Bethlehem University who came forward to help me. I really worked hard and prayed for this moment and will do my best to help others who seek to study at my university!" Arriving in Gaza to present Berlanty with her certificate, Vice-Chancellor of the Bethlehem University Brother Peter Bray said "the University has a commitment to help Berlanty –

and all our students in good academic standing – to graduate and succeed in life."

H.E. Archbishop Antonio Franco, Papal Nuncio and the highest ranking representative of the Pope to Israeli and Palestine, also traveled all the way to Gaza to award Berlanty her degree in Business Administration and to celebrate Mass at Holy Family Church in Gaza.

Brother Joe, Vice-Chancellor Emeritus and Trappist Abbott Thomas Davis accompanied Brother Peter to Gaza for meetings with some of the more than 400 graduates of Bethlehem University from Gaza as well as some of the current Bethlehem University students who continue to await for permission from the Israeli military to study at Bethlehem University.

As reported in the Washington Post, CNN, BBC, America Magazine, The Chronicle of Higher Education, Maan News and other media, Berlanty's case drew high-level attention: including inquiries from the State Department of the United States, members of the US Congress, members of Parliaments and Ministers of Foreign Affairs from Ireland, the UK, New Zealand, the Netherlands, and Australia, as well as Vatican officials, Cardinals, and Bishops Conferences in Canada, the UK, the United States, and Germany.

The Israeli human rights legal group Gisha took on Berlanty's case, seeking a ruling from the Israeli High Court to overturn the Israeli army's decision to not allow Berlanty the right to return to Bethlehem for the final two months needed to complete her bachelors degree. All attempts to seek justice, however, resulted in the Israeli High Court refusing to instruct the Army to allow Berlanty to return to the West Bank. Noting that the 22-year old female student had no security or other charges against her, and that she had been living in Bethlehem and dutifully pursuing her education at Bethlehem University for nearly four years without incident, dismay was expressed by many, including the Gisha lawyers who brought her case to theIsraeli High Court.

"I really wanted to be among my colleagues on such a day," Berlanty said as she lit a candle and kneeled after the homily and the readings as peace overwhelmed the church. "I still don't know why I was taken from Bethlehem and moved to Gaza while being handcuffed and blindfolded." She continued, "I am sad because I was not able to graduate with my colleagues in Bethlehem, but I was able to challenge the occupation and today I am graduating from Bethlehem University," her eyes filled with tears of joy.

Timeline of Events for Berlanty Azzam and the Israeli military's interference in her education: Sept 2005: Berlanty enrolls at Bethlehem University as a first year student 28 Oct 2009: Berlanty blindfolded, handcuffed, and taken from Bethlehem to Gaza by Israeli military:

> 12 Nov 2009: Israeli High Court Hearing, Court orders Israeli Military to hold due process hearing

> 18 Nov 2009: Israeli Military Conducts an Administrative Hearing with Berlanty at Erez Crossing

> 30 Nov 2009: Israeli High Court Hearing, Court orders Israeli Military to submit 2005 permission

> 9 Dec 2009: Israeli High Court issues ruling: Berlanty cannot return to Bethlehem

> 10 Jan 2010: Berlanty Graduates in Gaza at Holy Family Church

Other students from Gaza have been accepted at Bethlehem University and still await permission from the Israeli military to come to Bethlehem for their university education. Pray for them and help to support our "Gaza Student Initiative" efforts. Please send your gift check made payable to "Bethlehem University" noting support for the "Gaza Student Initiative" to:

Brother Dominic Smith, FSC Bethlehem University - USA Development Office Hecker Center, Suite 330 3025 Fourth Street, NE Washington , DC 20017 - 1102 A tax receipt will be issued for all donations.Email: dominicsmithfsc@yahoo.com

A Graduation in Gaza

by Sami El-Yousef – CNEWA's regional director for Palestine and Israel. ONE magazine

The Holy Family School celebrates its 12th commencement ceremony. (photo: Sami El-Yousef)

In many reports and blogs on Gaza, the tone is often negative, reflecting the very difficult circumstances in Gaza — for instance, the gas shortage or the usual challenges associated with the blockade. But this time, I want to write about a very joyous celebration: the 12th commencement ceremony at the Holy Family School in Gaza. I was privileged to attend this along with his Beatitude Patriarch Fouad Twal.

This was no ordinary ceremony, as the 17 graduates — including three Christians — started their schooling in 2000, just as the second intifada was beginning. There has not been a stretch of quiet since they started their studies; they've had to contend with closures, travel restrictions, a blockade, a full-fledged war, violence and counter-violence, and swift and forceful Israeli air strikes. In short, these young men and women have not had a normal childhood or education. Yet, sitting there for the celebration, I couldn't help but marvel: it was a grand, festive event with speeches full of hope and big dreams, just like any other commencement ceremony anywhere else in the world. Despite the bleak political situation, the valedictorian was full of energy and hope that tomorrow will be a better day.

Between each speech, there was a performance by the school's Dabkeh team, featuring traditional Palestinian dance. It was the largest I have ever seen, with some 50 members of all ages. The team was fully synchronized and disciplined. It was a great joy to watch. These students were proud to be performing for us all — as if they were passing on a message that, despite all the difficulties of these past 12 years, they learned how to have fun and how to keep the culture alive.

Congratulations to the class of 2012! May the future be kinder to you than the past.

Gaza Christian schools "back to normal"

Five Christian schools (including three Catholic schools) would have closed their doors for the academic year if the Hamas government followed a law banning mixed schools in the Gaza Strip. For the time being, the school year started without a problem.

Meeting of the Directors of the Latin schools

In April, Hamas (in power in Gaza since 2007) intended to implement legislation codifying the separation of sexes in schools and prohibiting a man to teach girls, and a woman to teach boys older than 9 years, according to Islamic law. However, only the Christian schools (as well as those held by the UN) have mixed classes, with a student population 3,500. This is good news for Father Faysal Hijazeen, director of the Latin Patriarchate schools in Israel and Palestine, who confirms that "back to school went well." He added that "all the students and teachers of the Christian Schools in Gaza have gone back to classes without changing any of the practices and routines of the previous years. Fr. Hijazeen hopes that "the situation will remain as it is."

In October Father Hijazen, Father Humam Khzouz, General Administrator of the Latin Patriarchate, will meet with the Minister of Education in Gaza. To date, the Ministry of Education requested increasing the number of students and teachers, male and female. Last April, Father Faysal said that "it will be a big problem to comply with the decision of Hamas to ban mixed schools in Gaza. We do not have the space and we do not have the money to divide our schools. In addition to finding additional spaces, schools should in this case hire and pay more teachers and staff."

Christophe Lafontaine, EOHSJ Newsletter 26, Oct. 2013
(www.lpj.org)

Catholic Schools Cancel Strike, Israeli Government Talks of 'Take Over'

Monday, 01 September 2014

Jerusalem - The past two years have been difficult for Catholic schools in Israel, particularly from the financial point of view: the Education Ministry has repeatedly reduced both subsidies to schools and grants to families. This caused considerable deficit for several schools last year. The Israeli authorities say Catholic schools there should become 'state' schools: this would allow them to survive but at the high price of loss of specificity and identity. The Catholic community in the Holy Land considers the government position discriminatory and unacceptable.

Fides learned from the Latin Patriarchate of Jerusalem that the Office for Catholic Schools had made many attempts at various levels to organize meetings and find a solution. The Assembly of the Catholic Ordinaries of the Holy Land sent several letters to the Israeli Ministry of Education requesting a meeting, but received no reply in the past two years.

Terra Sancta school, Jericho

This led to the announcement of a strike for Monday 1st September, first day of school after Summer holidays: an action decided unanimously by the local College of Headmasters, known as 'G 14' and chaired by Fr. Abdelmassih Fahim, in the presence of Bishop Boulos Marcuzzo.

The strike aimed to stigmatise silence on the part of the Israeli government, deaf to all forms of solicitation to tackle the problem and the present situation of difficulty and unease for Catholic schools in the Holy Land.

The announcement of the strike brought an immediate reaction from the Ministry of Education which gave a date for a meeting to discuss the difficulties and find solutions. Following this positive attitude, the G14 said it was ready to listen and that the strike was cancelled. The situation for Catholic schools in Israel is highly precarious and many are in danger of closing.

By: Agenzia Fides

Religious Freedom

"The Pope asks the faithful have free access to Holy Places"

Post-Synodal Apostolic Exhortation 2012

Religious Freedom

PATRIARCHS AND HEADS
OF LOCAL CHURCHES IN JERUSALEM

May 13, 2013

Statement concerning Israeli Police Measures on Holy Saturday

Fr. Arsanios of the Coptic Church, being prevented from entering the Holy Sepulchre by Israeli Police. (Eretz Zen)

We, the Heads of Churches in Jerusalem, watched with sorrowful hearts the horrific scenes of the brutal treatment of our clergy, people, and pilgrims in the Old City of Jerusalem during Holy Saturday last week. A day of joy and celebration was turned to great sorrow and pain for some of our faithful because they were ill-treated by some Israeli policemen who were present around the gates of the Old City and passages that lead to the Holy Sepulcher.

We understand the necessity and the importance of the presence of security forces to ensure order and stability, and for organizing the celebration of the Holy Fire at the Church of the Resurrection. Yet, it is not acceptable that under pretext of security and order, our clergy and people are indiscriminately and brutally beaten, and prevented from entering their churches, monasteries and convents.

We urge the Israeli authorities especially the Ministry of Interior and the police department in Jerusalem, to seriously consider our complaints, to hold responsibility and to condemn all acts of violence against our faithful and the clergy who were ill-treated by the police. We deplore that every year, the police measures are becoming tougher, and we expect that these accidents will not be repeated and the police should be more sensitive and respectful if they seek to protect and serve.

We also denounce all those who are blaming the churches and holding them responsible of the Israeli measures during Holy Week celebrations. On the contrary, the Heads of churches in Jerusalem condemn all of these measures and violations of Christians' rights to worship in their churches and Holy Sites. Therefore, we condemn all measures of closing the Old City and urge the Israeli authorities to allow full access to the Holy sites during Holy Week of both Church Calendars.

The Heads of Churches of Jerusalem

Christian High Holy Days

Sami El-Yousef, a native of Jerusalem. Sami is CNEWA's regional director for Palestine and Israel.

Police limit access to the courtyard of the Holy Sepulchre, where thousands typically greet the procession. (photo: CNEWA, Jerusalem)

Childhood dreams. I was 14 years old when my father decided I was ready to participate in the Holy Fire celebration on Holy Saturday, according to the Greek Orthodox tradition.

I belong to one of the 13 oldest Christian families in Jerusalem. Hundreds of years ago, locals commemorated these early Christians by placing in the Church of the Holy Sepulchre 13 banners, each named after one of these families. The only privilege the families' descendants enjoy is that once a year, on Holy Saturday, a representative from each family carries the banner in a procession that marches around Christ's tomb in the Church of the Holy Sepulchre three times.

After the procession, the Greek Orthodox patriarch enters the sealed tomb where the Miracle of the Holy Fire occurs, symbolizing the flame of the Resurrection. The fire is then passed out to the waiting crowds through a small window in the outer chamber of the edicule, which enshrines the tomb. Within seconds, the whole church lights up. This must be the most amazing surge of faith I experience throughout year. At that precise moment, I feel renewed as a Christian and prepared to face the many challenges we Arab Christians confront daily in the Holy Land. Since my first experience, I have never missed this amazing celebration except when I was out of the country.

Recent trends. Every year, as Easter approaches, we begin discussing who will represent our family on Holy Saturday. Though I must admit that, in recent years, with so many of us emigrating from the Holy Land, selecting our representative has become less of a problem. The number of adults still around who can carry the heavy banner has dwindled to a handful. As a matter of fact, about half of those 13 families have no one left in the Holy Land. For the last few years, three of my relatives have joined me in carrying the banners representing these families — an honor we deeply cherish.

These days, the discussion has shifted in my family from "who will carry the banner" to "who can even access the Church of the Holy Sepulchre." For the past few years, Israeli authorities have closed the Old City and the area around the Church of the Holy Sepulchre during Holy Week, preventing local Christian and pilgrims from attending the Holy Fire celebration.

My 88-year-old father remembers when Jordan controlled East Jerusalem. During Holy Week, fleets of buses packed with pilgrims from Lebanon, Syria, Egypt and Iraq would park along the road to Jericho. The crowds of pilgrims would walk to the celebration in the Old City. Their numbers far exceeded today's turnout at Easter time, yet the Old City never closed its gates and the streets inside were never blocked. Access was open to all.

A couple of years ago, Israeli authorities attempted to impose a permit system limiting the number of people who could attend the Holy Fire celebration. Incensed, local Christians demanded the government respect the church's centuries-old Status Quo, which prohibits any restrictions on the faithful visiting the church. After all, pilgrims naturally want to get as close as possible to Christianity's birthplace, especially during Holy Week.

Detained at St. Jacob's. This year, despite outcry from church leaders, members of civil society and the Christian community at large, Israeli authorities made it next to impossible to enter the Old City on Holy Saturday. In the early morning hours, police set up roadblocks at all the Old City's gates and dozens of manned checkpoints along the streets and alleyways leading to the church.

Religious Freedom

Authorities cooperated with church leaders only to the extent of allowing a limited number of local Christians access to the Church of the Holy Sepulchre, provided that police escort them. Israeli authorities also detained a small group of locals at Saint Jacob's Orthodox Church from early morning until just 15 minutes before the Holy Fire celebration began.

Since I live in the Old City, it was very strange to be escorted by Israeli police officers to my church. I felt ashamed to have capitulated to such treatment, but regretfully that was the only way to get to my destination. It was even stranger to witness St. Jacob's Church — my parish — transformed into a holding cell, a detention center if you will, for hours.

Though the group detained in the church numbered no more than 70, many panicked when they realized that its two doors were locked shut from the outside by Israeli police. Despite our loud cries from inside and numerous phone calls, the police refused to let us out. My frightened cousin asked a church elder and trustee what would happen if a fire broke out. Not sure himself, the wise man could only tell us to keep our faith.

Finally, St. Jacob's priest and the mukhtar were released, then the rest of us. We hurriedly made our way to the Christian Quarter to catch up with a troop of Boy Scouts and prominent members of the local community, who were waiting for us to begin the procession to the Church of the Holy Sepulchre.

Traditionally, the city allows 30 minutes for the Holy Saturday procession to march from the Christian Quarter to the Church of the Holy Sepulchre. This year it was reduced to 15 minutes. Who knows what next year will bring given recent trends.

Surprises. When the Boy Scouts, who led the procession, started playing the drums, the eager crowd began pushing and prodding one another along, in their usual way, from the Christian Quarter to the Holy Sepulchre. The Status Quo calls for us to be at the church's main entrance at precisely 12:30 p.m. For close to 30 years of my life, I participated in this celebration, and we never missed the deadline.

When we arrived in the church's courtyard, to our surprise, no one was there to welcome us but a long line of Israeli police officers. Normally, thousands of locals and pilgrims greet us in the courtyard. Our procession's leader alerted us that our scheduled time was fast approaching, and we had to advance to the church entrance to make room for similar processions from other Christian communities arriving in the courtyard behind us.

Once inside the church, we were surprised a second time to be welcomed by only a few worshipers. For as long as I can remember, the church was always filled to capacity, packed with hundreds if not thousands of pilgrims and tourists on Holy Saturday. This year, Israeli authorities prohibited entry to pilgrims so police could access it freely and easily. Has the formula changed? Is the church for worshipers or for the 1,500 police officers (according to Israeli police spokesman Shmuel Ben-Ruby) on the premises that day?

Police barricade the roof of the Holy Sepulchre, where thousands typically gather to receive the Holy Fire. (photo: CNEWA, Jerusalem)

What a strange world we live in. Instead of faithful pilgrims, armed police officers, with guns in plain sight on their waists, welcomed us inside the church on Holy Saturday. Where else on earth do hundreds of armed police officers patrol the inside of a church other than here in the Old City — the holiest of places for Christianity? What an ugly sight indeed.

Once the last of the procession cleared the threshold of the church's entrance, participants took their designated places, right outside the tomb adjacent to the small window, through which the Holy Fire would be handed to them about an hour later. For our part, the representatives of the 13 families rushed to the storage area to bring out the banners. As each of us held our respective banners, we proudly lined up and readied to lead the small procession around Christ's tomb. Upon the patriarch's signal, the 13 of us carrying the banners began to proceed around the tomb, followed by the choir from St. Jacob's Church, clergy and, lastly, the patriarch.

After the procession finished its third turn around the tomb, all lights in the church were shut off and the patriarch entered the sealed tomb. A few minutes later, he emerged holding the Holy Fire.

The mystified worshipers passed the fire from one to the other. In those moments, it seemed as though the skies opened up.It was a breathtaking experience. The church's bells were rung to announcethe arrival of the Holy Fire. The participants chanted as they passed the fire and hurriedly carried it to the roof of the Holy Sepulchre, which is the site of a Greek Orthodox monastery.

We encountered our third harsh surprise when we reached the church's roof. For centuries, thousands of Christians from Jerusalem, the Galilee, the West Bank and Gaza gathered on the roof to witness and receive the Holy Fire. They then would march through the streets and alleyways in the Christian Quarter with the fire in hand. This year, there was no enthusiastic crowd of faithful to greet us. In fact, the vast roof was all but empty apart from police barricades and police officers, who directed us immediately off the roof and out of the Greek Orthodox Convent.

Indeed, this year's Holy Fire celebration proved a strange one. First, roadblocks prohibited pilgrims from accessing the Old City and the Church of the Holy Sepulchre. Then, our procession arrived at an empty courtyard, entered a nearly empty church and, finally, ascended onto an empty roof. What was gained in making it so difficult for us Christians in the Holy Land to practice our faith?

Happy ending? There was, however, a happy ending. Once we arrived in the Christian Quarter, carrying the Holy Fire, the Israeli police withdrew and left us alone. At that moment, a festive feeling came over all of us there.

But what about the thousands of local Christians from the Galilee, West Bank, Gaza and even Jerusalem whom Israeli authorities impeded from joining us in this most holy celebration? I am sure they nonetheless celebrated Holy Saturday in their churches and within their communities. I am also sure it was not the same for them — unable to celebrate in Jerusalem as they have for generations — and to share with us the high point of the Easter holiday. It certainly was not the same for us. We missed them and truly hope they will be with us next year. The celebration will never be the same without our sisters and brothers in the faith.

Lessons to learn. The various authorities responsible for this year's excessive security measures have many lessons to learn.

Let the pilgrims back in the Old City on Holy Saturday. Rather than 1,500 police officers inside the Church of the Holy Sepulchre, let the pilgrims who come from near and far return to pray and witness the mystery of the Resurrection.

Instead of empty space in the church that marks the site of Jesus' death and resurrection, let it fill up to capacity again. Instead of an empty courtyard and roof, let the thousands of local Christians welcome us there again.

Facilitate their access, do not hinder it. Remove roadblocks and checkpoints and remember: Thousands upon thousands of local Christians and pilgrims have celebrated Holy Week in the Old City for centuries and we have always managed.

I fully understand concerns about crowd control, public safety and maintaining law and order, but there are other ways to do the job without infringing on the rights of Christians and, more important, treating us with dignity. After all, we come to pray.

Final thoughts. Did I feel renewed as a Christian this year, despite all the difficulties, and prepared to face the challenges I confront as an Arab Christian in the Holy Land on a daily basis? You bet I did. Otherwise, I would not be a true Christian. My only hope is that all the others did as well.

Finally, I look forward to the day when my youngest son, Michael, grows strong enough to carry the banner, and I can pass onto him the honor of carrying it on Holy Saturday. My father passed the honor onto me, and I have already passed it onto my eldest son, Rami. When the days come that I no longer carry the banner, but my sons do so in my place, I will know I have done what I could to keep the tradition and faith alive. Maybe peace will have prevailed in the Holy Land and the celebration will return to how it should be — free.

Visas for the Clergy

Several years ago and in accordance with the Vatican Israel Agreement priests, ministers, pastors and members of religious congregations both men and women of all Christian denominations were granted long term multiple entry visas, at certain occasions, those visas granted also social rights, such as health insurance and other allowances.

At a certain point, the ministry of religious affairs was dismantled, and the issues of the Christian clergy was moved under the authority of the Ministry of Interior. At about the same time as the Family Reunification Laws and Regulations began to assume more draconian limitations so also did the visa requirements for, in particular, Arabic speaking clergy of all Christian denominations.

But the Christian Community of the Holy Land is already too depleted to be self sustaining in vocations to the priesthood and the religious life. Therefore recruiting by necessity must take place in Arab speaking neighboring countries since the community that will ultimately be served is an Arabic speaking community.

It is difficult to avoid the conclusion gleaned from scores of cases that this visa system is a direct attack on the Arabic speaking Church and the Arabic speaking Christian Community. The Church holds the community together more than any other institution. Taking away native Arabic speakers from an Arabic community is destroying the relationship of trust and love and cultural understanding between the people and their Church. The impact we have been seeing for years in the steady emigration of Christians from the Holy Land.

The legal framework

The complexity and depth of the situation cannot be stated summarily. Religious visas are categorized into two types: A2 and A3

Religious Sponsored Visas. The A2 visa is a visa specific to students and covers those studying in the Minor Seminary and the (major) Seminary for studies for the priesthood. It also covers Postulants and Novices in religious orders of both men and women. This visa poses particular problems and is also subdivided by age and country of origin. The visa applies to students under 18 years of age and over 18 years of age, from Arabic speaking countries and from all other countries. All students from non Arabic speaking countries are NOT subject to one year single entry visas and may come and go as they please for the duration of the visa. Arabic speaking students are issued only one year single entry visas and must renew their visa abroad before returning and this process can take from four to eight weeks.

A number of factors are pertinent and critically important here:

- The Christian Community of the Holy Land is already too depleted to be self sustaining in vocations to the priesthood and the religious life.

- Recruiting by necessity must take place in Arab speaking countries since the community that will ultimately be served is an Arabic speaking community.

- Minor Seminary students range in age from 12 years to 18 years old.

- The policy of the Minor Seminary is to encourage a long period of "discernment" so that the young man can experience both the vocation to the religious life and also continue the vital and formative relationship with his family and thus frequent home visits were encouraged.

- The same is true for the religious orders and the recruitment and nurturing of Postulants in particular, both men and women.

- The Academic Year is some nine months in duration and the three months at home were divided into four or five home visits. But with each home visit now entailing a minimum of four to six weeks away due to visa applications which can only be made outside Israel or the Occupied Territories, the old four terms of the academic year is no longer tenable at all.

The **A2 student visa** also covers those studying in the (major) Seminary (and Novices in the Religious Orders of men and women) who have now committed to studies for the priesthood and the religious life. These students are subject to the same visa regulations as described above and because they are no longer minors (under 18 years of age), they are also subjected to rigorous and intensive "Security" checks which not only affect them but also their families and relatives. Before they are granted a new visa to return to the Holy Land **they are obliged to submit a comprehensive list of the names, addresses, telephones, mobile phones and Email addresses of all family members and friends**.

The results in the end are very similar with the academic year left in a shambles and fewer and fewer young men and women and their families remaining willing to make the sacrifices necessary to assist their children in reaching ordination or final profession.

The A3 Religious Sponsored Visa covers all ordained or professed religious and treatment under the visa also depends on age and country of origin. For priests and religious from non Arabic speaking countries there are few problems of multiple entry / exit visas and for the most part they may come and go as they please or their superiors direct.

Arabic speaking priests and religious are subject to the same requirements as those stated above for the A2 Student Visa and of course the consequences are doubly difficult since mature age, committed religious are more often than not in a position of responsibility for pastoral care activities. Thus they and their families and friends are submitted to stringent, discretionary and often arbitrary "Security" checks while the priest or religious is forced into prolonged periods of absence from pastoral care duties which causes inconvenience and often hurt and injury to parishioners, orphans, students or the elderly and infirm under the care of their pastoral duties and responsibilities

Society of St. Yves

Christian Relations in the Holy Land

"Christians are ideally placed as bridge builders in a land associated with conflict. They share the Old Testament with Jewish people. They share the culture, language and national aspirations with the Islamic peoples of the Holy Land. They also act as a conduit between the Churches and culture of the East and West. They provide a buffer between the growth of both Jewish and Islamic fundamentalism in the region. They are the "Living Stones."

Fr. Firas Arideh, Catholic Priest, Holy Land, 2012

Christian/Christian Relations - The Jerusalem Declaration on Christian Zionism

Religious Leaders' Statement on Christian Zionism

Latin Patriarch Emeritus Michel Sabbah

"Blessed are the peacemakers for they shall be called the children of God." (Matthew 5:9)

Christian Zionism is a modern theological and political movement that embraces the most extreme ideological positions of Zionism, thereby becoming detrimental to a just peace within Palestine and Israel.

The Christian Zionist program provides a worldview where the Gospel is identified with the ideology of empire, colonialism and militarism. In its extreme form, it laces an emphasis on apocalyptic events leading to the end of history rather than living Christ's love and justice today.

We categorically reject Christian Zionist doctrines as false teaching that corrupts the biblical message of love, justice and reconciliation.

We further reject the contemporary alliance of Christian Zionist leaders and organizations with elements in the governments of Israel and the United States that are presently imposing their unilateral preemptive borders and domination over Palestine.

This inevitably leads to unending cycles of violence that undermine the security of all peoples of the Middle East and the rest of the world.

We reject the teachings of Christian Zionism that facilitate and support these policies as they advance racial exclusivity and perpetual war rather than the gospel of universal love, redemption and reconciliation taught by Jesus Christ.

Rather than condemn the world to the doom of Armageddon we call upon everyone to liberate themselves from the ideologies of militarism and occupation. Instead, let them pursue the healing of the nations!

We call upon Christians in Churches on every continent to pray for the Palestinian and Israeli people, both of whom are suffering as victims of occupation and militarism. These discriminative actions are turning Palestine into impoverished ghettos surrounded by exclusive Israeli settlements.

The establishment of the illegal settlements and the construction of the Separation Wall on confiscated Palestinian land undermine the viability of a Palestinian state as well as peace and security in the entire region. We call upon all Churches that remain silent, to break their silence and speak for reconciliation with justice in the Holy Land. Therefore, we commit ourselves to the following principles as an alternative way:

We affirm that all people are created in the image of God. In turn they are called to honor the dignity of every human being and to respect their inalienable rights.

We affirm that Israelis and Palestinians are capable of living together within peace, justice and security.

We affirm that Palestinians are one people, both Muslim and Christian. We reject all attempts to subvert and fragment their unity.

We call upon all people to reject the narrow world view of Christian Zionism and other ideologies that privilege one people at the expense of others.

We are committed to non-violent resistance as the most effective means to end the illegal occupation in order to attain a just and lasting peace. With urgency we warn that Christian Zionism and its alliances are justifying colonization, apartheid and empire-building.

God demands that justice be done. No enduring peace, security or reconciliation is possible without the foundation of justice. The demands of justice will not disappear. The struggle for justice must be pursued diligently and persistently but without violence.

"What does the Lord require of you: To act justly, to love mercy, and to walk humbly with your God." (Micah 6:8)

This is where we take our stand. We stand for justice. We can do no other. Justice alone guarantees a peace that will lead to reconciliation with a life of security and prosperity for all the peoples of our land. By standing on the side of justice, we open ourselves to the work of peace -- and working for peace makes us children of God.

"God was reconciling the world to himself in Christ, not counting men's sins against them. And he has committed to us the message of reconciliation." (2 Corinthians 5:19)

Patriarch Michel Sabbah
Latin Patriarchate, Jerusalem

Archbishop Swerios Malki Mourad,
Syrian Orthodox Patriarchate, Jerusalem

Bishop Riah Abu El-Assal,
Episcopal Church of Jerusalem and the Middle East

Bishop Munib Younan,
Evangelical Lutheran Church in Jordan and the Holy Land

Christian-Jewish Relations in the Context of Israel-Palestine

by Fr. David Neuhaus, Latin Patriarchal Vicar for Hebrew Speaking Catholics in Israel and Coordinator of the Pastoral among Migrants. He is a member of the Society of Jesus and teaches Scripture at the Seminary of the Latin Patriarchate of Jerusalem and at Bethlehem University.

Perspectives on Christian-Jewish relations in Israel/Palestine in particular and in the Middle East in general are clearly distinguishable from perspectives that are current in Europe and North America. From the European and North American perspective, Jews and Christians have been in a fruitful and passionate dialogue for the past six decades, following a fundamental rethinking of the relationship with Jews and Judaism in the Western Churches. In fact, a deep dialogue has developed between Western Christians and their Jewish neighbors. This dialogue has been powered by two strong motors. One is the awakened sense of contrition among Christians with regard to the tragic fate of the Jews during periods when anti-Judaism and anti-Semitism dominated, culminating in the catastrophe of the Shoah (Holocaust). The other is the embrace of the Biblical and, by extension, the Jewish heritage of the Church and at its center the fact that Jesus, his disciples and the early Church are part of a Jewish world that has bequeathed to us a rich shared heritage, most importantly the Old Testament.

Clearly, the context, and thus the perspectives in Israel/Palestine and in the Middle East are quite different.

In the Middle East today, Jews are not generally perceived as victims of marginalization and persecution but rather as the face of a problematic political reality in the Middle East in the form of the State of Israel and its occupation of Palestinian lands. Arab Christians, and Palestinian Christians in particular, challenge those engaged in the European and North American Jewish-Christian dialogue, asking whether a sense of guilt for the iniquity of anti-Semitism has not promoted an unhealthy dialogue where some Christians seek to assuage this sense of guilt by naively approving anything Jews say or do. This is particularly dramatic when Christians side with the political claims of the State of Israel and ignore Palestinians, their suffering and their legitimate demands for justice. Furthermore, the Old Testament, rather than being held up as "a shared heritage", provokes concern, particularly with regard to texts about election, promise and land. Many Middle East Christians fear fundamentalist exploitation of these texts in the conflict between Arabs and Jews over Israel/Palestine.

I would like to underline five characteristics of the particular context for Christian-Jewish relations in Israel/Palestine and by extension in the Middle East in contrast to the European context:

Not part of the Christian world

Contemporary dialogue between Jews and Christians has focused almost exclusively on historical relations between Jews and Christians in the lands where Christians are the majority and where they have defined culture, society and power relations. In relation to these lands, Christians have realized that certain modalities of thought, action and political practice marginalized and even excluded Jews, often accused of being outsiders because of their refusal of the Christian faith and their adherence to religious practice other than Christianity. Middle Eastern society and politics are not derived from this same Christian tradition. On the contrary, the modern Middle East is formed in the shadow of the creation of a Jewish state with a Jewish majority in 1948, perceived by many Middle Easterners and by Palestinians in particular as the last remnant of a colonial domination that ignores the aspirations of the indigenous population.

The presence of Islam

Islam is the dominant religion in historical Palestine and the Middle East and Muslims are the majority in all of the countries in the Middle East today (except for Israel). The Christian Arab and the Muslim Arab, whatever their religious differences might be, live in one society, speak one language, share one culture and experience one socio-political reality. Thus, dialogue with Muslims is a priority for Middle East Christians in a way that is not self-evident in interreligious dialogue in Europe. Dialogue with Jews, in fact, almost always becomes a trialogue within the Middle East context because Muslims cannot be ignored.

The reversal of power relations

The teaching of many Western Churches, profoundly cognizant of the European and North American context, is extremely sensitive to the marginalized and vulnerable status of the Jews in the history of the West. However, Middle East Christians reflect on Christian-Jewish relations from the experience of the sovereignty of a powerful Jewish polity - Israel. Never before in history have Christians experienced Jewish sovereignty (this having been established in 1948 with the creation of the State of Israel). For many Middle East Christians, the Jew is often, first and foremost, a soldier, a policeman or a settler. Whereas Western Christians engage with Jews as a minority, marginalized and often traumatized, Palestinian Christians are in a situation where power relations are reversed. They do not feel responsible for the fate of Jews in Europe; on the contrary they often sense that they themselves are the victims of that very same history, having lost their homeland when the State of Israel was established.

The Israel-Palestine conflict as definitive

Whereas from the European and North American perspective, the watershed in Christian-Jewish relations was the Shoah, which provoked an awakening to a certain teaching of contempt for Jews in Christian circles, from the Middle East perspective, the question of Palestine is at the center of relations with Jews. Whereas dialogue from the Western perspective often includes a focus on the struggle against anti-Judaism and anti-Semitism, the focus on justice and peace is an essential element of any prospective dialogue between Christians and Jews within the Middle East context.

The place of the Bible

The shared Biblical heritage is a fundamental principle in the decades of Christian-Jewish dialogue that has flourished over the past century. However, the experience of the shared Biblical heritage within the context of Israel/Palestine is not without its ambiguities. The Bible has been used as a foundational text when it comes to establishing a contemporary Jewish claim to the land that Palestinians see as theirs. Zionism, the ideology of Jewish nationalism, often reads the Bible as a legal, historical or even divinely revealed title deed to the land. For many Middle East Christians, a major problem is the use of the Bible to dispossess Palestinians and legitimate injustice. This is particularly evident in certain forms of Christian Zionism that offer Biblical justifications for the dispossession of the Palestinians and hostility towards Muslims.

Conclusion

Whereas Christians and Jews frequent one another in Europe and North America, Jews are no longer present in the majority of the Middle East countries, where they had once constituted vibrant communities before 1948. Only in Israel/Palestine are there substantial communities of both Christians and Jews today. Here we might suggest some practical initiatives to promote dialogue between Jews and Christians within the context of Israel/Palestine:

1. Encourage a dialogue of daily life focused on the concrete conditions of life in this land called holy. Jews and Christians together with Muslims are called to develop a shared commitment to justice and peace for all inhabitants of the Holy Land. They do come together in the NGOs that promote shared values but often the religious and spiritual elements of the relationships established are ignored. Justice, peace, freedom, reconciliation, pardon, respect

for human life and human rights are all concepts that can and must be rooted in the spiritual traditions that are rooted in the Holy Land. Religious discourse should not be left to fanatics and fundamentalists.

2. Jews and Christians must begin to study their shared textual heritage, the literature of the Old Testament, together. Joint study can throw light on the meaning of the religious text and its consequences in the here and now. Challenging violent, exclusivist and discriminatory interpretations of sacred texts is an important part of educating for justice and peace.

3. Jews, Christians and Muslims are invited to recover a memory of a time when Jews lived integrated in the Middle East. In fact, before 1948, Jewish Arabs were as significant a part of the Middle East as Christian Arabs. Traces of this Jewish presence include the contributions of prominent Jewish figures within Arab culture whether in the medieval period (eg. Saad bin Yusuf al-Fayoumi known as Saadia Gaon, great biblical commentator and translator of the Bible into Arabic) or the philosopher Moussa bin Maymoun (Maimonides) or in modern times (eg. musicians like Leyla Mourad, Daoud Housni and Feirouz al-Halabiyyah). Sadly, the once illustrious Jewish communities of Iraq, Egypt, Syria and Lebanon have all but disappeared whereas those of Iran, Turkey and Yemen have been dramatically reduced, yet another victim of the conflict that has plagued the Middle East since 1948.

4. Religious people are called to lives of faith and hope. What more hopeful sign can there be than religious people in understanding and acceptance, speaking a language of mutual respect and esteem rather than the language of contempt that dominates much of the political discourse in Israel/Palestine today. Prophetic discourse must be appropriated afresh so that "God-talk" reminds all human creatures of their fundamental duty to honor one another as created in the image and likeness of God. This prophetic discourse must point out the iniquity of human sinfulness in the dispossession, repression, discrimination and violence that surrounds us and open up the human imagination to the possibility of a society where men and women recognize one another as belonging to one family.

PATRIARCHS AND HEADS
OF LOCAL CHURCHES IN JERUSALEM

Are Christians being Persecuted in the Middle East?

Persecution! In many parts of the Western world, this word is people's lips. It is said that Christians are being persecuted in the Middle East today! However, what is really happening? How should we speak in truth and integrity as Christians and as Church about the suffering and violence that are going on in the region?

There is no doubt that the recent upheavals in the Middle East, initially called the Arab Spring, have opened the way for extremist groups and forces that, in the name of a political interpretation of Islam, are wreaking havoc in many countries, particularly in Iraq, Egypt and Syria. There is no doubt that many of these extremists consider Christians as infidels, as enemies, as agents of hostile foreign powers or simply as an easy target for extortion.

However, in the name of truth, we must point out that Christians are not the only victims of this violence and savagery. Secular Muslims, all those defined as "heretic", "schismatic" or simply "non-conformist" are being attacked and murdered in the prevailing chaos. In areas where Sunni extremists dominate, Shiites are being slaughtered. In areas where Shiite extremists dominate, Sunnis are being killed. Yes, the Christians are at times targeted precisely because they are Christians, having a different set of beliefs and unprotected. However they fall victim alongside many others who are suffering and dying in these times of death and destruction. They are driven from their homes alongside many others and together they become refugees, in total destitution.

These uprisings began because the peoples of the Middle East dreamed of a new age of dignity, democracy, freedom and social justice. Dictatorial regimes, which had guaranteed "law and order", but at the terrible price of military and police repression, fell. With them, the order they had imposed crumbled. Christians had lived in relative security under these dictatorial regimes. They feared that, if this strong authority disappeared, chaos and extremist groups would take over, seizing power and bringing about violence and persecution. Therefore some Christians tended to defend these regimes. Instead, loyalty to their faith and concern for the good of their country, should perhaps have led them to speak out much earlier, telling the truth and calling for necessary reforms, in view of more justice and respect of human rights, standing alongside both many courageous Christians and Muslims who did speak out.

We fully understand the fears and sufferings of our brothers and sisters in Christ, when by violence they lose members of their families and are driven out of their homes. They have the right to count on our solidarity and prayers. In certain circumstances their only consolation and hope is to be found in Jesus' words: "Happy are those who are persecuted in the cause of right: theirs is the kingdom of heaven" (Mt 5:10). However, the repetition of the word "persecution" in some circles (usually referring only to what Christians suffer at the hands of criminals claiming to be Muslims) plays into the hands of extremists, at home and abroad, whose aim is to sow prejudice and hatred, setting peoples and religions against one another.

Christians and Muslims need to stand together against the new forces of extremism and destruction. All Christians and many Muslims are threatened by these forces that seek to create a society devoid of Christians and where only very few Muslims will be at home. All those who seek dignity, democracy, freedom and prosperity are under attack. We must stand together and speak out in truth and freedom.

All of us, Christians and Muslims, must also be aware that the outside world will not make any real move to protect us. International and local political powers seek their own interests. We, alone, can build a common future together. We have to adapt ourselves to our realities, even realities of death, and must learn together how to emerge from persecution and destruction into a new dignified life in our own countries.

Together, we must seek out all those who dream as we do of a society in which Muslims and Christians and Jews are equal citizens, living side by side, building together a society in which new generations can live and prosper.

Finally, we pray for all, for those who join their efforts to ours, and for those who are harming us now or even killing us. We pray that God may allow them to see the goodness He has put in the heart of each one. May God transform every human being from the depth of his or her heart, enabling them to love every human being as God does, He who is the Creator and Lover of all. Our only protection is in our Lord and like Him we offer our lives for those who persecute us as well as for those who, with us, stand in defense of love, truth and dignity.

The Calvary of The Middle East Church

Fr. Drew Christiansen is former editor of America magazine and a professor of ethics at Georgetown University. Ra'fat Aldajani is a Palestinian-American writer and commentator. NCRonline.org

As yet another week of apocalyptic violence swept across Gaza, Fouad Twal, the Latin Patriarch of Jerusalem, has been making the rounds in Washington, advancing the cause of Palestinian Christians and of peace in the Holy Land. His itinerary has included the U.S. Commission on International Religious Freedom, the White House National Security Council, the U.S. bishops' conference, Catholic News Service, and supporters in the Holy Land Christian Ecumenical Foundation (HCEF). In a moving plea to diners at an HCEF-sponsored dinner Wednesday, the patriarch made an eloquent plea: "Do not leave me alone. Do not leave us alone."

Twal pleaded for the church across the region. The church of Jerusalem, he explained, understands it has a vocation to suffering. It is "a church of Calvary," he said. "The church of Iraq," he added, where Christians have been expelled by the jihadist ISIS, is "a church of Calvary. The church of Syria is a church of Calvary," too, where civil war has destroyed one of the last remaining refuges for Christians in the region and driven tens of thousands into encampments in Jordan.

The church in the Holy Land suffers its own Calvary. In Gaza, though the parish priest remains, the patriarch reported to another group, the three religious communities staffing schools have fled the fighting in the Palestinian enclave. "The whole church of the Middle East is a church of Calvary. Do not leave us alone," Twal concluded.

Pressed on what contribution the church can make to peace in the region, the patriarch explained its primary efforts come through education, where Christians, Muslims and sometimes Jews mix with one another in the classroom. The Latin Patriarchate runs 118 elementary and high schools in Israel, Palestine and Jordan. This co-religious education makes for lifetime friendships, knowledge of Christianity, and a set of values that bring respect for Christians despite their minority religious status.

Twal also made the case for his special initiative, the American University of Madaba in Jordan. AUM, he argued, will be a force for moderation, bringing Muslims and Christians together, not just from Jordan but from across the region, at a time when the havens of moderation are harder and harder to find.

In meetings with concerned Catholics and public officials, the patriarch pursued an updated agenda of religious liberty issues. The newest of these is the efforts of the Israeli government to create a special identity for Arab Christians in the Jewish state. According to legislation making its way through the Knesset, the Israeli parliament, Arab Christians in Israel will be required to carry an ID card marking them as Christians. Young Christians will also be eligible to be drafted into the Israeli Defense Forces.

The Christians regard the ID as discriminatory because, contrary to Israel's own democratic aspirations, it makes their religion something that singles them out in Israeli society. Politically, it also has the insidious effect of dividing them from the Muslim Arab citizens of Israel. For propaganda purposes, it then becomes easier for the narrative of the Israeli-Palestinian conflict to be presented as a strictly Jewish-Muslim one. By contrast, for decades, the Christian leaders in the Middle East, like the Council of Catholic Patriarchs and the former Latin Patriarch Michel Sabbah, have endeavored to articulate their bridging role as Arab Christians whose unique self-definition has been colored by 1,400 years of coexistence with Muslims.

Another long-term issue affecting young people concerns family formation, especially in Jerusalem. For many years, Israel has refused to approve residency permits for Jerusalemites who marry spouses from the West Bank. To form a family in such a relationship, a couple must move to the West Bank. In addition, residency permits for Arabs living in Jerusalem may be pulled for any number of reasons, including study or work abroad.

Finally, there is the lack of access to the holy places affecting all Arab Christians and Muslims, which has a notably deleterious effect on young Palestinian Christians, who are unable to visit the holy places so central to the religious life of Holy Land Christians. This is a long-lingering problem, but the separation wall between Israel and Palestinian territories has made it increasingly difficult for Palestinian Christians from Bethlehem and the nearby Christian towns to visit. Indeed, Bethlehemites are now constrained by a maze of walls, which put a stranglehold not only on religious observance, but on everyday life.

Christians In Israel

"From this holy place, I wish to extend my heartfelt greetings to all Christians in Jerusalem: I would like to assure them that I remember them affectionately and that I pray for them, being well aware of the difficulties they experience in this city. I urge them to be courageous witnesses of the passion of the Lord but also of his resurrection, with joy and hope."

Pope Francis, Jerusalem, 2014

Christian Palestinians in Israel: a Threatened Identity?

19 March 2014

HOLY LAND – March 2014. The Assembly of the Catholic Ordinaries has approved a document published by the Justice and Peace Commission about the Knesset law project which is about to introduce a distinction between Christian and Muslim Palestinians, stating that Christian Palestinians are Christians and not Palestinians. One of the consequence of this campaign will be to draft Christian Palestinians into the Israeli military.

Israeli policy makers are increasingly insisting that Christian Palestinians are not Arabs and not part of the Palestinian people. This has been expressed in the campaign to draft Christian Palestinians into the Israeli military and most recently in a law proposed by Member of Knesset Yariv Levin, which introduces a distinction between Christian and Muslim Palestinians and states that Christian Palestinians are Christians and not Palestinians.

We, the heads of the Catholic Church in Israel, would like to clarify that it is not the right or the duty of the Israeli civil authorities to tell us who we are. In fact, most of our faithful in Israel are Palestinian Arabs. They are obviously Christians too. They are also citizens of the State of Israel. We do not see any contradiction in this definition of identity: Christian Palestinian Arabs who are citizens of the State of Israel.

We address our words to all Christian Palestinians, whether in Israel or in Palestine and wherever they are in the world. They are, all, wherever they are, Palestinians and Christians and citizens. Indeed, there are some Christians in Israel, a small, marginal minority, who are supporting this campaign to redefine our identity. Whether they do so out of self-interest, fear, dreams of having full equality, we cannot say. However we must point out that they cannot pretend to be the spokespeople of the Christian Palestinians in Israel.

The people of this land, Jews, Christians, Muslims and Druzes, have lived here for centuries and have known successive governments. Christians and Muslims and Druzes together (and some Jews too who always lived in the land) insist that their shared common identity, which has developed over centuries, is Palestinian.

This campaign clearly has as its aim to divide Christians from their Muslim compatriots. However, it is equally dangerous because it will divide Christians among themselves even further.

If the Knesset indeed seeks the good of the citizens of Israel, it should invest every effort to legislate laws that remove discrimination, whether it be against Jews or Arabs, Christians, Muslims or Druze. In creating a society that unites all citizens in equality and strives for justice and peace, there will remain no reason to fear for anybody and Israelis and Palestinians, Christians, Muslims and Druze, can live together in mutual respect and dignity, working together to build a better future.

By: Justice and Peace Commission, and the Assembly of the Catholic Ordinaries in the Holy Land.

The Plight of Palestinian Christians

Fr. Hijazeen is Head of Latin Patriarchate Schools in Palestine
Fr. Shomali is priest of Annunciation Parish in Beit Jala.
A Sister of St. Francis tending the convent grounds, Jericho, Palestine

Based on our years as parish priests in Palestine, we were appalled by the false allegations regarding Palestinian Christians made in recent weeks by Israeli spokespeople, such as Ambassador Michael Oren.

We were perplexed not because of their position, which has been part of the official Israeli narrative for many years, but by how openly they have distorted facts and misconstrued the plight of Palestinian Christians pursuing justice and peace.

These spokespeople have wrongly propagated a cynical discourse misleadingly touting "Christian persecution by Muslims." Every Friday, we celebrate the holy mass attended by hundreds of Palestinian Christians from Bethlehem, Ramallah and Jerusalem in the Cremisan Area of Beit Jala. The holy service, celebrated among ancient olive trees, was not a prayer to end a "Muslim-led persecution" but to prevent Israel from confiscating this area of land that belongs to 58 Palestinian Christian families – Israel's latest attempt to consolidate its ring of settlements that aim to sever Bethlehem from Jerusalem. This is one last attempt to prevent a land confiscation that would have catastrophic consequences for the local Christian population.

Since the Israeli occupation began in 1967, Israel has confiscated thousands of acres belonging to Palestinian Christians and Muslims. In the Jerusalem and Bethlehem areas, Christians have been severely affected by Israel's colonization policies. As an example, approximately 5,436 acres of land from northern Bethlehem were unilaterally annexed by Israel to create the illegal settlements of Gilo and Har Homa – which Israel now cynically calls new Jerusalem "neighborhoods."

These "neighborhoods," aim to physically separate Jerusalem from Bethlehem and, for the first time in history, prohibit Palestinian Christians from worshipping in the holy city of Jerusalem.

It is also completely disingenuous for Israeli spokespeople to argue that the population of Christians in Israel has "tripled since 1948." In fact, figures show that the percentage of Christians in the area began to decrease in 1948, when Israel was created.

Much of the so-called "growth" in Israel is due to the immigration of foreigners and while it is true that in numbers Christians have grown in both Israel and Palestine due to natural increase, the percentage would be much higher in absence of the ongoing Israeli displacement policies against the indigenous Palestinian population.

In fact, Israeli spokespeople "forget" to mention that in 1948, 75 percent of the Palestinian Arab population, including Christians, of what is now the State of Israel became refugees. Entire Christian villages were destroyed by Israel; and tens of thousands of Christians were expelled. Some areas of today's west Jerusalem, such as Talbiya and Katamon, were home to thousands of Palestinian Christians whose homes were looted and private property confiscated.

Since the occupation of the West Bank in 1967, Israel has implemented a policy of taking as much as land as possible and as few as Palestinians as possible. Palestinian Christians, particularly in Jerusalem, have suffered the consequences of this policy. Considering the hundreds of cases put forth by Palestinian Christians living in occupied east Jerusalem, if Israel continues its policies of residency revocations and home demolitions, within a few years the Christian community in Jerusalem will not count more than 6,000 faithful. Next week, thousands of Palestinian Christians from the Gaza Strip and the West Bank will once again be denied their right to worship in the Church of the Holy Sepulcher for Easter celebrations. And, if they are lucky enough obtain a permit from the Israeli military to enter Jerusalem, they will have to cross through humiliating security checks to cross from one part of their occupied homeland to another.

We still have to live with the irony that Christians tourists from all over the world will freely access the Church of the Holy Sepulcher, located just a few kilometers away from our homes, while we cannot enjoy the same right. As Easter brings its message of resurrection, we will be praying for the resurrection of justice for everyone on this land.

During our years of priesthood, we have paid visits to many Palestinian Christian political prisoners jailed in Israeli prisons, participated in funerals of Christians who have lost their lives in this bloody conflict, assisted families divided by the Israeli policy of stripping Palestinian residency rights, and lobbied on behalf of our parishioners whose property was confiscated by Israel.

In the West Bank Israel does not differentiate between Palestinian Christians and Muslims in its policies. Several studies have shown that the Israeli occupation and settlement activities are the main reason for Christian emigration

These claims are not Palestinian "propaganda" but have been largely researched by the US government, the European Union and the United Nations. In fact, all the recent International Religious Freedom Reports published by the US Department of State highlight this issue.

To conclude, Palestinian Christians are not persecuted by Palestinian Muslims. The end of the Israeli occupation would allow all our people, Christians and Muslims, to develop all our potential living side by side.

Christian Migrants: Faithful of the Diocese

JAFFA-TEL AVIV —The Christian community in the Holy Land expands, officially: so attests the first pastoral visit by the Patriarch of Jerusalem to Christian migrants in southern Tel Aviv. On Saturday, April 26, 2014, an important meeting for the Hebrew speaking community which needs the Church's support and which supports the Church in return by its faith and influence.

The opportunity to practice the faith has not always been easy for all Filipino, Sri Lankan, Ethiopian, Eritrean, Indian, Sudanese, and all the people who have recently arrived in Israel and south of Tel Aviv to find work or escape authoritarian political regimes. About three months ago, an air-raid shelter acted as a chapel, rented at exorbitant prices, and entirely financed by migrants who, despite their poverty, invest everything they can in order to live their faith.

Thanks to the help of generous donors, a home was acquired by the Pastoral Care of Migrants Ministry of the Diocese. After much necessary work, the center welcomes each Saturday and Sunday all the children en masse to the Sacred Liturgy of the Eucharist who are enrolled in catechism classes to prepare for the sacraments. The center also serves as home to two religious sisters who live among migrants, visit and share their lives. Located in the heart of a poor neighborhood in southern Tel Aviv, the center is not yet in its final location. For Father David Neuhaus, Head of Pastoral Care of Migrants, "the center will move the day the area becomes a middle-class neighborhood. Because we necessarily *live among people* that we welcome.

The "Divine Mercy" community which cares for the center has chosen to name the center "Our Lady Woman of Valor" (for more details, click here), represented in an iconographic style painting, made especially for the chapel. The center is not a parish, but the large number of Christian migrants who participate there actually occupy an essential place in the life of the diocese: indeed all intend to stay in the country for several years and have children who are part of the country. They obviously transform the sociology of the diocese and reinforce the weight of the Hebrew-speaking Catholic community.

Since the birth of the community in 2009, it became imperative that they receive the pastoral visit of Patriarch Fouad Twal, whose jurisdiction extends over all Latin Catholics of Jordan, Palestine, Cyprus and Israel. The community is a very enthusiastic crowd, compressed in the small chapel of the center, which hosted its pastor, and with him the Apostolic Nuncio, Archbishop Giuseppe Lazzarotto, Bishop Marcuzzo, Patriarchal Vicar for Israel, and Bishop Shomali, Patriarchal Vicar for Jerusalem.

"You are welcome in your center, yours," insisted the Patriarch several times in his homily. *"I encourage the different communities of our Patriarchate to develop a true sense of unity in diversity. Do not stand independent of the others. Gather to share with each other your wealth of religious, social and cultural life. It is most important to create a genuine unity."*

He continued giving support to those who are *"uncertain of time-length of their stay, and who are vulnerable to unjust treatment, facing the possibility of expulsion. With them, we, as Church, raise our voice publicly and effectively to ensure the full recognition of their rights as persons and to see that they are treated fairly."*

After Mass, a colossal feast was served to all participants. Dishes from everywhere on the color-clothed tables. A time of music and dance followed to crown this visit during which the joy of community, the sense of home, and love of the Church impressed the distinguished guests, bishops, priests and others.

Pierre Loup de Raucourt (www.lpj.org)

"The Presence of Christian Migrants Is an Asset for the Local Church"

17 September 2014

TELAVIV-JAFFA — On Saturday 13 and Sunday, September 14, 2014, Patriarch Fouad Twal made a pastoral visit to the Catholic community in Jaffa. He came to meet a suffering Catholic Arab community, but also a vibrant and large community of Catholic immigrants. This visit is part of the pastoral visitations of the Patriarch to each parish in the diocese, which began two years ago and continues.

The Patriarch met a suffering and numerically small Arab Christian community that is struggling to find or keep its identity at the heart of the bustling major Israeli city. "Many children do not speak Arabic and most young people do not go to Mass," lamented His Beatitude.

Nevertheless, he warmly welcomed the presence of a group of young Arab Christians who came to the celebration. The Patriarch was very touched by the Indian and Filipino community: "They are very loyal to their faith and tradition. There are those who live in fear of being deported from the country, but they have found a refuge, a shelter and a place to get together in the Church." Several times a week, this migrant community, is found in the church or in the center of Our Lady Woman of Valor in Tel Aviv, for fraternal meeting times around a typical meal or time of prayer and Eucharistic adoration. "Some are found in prayer at ten o'clock in the evening having started for work that day at two in the morning. Their presence is a treasure for the Church, a testament to the local Christians often too busy with politics," stressed Patriarch.

He also met with the civil authorities of the Jaffa Municipality and Police, who affirmed their commitment to do everything possible to ensure that all can live in peace. They further discussed the coexistence of the different communities.

After some traditional Philippine and African dances, various groups of diplomats from Africa and Latin America came to greet the Patriarch, who, in turn, thanked them for their support and the their country's stand during the war in Gaza.

On Sunday, the Patriarch presided at Mass in the Latin parish of Jaffa, St. Anthony of Padua, which completed his pastoral visit. Concelebrating the Mass at his side was his Vicar in Israel Bishop Marcuzzo and the parish pastor, Father Zaher Aboud OFM. Heads of the Melkite Greek and Orthodox communities came to meet the Patriarch and they also attended the mass.

During his homily, the Patriarch stressed the mystery of the cross is a mystery of joy, intimately linked to the hope of the Resurrection.

He pondered the characteristics of the first Christian community in Jerusalem. He urged the faithful to rediscover the values that have marked the first Christian community who persevered in prayer, the teaching of the apostles, brotherly love and the breaking of bread. He recalled as well the importance of "Christian fellowship", unity among different communities living sometimes isolated from each other when they are called to discover and enrich each other:"We are a single Church, the Church of God."

During the Mass, a group of women members of the Legion of Mary, whose main apostolate is prayer and home visitation, were able to renew their promises.

At the end of the celebration, a delightful buffet awaited the guests and the Patriarch took the time to greet everyone.

Before leaving Sunday night for Jerusalem, Patriarch was able to meet some members of the movement of the Legion of Mary and their two Jaffa groups: Help of Christians and Cedar of Lebanon. He then met with the pastors of various parishes in the city of Jaffa – Maronite, Melkite, Armenian and Greek Orthodox – and with the Christian Brothers who staff a school in Jaffa.

By: Myriam Ambroselli- LPJ

The Plight of Eritreans in Israel

Jun 16, 2014 on LPJ

ISRAEL – *Eritrea celebrated on May 25 the anniversary of its independence. On this occasion, the Church has responded to the crisis of Eritreans. A pastoral letter of 36 pages written by the Eritrean bishops lists the serious problems they face: the disintegration of families (whose members are scattered because of military service, imprisonment or placement in rehabilitation centers), a ruined economy, a poor quality educational system, the arbitrariness of the law, and a lack of prospects.*

Father David Neuhaus, director of pastoral care of migrants in Israel, was interviewed by Vatican Radio:

"All this creates a desolate country" and forces young people to flee. Some of these young Eritreans arrive in Europe or Israel, where they are now taken to camps in the desert.

They are Eritreans but unfortunately they are not recognized as refugees and for that reason they live without any rights. And they are treated almost like criminals. It is a horror, a great suffering for the people trying to live here. We are talking about a population of just over 50,000 people. Presently, the big drama is that three months ago Israel began to deport young unmarried men to a huge camp in the Negev desert, 80km from the nearest city. Authorities say this is not a prison but people have to sleep there, they must be counted three times a day and they do not have money to travel elsewhere. We went there and we saw that the conditions are super difficult. There are too many people in these places and the food is awful. There is insufficient medical treatment but the most terrible of all is the boredom. There is nothing to do. Today, in these places, there are 2,300 young men who have nothing to do. The authorities still plan to expand the space to hold 7,000 people, that is to say a real horror.

What the Church seeks to do for these people?

I think the first thing that is important is to speak somehow, to tell their stories, stories of sadness and suffering because many came through the Sinai. On their way here some have experienced the torture camps in the Sinai, and the traffickers who kidnapped and tortured people. Others came here and lived in extreme poverty. This all happened with the great migrations around 2007. The Church must be like a spokesperson, a voice for those who do not have a one. Second, the Church can and must demand rights for these people. We are now also looking for creative ways to help those who are incarcerated there by collecting books, trying to see if we can mobilize teachers who are willing to teach. We have been given free access to enter.

I asked, "Can we bring books? Can bring teachers? Can we organize classes?" All of that remains to be seen because it is a new situation and the ways of the Church are very limited. We are very few people and many are they who are in need. In any case, the priority is to speak about this story and try to help NGOs, Israeli people, who are also trying to aid these people.

At the same time, in Israeli public opinion, they are not highly regarded.

That is true. It starts of course with the way people talk about this world. They are treated like criminals who have illegally entered the country but Israelis do not know that they have fled horrific situations. Israelis are not aware that they do not have the right to work. It starts with the language used and the attitudes held, and, once again, I say "the Church must speak very loudly and with another language by showing our humanity and emphasize that they are not so many. When Israelis speak, they tend to think they are really a lot. But we have just a little over 50,000 people.

Source: Vatican Radio

The Case of Christian Arab Citizens of Israel

The following is a response drafted by the Justice and Peace Commission June 18, 2013, in response to Israeli military plans to recruit Palestinian Christians holding Israeli passports. Founded in 1971, the Commission for Justice and Peace functions under the auspices of the Assembly of Catholic Ordinaries of the Holy Land as a Catholic resource, liaison, and animation center to further the social mission of the Church.

- Introduction

According to Israeli law, all permanent residents of Israel, male and female, are eligible to be called up to serve in the Israeli military.1[1] In fact, after 1948, two populations were not mobilized: ultra-Orthodox Jews and Arabs. Ultra-Orthodox Jews were not mobilized because of agreements reached between the rabbinical leaders of the community who opposed their young people being drafted because they would be exposed to modern, non-religious society and would not pursue lives of Torah study. In practice, young men enrolled in Torah study were not drafted. This situation was formalized in the Tal Law in 2002. Arabs were not drafted because they were seen as identified with "the enemy" and unlikely to be loyal.

---

[1] This includes Jerusalem Arab residents. The past months have seen a rise in the attempts to draft some Jerusalem Christians into the military. Here we deal only with Arab citizens of Israel.

Recent talk of drafting ultra-Orthodox and Arabs has been the result of the ruling (2012) that determined that the Tal Law was not in accord with the Basic Laws and the ensuing popular movement among Israeli citizens that all should serve in the army.

In 1956, Israeli reached an agreement with the Druze religious leadership by which young non-religious Druze (the *juhhal* being those ignorant of religious teaching) would be drafted whereas the religious youth (the *uqqal* being those initiated into religious teaching) would be exempt, under a similar understanding as that with the ultra-Orthodox community. In return, the Israeli authorities recognized the Druze religious leadership as totally independent from Muslim leadership and instituted a separate religious court system. Circassian Muslims were drafted in 1958. Various Bedouin tribes from the Galilee and from the Naqab also agreed to the mobilization of their young men although no general conscription of Bedouin exists.

As early as the 1950s, some Israeli officials promoted the mobilization of all Arabs. Others focused on the Christian Arabs. Draft orders were in fact served to the young Christians in Jish (a village with a large Maronite population). The draft orders were not followed up, probably because the Arab Christians were still seen as a security threat, being part of the general Arab population and enjoying a high level of education.

- *Why does Israel seek to mobilize the Christians today?*

Israel does not need more soldiers in an age of technological warfare however the military is seen as an institution that promotes social cohesion – a very important melting pot in the Israeli reality of diversity. The army is seen as a principal place of forming "national (Israeli-Zionist)" consciousness and participating in the nation building project as conceived by the authorities, i.e. promoting Israel as a Jewish national state. Army service is seen as a tool to promote the Israelization of the Arab minority. Identification with Israel rather than with Palestinian Arab society is clearly an important goal.

The mobilization of minorities is undoubtedly also motivated by the will "to divide and rule" the Arab minority. By drafting some segments of the population, the authorities succeed in dividing the society. This was clearly the case with the mobilization of Druze, Bedouin and Circassian minorities who were defined by government offices as "non-Arab". Talk about drafting the Christian Arabs rather than the Arabs in general (Muslims and Christians) is clearly an attempt to drive a wedge between Christian and Muslim Arabs in Israel.

- Why do some Christians serve in the Israeli army?

Non-Arab Christians are regularly drafted into the military. Since 1996, with the increase of non-Arab Russian speaking Christians being drafted, Christian soldiers were even allowed to swear the oath of loyalty on a copy of the New Testament. Christian soldiers can ask for leave on Christian holidays. It is also true though that extensive pressure is exerted on non-Jewish soldiers (particularly those integrated into the Hebrew speaking, Jewish population) by the rabbinate within the military to convert to Judaism and extensive conversion courses are offered.

Some Christian Arabs do volunteer for army service as do some Muslim Arabs. Their motivations are usually either economic (the army provides well paid employment to professional soldiers) or professional (the belief that educational, occupational and other social opportunities, otherwise off limits to Arabs, will open up after army service). There is also a belief among some who serve in the army that if Arabs fulfill this duty they will receive equal rights to those of the Jewish population. This will be strengthened if the parliament passes proposed legislation now being debated that offers certain privileges to those who serve in the army (particularly employment in the bureaucracy of the state).

It is important to note that the drive towards volunteering for army service among Christian Arabs is particularly strong after manifestations of confessional (Christian-Druze or Christian-Muslim) tension. This can be seen in the relatively higher number of Christians being drafted in certain areas like Kafr Yassif (bordering on the Druze village of Julis, where the residents are Druze who serve in the military) or in Maghar (where tensions within the village between Druze and Christians have erupted in violence in recent years).

- What should be the position of the Church?

Clearly the Church teaches that Christians should be good citizens and participate actively in society to promote the common good. The Church is committed to raise consciousness about issues of justice, reconciliation, love of enemies and non-violence as well as the ethical problems of war.

In her promotion of awareness of justice issues, the Church should point out that the Israeli army is used as an instrument promoting the interests of only one part of the population, the Jews, to the detriment of the Palestinians. The army is used as a means of imposing and maintaining the occupation of Palestinian lands and thus preventing the Palestinians from achieving dignity and independence. The army is primarily an army of aggression rather than an army of defense as is clear in its patrolling of the Palestinian areas and its defense of the settlers [2].

Furthermore, in promoting an awareness of the rights to equality, the Church can point out that Israel discriminates against her Arab citizens. The case of the Druze and Bedouin is a particularly powerful testimony to the fact that army service does not bring equality. The Druze and many Bedouin have been serving for decades in the Israeli army and yet their villages are still grossly underdeveloped when compared with neighboring Jewish areas. [3] In fact, as Druze became better educated, so did their resistance to the draft grow and since 1972 the Druze Initiative Committee has been actively promoting refusal to serve in the army, assisting Druze youngsters who are imprisoned for this refusal.

The Church promotes good neighborly relations within the Arab minority: among Christians, Muslims, Druze and all others. The use of army service to divide the Arab population against itself is detrimental to the interests of the Arabs as a community. The promotion of army service among the less educated and more impoverished must be countered with the promotion of better education, improved social conditions, more cohesion within the Arab minority in Israel and a concerted struggle for equality in the State of Israel.

Furthermore, the Church is also aware that many of the Arab youth in Israel are losing their national, cultural and religious identity and many no longer identify themselves as Arabs. In some places like the mixed cities (Jaffa, Ramleh, Haifa, Lydda, etc) many young Christian Arabs try their best to assimilate into the Jewish majority and identify with it. The Church sees her task as one of educating our young people to accept themselves as they are, giving them a balanced human, national and Christian education and an awareness of their history, their rootedness in the land and a sense of identity that integrates the different elements (Palestinian Arab, Christian and citizen of Israel) rather than repressing any one of these elements. The bishops and priests must help the faithful in the midst of this "crisis of identity".

- What about proposals regarding civil rather than military service?

Faced with the understandable reticence of some Arabs to take up arms against their brothers and sisters, the Israeli authorities have been proposing some kind of civil service for Arab residents. What needs to be made clear is:

> *- Civil service in the format proposed is equivalent to military service and therefore equally problematic along the lines underlined above.*

- The military authorities are those initiating the option to do civil service with the same goals: legitimizing the status quo and promoting a "national" consciousness that is opposed to the aspirations of the Palestinian Arab people.

Despite the benign appearance of the forms of civil service proposed, the underlying principle is the defense and legitimation of the so-called "Jewish" state.

The members of the Commission of Justice and Peace of the Assembly of Catholic Ordinaries in the Holy Land ask that the Catholic Ordinaries address the many issues that face the faithful in their day to day lives, including the complex socio-political issues in the state of Israel.

Christian Leaders tell Youth to 'tear up' Israeli Army Forms

26/04/2014

Orthodox Archbishop Atallah Hanna and former Latin Patriarch Michel Sabbah (MaanImages)

JERUSALEM (Ma'an) -- Orthodox Archbishop Atallah Hanna and former Latin Patriarch Michel Sabbah on Friday urged Christian youth not to enlist in the Israeli military and to ignore Israeli "propaganda" encouraging them to do so. The statement came after a meeting between the two religious figures on Friday, which followed reports on Tuesday that Israeli authorities would distribute military enlistment papers to Palestinian Christian youth who are citizens of Israel in order to encourage them to voluntarily sign up for military service.

The leaders called upon Christian youth who have received the enrollment papers to "tear them up and throw them away and not to engage with them in any way." The leaders also stressed the "firm national position of the Christians in refusing to join a military that exercises violence against the rights of the Palestinian people." The forms to be sent to Christian youth resemble the mandatory enlistment forms distributed to Jewish and Druze Israelis, and the army hopes that by sending these papers more youth will voluntarily sign up to enlist.

Although Christian Palestinian citizens of Israel are currently exempt from military service along with Muslims, a government decision made in February to re-classify Christians as a separate ethnicity distinct from "Arab" raised fears that mandatory enrollment would follow, as it did for Palestinians of the Druze religion in the 1950s.

About 10 percent of Palestinian citizens of Israel, also called "Arab-Israelis," are Christians, while the majority of the remaining are Muslims and Druze. Although the majority of Palestinians were expelled from their homes inside Israel during the 1948 conflict that led to the creation of the state of Israel, some managed to remain and their descendants today make up around 20 percent of Israel's population.

Report - Maan News

Peace for the Holy Land:

The Promised Land and the Chosen People

The Two-State solution

By Archbishop Cyrille Salim Bustros

From 10 through 24 October 2010 a special Assembly of the Synod of Bishops took place at the Vatican with the title: "The Catholic Church in the Middle East: Communion and Witness: Now the company of those who believed were of one heart and soul" (Acts 4:32). Participating in this Assembly, gathered around His Holiness Pope Benedict XVI, were the Patriarchs and the Bishops of the Eastern Catholic Churches of the Middle East, cardinals and archbishops who are heads of the various offices in the Roman Curia, presidents of Catholic episcopal conferences around the world, who are concerned with the issues of the Middle East, representatives from the Orthodox Churches and Ecclesial Communities, and Jewish and Muslim guests.

In its final message the Synod developed the issue of "Communion and Witness" first through history, then in the present time within the Catholic Churches of the Middle East, and with the Orthodox and Protestant Communities in the Middle East. After that, it addressed the issue of the cooperation and dialogue with our fellow-citizens the Jews and the Muslims.

In paragraph 8 of the final message concerning the Jews, after explaining what Christianity and Judaism have in common—the Old Testament, "all that God revealed there, since he called Abraham, our common father in the faith, Father of Jews, of Christians and of Muslims"—the Synod stressed the necessity to continue "the dialogue which is taking place between the Church and the representatives of Judaism." The statement then goes on:

"We hope that this dialogue can bring us to work together to press those in authority to put an end to the political conflict which results in separating us and disrupting everyday life in our countries. It is time for us to commit ourselves together to a sincere, just and permanent peace. Both Christians and Jews are called to this task by the Word of God. Both are invited to listen to the voice of God "who speaks of peace: "Let me hear what God the Lord will speak, for he will speak peace to his people, to his holy ones" (Ps 85:9)

Then adds: "Recourse to theological and biblical positions which use the Word of God to wrongly justify injustices is not acceptable. On the contrary recourse to religion must lead every person to see the face of God in others and to treat them according to the attributes of God and his commandments, namely, according to God's bountiful goodness, mercy, justice and love for us."

The Promised Land

During the press conference which was held at the end of the Synod, I presented this message in my role as president of the commission that drafted the message. I was then asked by a journalist: "What do you mean by this sentence: 'Recourse to theological and biblical positions which use the Word of God to wrongly justify injustices is not acceptable'?" I answered: "Israel cannot use the Biblical concept of a promised land to justify its occupation of Palestinian territory and the expulsion of Palestinians who have been living there for centuries. We Christians cannot now speak about the Promised Land for the Jewish people. With Christ the Promised Land became the Kingdom of God": Jesus referred to this land in His Sermon on the Mount and gave it a spiritual interpretation: "Blessed are the poor in spirit, for theirs is the Kingdom of God... Blessed are the meek, for they will inherit the land." (Mt. 5:3.5)

In my answer I was thinking in particular of Jewish settlers who claim their right to build on Palestinian territory by saying it forms part of biblical Israel, the land promised by God to the Jews according to the Old Testament. I also warned against the risk of Israel becoming an exclusively Jewish state, with a consequent threat to the 1.2 million Muslim and Christian Arabs living in Israel. The Synod is acknowledging the separation between religion and politics, in stating that recourse to the Bible cannot be used to justify political events: "Give to Caesar what belongs to Caesar and to God what belongs to God." (Mt. 22:21)

As a Christian, and especially as a Middle-Eastern Christian—and this is the unanimous opinion of the Middle-Eastern Christians, Catholics, Orthodox and Protestants—I see that the concept of the Promised Land cannot be used for the justification of the return of Jews to Israel and the displacement of Palestinians. The creation of the State of Israel in 1948—after the resolution of the UN in 1947 regarding the partition of Palestine which was under the British mandate between Arab and Jews—is a political issue not a religious one. It is a fact of history like other facts: Jews who were persecuted in Europe and suffered the horrors of the shoah decided to come to Palestine and build, with the Jews who were there, a country for their own. They could have chosen another place. But they chose Palestine, some of them relying on the theme of the Promised Land, and others only because of the memory of the Jews who lived there 2000 years ago. So they came in great numbers; a war arose between them and the Arabs living there, and they won the war; hundreds of thousands of Palestinians were forced to leave their homes and flee to the surrounding Arabic countries: Lebanon, Syria and Jordan. If some of the Jews based their return on the Old Testament theme of the Promised Land, this does not mean that God is behind their return and their victory against the Arabs. It is a religious interpretation of an historical event.

We find this same religious interpretation of historical events in the Old Testament: A religious people believing in God wins a war, they interpret their war as God's war and their victory as God's victory. The idea of a "Warrior God" which we find in the Old Testament, a God who fights with his chosen people and condemns to death all his enemies cannot be accepted in Christianity. We have to read the Old Testament in the Spirit of Jesus Christ and in the light of His teachings. Jesus did not allow Peter to draw even a sword to fight for Him (Cf. John 18:10-11). According to Jesus' teachings, God is a God of love, peace, justice and mercy. How can we figure Him at the head of an army fighting with a particular people against other peoples? This idea may have infiltrated Christian thought during the first centuries and the Middle Ages; it can be found today in some extremist Muslims groups, who still say that the land of Palestine is a Muslim land given to Muslims by God who was fighting with them during the Arab conquests, and that they will oppose God's will if they give up a part of it to the Israelis. But, as Christians, we cannot today accept such an idea. It is against the image of God revealed to us by Jesus Christ in the New Testament.

The Chosen People

As for the idea of the chosen people, it is clear, according to Christian theology and especially to St. Paul, that after Christ there is no longer one particular chosen people! With Christ and in Him, all men and women of all countries are called to become children of God and unite in one body, the Body of Christ.

Being the chosen people was not a privilege, it was a mission: Israel was chosen by God in the Old Testament to live in holiness, to proclaim His name among the nations, and to prepare the coming of the Messiah. St Paul does not deny the role of the Jewish people in the history of salvation. He writes to the Romans: "I have great sorrow and unceasing anguish in my heart. For I could wish that I myself were cursed and cut off from Christ for the sake of my people, those of my own race, the people of Israel. Theirs is the adoption to sonship; theirs the divine glory, the covenants, the receiving of the law, the temple worship and the promises. Theirs are the patriarchs, and from them is traced the human ancestry of the Messiah, who is God over all, forever praised. Amen." (Rom. 9:1-5)

But in his letter to the Ephesians, he declares that Jesus has united all the peoples in one people and one body:

"Therefore, remember that at one time you, Gentiles by birth, called 'the uncircumcison' by those called 'the circumcision', which is done in the flesh by human hands, remember that you were at that time without Christ, being aliens from the community of Israel and strangers to the covenants of promise, without hope and without God in the world. But now in Christ Jesus you who once were far off have been brought near by the blood of Christ. For he is our peace; in his flesh he made both groups into one and has broken down the dividing wall, that is the hostility between us. He has abolished the law with its commands and ordinances, that he might create in himself one new humanity in place of the two, thus making peace, and might reconcile both groups to God in one body through the cross, thus putting to death that hostility through it. So He came and preached peace to you who were far off and peace to those who were near. For through him both of us have access in one Spirit to the Father." (Eph 2:11-18)

In his letter to the Galatians also, Paul affirms this unity of all peoples in Christ: "So through faith you are all children of God in Christ Jesus. For all of you who were baptized into Christ have clothed yourselves with Christ. There is neither Jew nor Gentile, neither slave nor free, nor is there male and female; for you are all one in Christ Jesus. If you belong to

Christ, then you are Abraham's descendant, and heirs according to the promise." (Gal 3:26-29)

And St Peter, in his first letter, applies the concept of chosen people to all who became Christians, Jews and non-Jews: "But you are a chosen people, a royal priesthood, a holy nation, a people of His own, so that you may announce the praises of Him who called you out of darkness into his wonderful light. Once you were 'no people', but now you are God's people; once you had not received mercy, but now you have received mercy." (1 Pet. 2:9-10)

So in the New Testament the concept of "chosen people" has been extended to all those who believe in Jesus and become through him God's people. So we ask with St. Paul: "Has God rejected his people?" and we answer also with St. Paul: "Of course not!... God has not rejected his people whom he foreknew." (Rom. 11:1-2) This we can call the inclusive theology of St. Paul: the Jews are included in this people of God. They still remain the people God has chosen, but they are no more the only chosen people. This is clear when St. Paul says: "you are all children of God in Christ Jesus."

Sometimes in our limited human thought we think when a favor was given to a special group then extended to other groups, it ceases to be a favor; in the same manner some think that when the grace of "chosen people" and "God's people" was given to the Jews, and then extended to all peoples, it ceases to be a grace to the Jews. But the grace still remains a grace, even if it is extended to all peoples. In this sense we can understand Jesus' saying: "Do not think that I have come to abolish the law or the prophets. I have come not to abolish but to fulfill" (Mt. 5:17) The Old Covenant with the Jewish people, according to which they are God's chosen people, is not abolished, but it is fulfilled with the entrance of all peoples in this chosen people.

In its Message the Synod says to the Jews: "The same Scriptures unite us. The Old Testament, the Word of God is for both you and us. We believe all that God revealed there, since He called Abraham, our common father in the faith, father of Jews, of Christians and of Muslims. We believe in the promises of God and his covenant given to Abraham and to you. We believe that the Word of God is eternal." (paragraph 8)

So there is nothing offending to the Jews to say that they are no more the only "chosen people" of God and that "God's mercy" has been extended to all peoples. They must be proud, as was St. Paul, to be the people that God has chosen to be the first people God has chosen to be holy and to proclaim his name among all the nations of the earth. But at the same time they must also be humble, as St. Paul also was, to see that to be God's chosen people is a grace, and finally they must glorify God, as it pleased to St. Paul and St. Peter to do, that this grace has been extended to all peoples.

The Two-State Solution

After this theological issue we come now to the political issue, and these two levels must be clearly distinguished. Now in the Israeli-Palestinian issue, besides the moderates among both the Palestinians and the Jews, we are in presence of two opposed religious extremist ideologies: from one part extremist Jews who say that Palestine is the Promised Land given to them by God, and that they cannot give up any part of it to the Arabs; and from the other part extremist Muslims who say that Palestine is a Muslim land given to them by God during the Arabic conquests, and that they cannot give up a part of it to the Israelis. With these two opposed religious ideologies it is impossible to find a compromise in order to reach a lasting peace.

The message of the Synod for the Middle East takes a moderate position and clearly advocates, regarding the Israeli-Palestinian issue, the two-State-solution:

"The citizens of the countries of the Middle East call upon the international community, particularly the United Nations, conscientiously to work to find a peaceful, just and definitive solution in the region, through the application of the Security Council's resolution and taking the necessary legal steps to put an end to the occupation of the different Arabic countries. The Palestinian people will thus have an independent and sovereign homeland where they can live with dignity and security. The State of Israel will be able to enjoy peace and security within their international recognized borders. The Holy City of Jerusalem will be able to acquire its proper status, which respects its particular character, its holiness and the religious patrimony of the three religions: Jewish, Christian and Muslim. We hope that the two-State-solution might become a reality and not remain a dream only." (Paragraph 11)

Then the message explicitly condemns all kinds of violence and religious extremism: "We condemn violence and terrorism from wherever it may proceed as well as all religious extremism. We condemn all forms of racism, anti-Semitism, anti-Christianism and Islamophobia and we call upon the religions to assume their responsibility to promote dialogue between cultures and civilizations in our region and in the entire world."

By dialogue only – a dialogue which requires compromises from both sides, not by war, and especially not by a war based on religious assumptions – can the Holy Land reach a just and lasting peace.

+ Archbishop Cyril S. Bustros - Eparch of Newton

Defending the Palestinians did not mean being against Israel

By: Agenzia Fides Feb. 2014

Jerusalem- The problems and conflicts between Israelis and Palestinians will end only when we recognize the crucial role of religion in the peace process, because "we cannot indeed claim to find a solution without taking into account the spiritual dimension of this land".

This is what the Patriarch of Jerusalem Fouad Twal Latin said to the U.S. official Shaun Casey during a meeting focused on the vital contribution that religious communities are called to offer to bring peace to the Holy Land.

Casey is the head of the Office of Faith-Based Community Initiatives, an organization linked to the U.S. State Department and set up by the Secretary of State John Kerry with the mission to renew and strengthen the role of religious communities in the foreign policy of the United States. In the meeting, which took place on Monday, February 17 - and whose contents were released from sources of the Latin Patriarchate of Jerusalem - both the U.S. envoy and the Patriarch expressed high expectations with regards to the upcoming visit of Pope Francis to the Holy Land. Casey reiterated that the protection of Christians and freedom of worship and access to the holy places are at the heart of the concerns of the Vatican and the United States.

In particular, the current U.S. Secretary of State - assured Casey - "is aware of the power of faith in the peace process", and has been "attentive to the concerns of the Christians in the Holy Land" and hopes even to put in place the framework of the agreement before the Pope's visit . "Of course", said Casey, "speaking to the Pope during his next visit will be important to help the two peoples to move in this direction". On his behalf, the Patriarch welcomed the establishment of the faith-based initiatives office whose role will be crucial in the peace process. For His beatitude Twal, Jerusalem must remain "an open city for the two peoples and three religions".

"Defending the Palestinians", said the Patriarch, "did not mean being against Israel". "Everyone should realize how peace would be beneficial not only for human rights, but also economically for both parties", declared Shaun Casey.

Christians in Gaza

"Look at the conditions in Gaza: more and more, it resembles a big concentration camp."

Cardinal Renato Martino, Papal Minister of Justice, 2009

Bishops tell Christians of Gaza "You Are Not Alone"

Bishops from Europe and North America celebrated mass with the Catholic community in Gaza on the Feast of the Lord's Baptism, 8 January, 2012 as they started this year's Holy Land Coordination in support of the local Church.

The Christian community of Gaza is made up of 2,500 people, of whom Catholics number around 300, in a total population of 1.5 million. Religious sisters run a home for the elderly, a centre for the disabled and a kindergarten and with the parish of the Holy Family are also involved in the running of the Catholic schools for the community.

Greeted by a band of 40 scouts, the Bishops brought messages of support from their Dioceses and respective Bishops' Conferences. After mass, there was an open meeting, during which the parishioners shared their experiences of living in Gaza, where the economic blockade and security situation make work and freedom of movement extremely difficult.

Bishop William Kenney, Auxiliary Bishop in Birmingham told the parishioners: "What I want to say to you is 'you are not forgotten'."

Bishop Michel Dubost, Bishop of Evry, Paris, said: "Today everyone in my Diocese is praying for you as they know we are making this visit. Last week, I asked prisoners in the largest prison in Europe [in Evry] to pray for you."

The Apostolic Nuncio, Archbishop Antonio Franco said in his homily that in celebrating the feast of the Baptism of our Lord, there was a call to act as Christians at all times as we share this Baptism.

"This is a faith that should always inspire us to act in love. Jesus inspires us to overcome difficulties in life and this shared celebration is a signal of hope. The Universal Church, led by the Holy Father shares its faith with you in this Church in Gaza and is united with you as you go through particularly difficult times.

"You are not alone and with faith in the Lord we can together overcome difficulties. This mass is a renewal of our faith and we ask for Mary's blessings that we should always be Christian in the way we act and the way we live."

Since 1998, the Bishops' Conference of England and Wales has organised the annual meeting of the Coordination of Episcopal Conferences in Support of the Church of the Holy Land and at the invitation of the Assembly of Catholic Ordinaries of the Holy Land. It is often more simply called the Holy Land Co-ordination.

Mandated by the Holy See, the Holy Land Co-ordination meets every January in the Holy Land, focusing on prayer, pilgrimage and persuasion with the aim of acting in solidarity with the Christian community there and sharing in the pastoral life of the local Church as it experiences intense political and social-economic pressure.

With the Assembly of Catholic Ordinaries of the Holy Land, the opening session of the Coordination will take place on Monday 9 January. During the four days of the meeting, there will be addresses from His Beatitude Patriarch Fouad Twal and the Apostolic Nuncio, presentations from academics and a view from both Israelis and Palestinians about the impact of the "Arab Spring" and the socio-political changes in the region.

In addition to the prayers, liturgies and formal visits to other Catholic rites and Christian denominations, on Tuesday 10 January, there will be a visit to Haifa, during which there will be an inter-religious exchange with Jews, Muslims, Druze and Bahai. Political meetings will take place with both Israeli and Palestinian ministers and other politicians.

Children of Gaza greet the Patriarch

Photos and article by Andres Bergamini, Christmas 2011

His Beatitude Fouad Twal, Latin Patriarch of Jerusalem visited the Latin parish in Gaza on Sunday, December 18th for an early Christmas celebration. Some children received the sacraments of Confirmation and First Communion. The young Christians in Gaza are the best example of this year's Christmas, and a beautiful Sunday message for the small Catholic community of the Strip. The Patriarch was welcomed by the local Christians led by the parish priest, Fr. Jorge Hernandez. Mass was celebrated, seven children were confirmed and three received first holy communion.

The Latin Patriarchate delegation was greeted in the courtyard of the parish to the rhythm of drums of the scout group of 60 members. About 300 people filled the church. The children were at the heart of the Patriarch's homily drawing the attention of the faithful to the Advent of Christmas. "A child, innocent and defenseless, was born in Bethlehem, in our beloved Holy Land. He brings peace and salvation to all men. We look up to him as a model and example, to be like him, to be witnesses of the love and mutual acceptance. In a world torn by conflict and hostility, the Child Jesus is an extraordinary sign of newness and hope. "The Patriarch continued by stating that "the children of the parish, who for the first time receive the Body and Blood of Christ, or marked by the Holy Spirit are for us the image of the nativity in Bethlehem." He concluded by saying that, "Peace begins in our hearts and extends to our families, and then silently spreads to our cities and in our land.After the celebration, His Beatitude gave interviews to the local press. He insisted that every Christian has the right to go to Bethlehem to celebrate Christmas. This year, Israeli authorities issued about 500 permits for Christians from Gaza to travel to the city where the Savior was born. However, excluded are those between 16 and 35. Families are not together, not for Christmas. Christians suffer like all Palestinian people who still do not enjoy the right to live in an independent free and peaceful state.

In the parish hall, families exchanged Christmas greetings and wishes for the new year in a joyful atmosphere. Members of the Patriarchate delegation were: Fr. Pietro Felet, Secretary General of the Celra; Fr.  Humam Khzouz, Patriarchate Director General; Fr. Marcelo Gallardo, Vice Chancellor of the Patriarchate; Fr Mario Corniole and Fr. Gabriel Romanelli. Cris El-Bandak, a Christian from Bethlehem released by the State of Israel on October 18 in exchange for soldier Gilad Shalit, was present during the celebration. After the big meal, the two cars of the delegation of the Patriarchate returned to Jerusalem. Control procedures and security at the Erez checkpoint were particularly quick and easy, thanks to coordination with the Israeli authorities.

Suffering and Consolation in The Parish of Gaza

GAZA – Around midnight on February 26, the feast day of St. Porphyry, unidentified assailants placed an improvised explosive device in the Churchyard of the Holy Family Parish of the Latin Church in Gaza. The explosion awoke the pastor, Fr. Jorge Hernandez, who immediately extinguished the initial fire that was developing near his car. The suspects also scribbled some writing on the facade of the Church.

Overall, the damage is modest. From the initial police investigation it seems that the perpetrators are not skilled people, but criminals who wanted to make a statement. The explosive was not placed near the Church door but on the side of the churchyard and the words did not desecrate the Cross that stands out in plain sight on the building. The event, however, has deeply shaken the small Christian community, and, in particular, the religious sisters who reside in the parish. The coexistence of Christians and Muslims in the Gaza Strip has been peaceful, for the most part. Apart from some rare episodes, there were no serious events of intolerance and persecution in the past. However, the balance is delicate, and any false or hyped news can endanger the lives of people.

The Pastor, concurring with the Latin Patriarchate, did not want to give too much prominence to the news, in order to protect the community from further similar actions. The social and economic situations in the small and densely populated Gaza Strip are sorely tested by the siege,

which has lasted for too many years, and by the almost-total closure of the checkpoints with both Israel and Egypt.

In the days following the attack, the highest civil and religious authorities and a number of delegations visited the parish to show their solidarity and closeness to Christians and to firmly condemn this deplorable act of intimidation.

The **life** of the parish – the schools, the sacred liturgies, the youth club, family visitations, and welcoming guests – immediately resumed normalcy, with the strength and enthusiasm that characterizes our beloved Gaza Christians. A young couple's engagement and the birth of a child, Julia, are some of the more beautiful and strong signs of the **witness** that bring **comfort** to the Christian family, despite the hardships to which they are subjected.

Article and photos of the LPJ correspondent in Gaza, Andres Bergamini.

A Letter from a Priest in Gaza

Written on November 19, 2012 in LPJ

GAZA - On the sixth day of the military operation launched by Israel against the Gaza Strip, the parish priest of the Latin parish, Father Jorge Hernandez, IVE, back among his parishioners tells the continuous and growing fear that everyone tries.

I write to you from our parish of the Holy Family in Gaza as part of the Latin Patriarchate of Jerusalem and has about 200 Catholics. The place is known by everyone and even the parish complex that houses school children - Christians and Muslims - as one family.

The tension that exists in the Gaza Strip Saturday, November 10th is already known. It has intensified, especially since Wednesday 14 The situation has not changed, but rather worsening day by day. The pressure of the bombing continues night and day, is amplified more and more with the continuation of the conflict.

The deafening noise of the bombs, insecurity and fear make people suffer torture, not only bloody, but also cruel and ruthless both spiritually and mentally. Just look at the case, for example, of a young girl in our parish who has had a nervous breakdown because of the bombing. It is not the first case, there is only one example among others. You may also remember the young Cristina Wadi Al Turk, Christian killed by a heart attack due to the cold and fear during the war of 2008-2009.

We call on all leaders to leave Gaza to live in peace!

The careful reader will ask: How are the people? What are they experiencing? In a word, they are afraid and cannot be otherwise. The missiles do not understand nor ethics, nor morals. Do not distinguish between young and old, between Christians and Muslims, between men and women ... Just fall down and then destroy it. When we hear the planes and missiles then try a very large inner sadness and some relief to see that were not affected. With the same question: "how long?" The people want nothing more than to simply live their lives. We ask all the leaders to leave Gaza to live in peace!

We wonder about Christians who are suffering. Yes, they suffer as Christians, but also suffer because the Palestinians. As Palestinians suffer for the unjust aggression, in the same way as their Muslim brothers, but, as Christians, they resign themselves and rely on divine providence of God the Father, with a simple *"Alhamdu Lil'a" (Laus Deo! God be praised)*. It is recognized as an extraordinary force that characterizes them and that builds up when paradoxically emerges from this suffering.

Our mission is to be close to the Christians of Gaza

And you missionaries? We give thanks to God, we're fine. Our mission is to be close to the Christians of Gaza. Accompany them, carry this cross with them. Call them, encourage them and be comforted them, and teach them the true Christian meaning of suffering, namely participation in the sufferings of Christ. And this gesture, which is our own, recognize him, give him value and appreciate. We plead: *"Do not leave ... We understand that you are tempted to leave, but it is better that you stay with us"* ... These are the phrases with many others we are confident that our parishioners. The mere fact of knowing that accompanied the suffering is a huge relief. And 'this is our task.

But it would be too long to describe what is the inner attitude of the pastor, religious and missionaries in such circumstances as are present. During the celebration of the Mass, in the silence of Eucharistic adoration during the recitation of the Holy Rosary we present all those who suffer. We also learn to be ready at any moment to put our lives in the hands of the Lord and meditate on eternal life. For every bomb that falls stands a prayer to God that embraces these poor souls, have mercy on them. We think: How many unnecessary deaths! How many innocent deaths for a reason I do not know! How many orphans and widows because of these attacks! For each and every one of them stands a prayer to heaven.

Consular and pity is the duty of the Mother Church

We are not pioneers in this. Consular and pity is the duty of the Mother Church, it is also the duty and the task of the priest. And among many others of Father Manuel Musallam, who was pastor of this community in difficult times and in times of war and is now with us and teaches us.

It 'worth noting the edifying example of courage and submission of complete and unconditional religious who are in our parish and who like to stay here and carry this cross with others. Three religious congregations are present in the Gaza Strip: the Sisters of the Rosary (Jerusalem), the Missionaries of Charity of Mother Teresa and the Servants of the Lord and the Virgin of Matara. Their prayers and the prayers are a blessing and God will reward them for their generosity.

Finally, finally, do not forget how the war is always terrible. No one gains in a war. I would say even more, is lost forever. Each party shall pay, in its way, the consequences of the war. The consequences of all types, including the consequence of having lost what is most proper to man "his humanity."

May our Lord Jesus Christ "Prince of Peace" and the God of mercy protect these people who welcomed him during his The Flight into Egypt, to enlighten its leaders and bless this land with the gift of peace.

We entrust to your prayers in Christ and the Blessed Virgin.

Jorge P. Hernandez
Religious Institute of the Incarnate Word
Parish Priest of Gaza

Meeting with a Delegation of United States Catholic Bishops: "We Cannot Keep Silent!"

Monday, 15 September 2014 LPJ

JERUSALEM– On Friday, September 12, 2014, a delegation of twenty bishops from the United States on a pilgrimage in the footsteps of Pope Francis to promote peace, accompanied by members of CRS (Catholic Relief Services), gathered with His Beatitude Fouad Twal the Latin Patriarchate. The countless challenges of the Christian community in the Holy Land were discussed, and the Patriarch and various speakers called for prayer and support of the Mother Church in its most concrete needs.

The director of schools, Father Faysal Hijazen, then spoke and stressed the **importance of education for the formation of a new generation of peace**, recalling the words of Pope Francis in Bethlehem:*"The Child is the sign Peace."*The director of the school in Beit Jala presented all the challenges faced by schools in the Holy Land, which have worked in the region for over 160 years, and currently devoted to the education of over 17,000 students spread over 45 schools. Schools are indeed the essential breeding ground for transmission of the faith, of universal Christian values, and teaching mutual respect and coexistence between different faiths welcomed on equal terms. They also help to preserve the identity and the Christian presence in this troubled region of the world. In the very long list of challenges that schools must face, there are two priorities: social security for teachers, as yet non-existent, and the restoration of schools in Gaza. Faced with these challenges, Father Faysal suggested to American bishops that each diocese of their country could adopt a school in our country.

Fr.Raed Abusahlia, general director of Caritas Jerusalem, also presented the needs of the people of the Holy Land, specifying concrete and current needs of the Gaza Strip. After intensive emergency interventions during the war, now it is necessary to face a long process of rebuilding and continue to meet the immediate needs of the displaced and homeless. Father Raed highlighted how Caritas works for peace and coexistence. At a recent initiative called *"Footballs not bombs"*, the organization distributed more than 7,000 soccer balls to the children of Gaza. And in response to 4564 rockets sent by Hamas, 4564 balloons were sent to children in southern Israel. *"This is a very symbolic message. On both sides, children have suffered. These children should play"* said Fr. Raed while stressing how, during the war, he was touched by the solidarity of many Israeli associations for peace and individuals who provided assistance and expressed their support for the people of Gaza. The director of Caritas Jerusalem concluded by suggesting to the delegation, like the Fr. Faysal, that the various dioceses of the United States sponsor activities and projects of Caritas.

Father Jorge Hernandez, parish priest of Gaza, with Msgr. Shomali, Vicar for Jerusalem and Palestine

Next, the **parish priest of Gaza, Father Jorge Hernandez** spoke, thanking Catholic Relief Services and Caritas for their valuable support during the war. Father Jorge explained the urgency of finding **a political and not only an economic solution for Gaza.** *"We need a solution to the Gaza blockade, otherwise we are going to just rebuild before the next war."* Many Christians choose to leave, and the number of Christians in Gaza continues to decline, recounted Father Jorge. A humanitarian emergency that will only become more acute with the approach of winter is the insufficient number of tents to shelter the displaced, coupled with serious injuries and psychological trauma suffered:**"a six year old child in Gaza has already experienced three wars"** lamented Father Jorge, launching an urgent call to prayer.

Then, Bishop Shomali, Patriarchal Vicar for Jerusalem and Palestine referred to the two main demands made by Pope Francis during his visit to the Israeli government: a solution for the **reunification of families** divided by the wall of separation, and the **facilitation of clergy movements** between Israel and Palestine. The Patriarch concluded the meeting by reminding that *" Peace will never happen by building walls,"* and he encouraged the American bishops to advocate loudly the cause of a just peace in the country. The meeting was then followed by a Mass at the Co-Cathedral of the Patriarchate, after which all were invited to lunch.

Myriam Ambroselli- LPJ

Bishops call for Leaders of Hope

Statement of the Co-ordination of Bishops' Conferences - 15 January 2014 (This date is prior to the latest war)

GAZA – The Bishop representatives of the Episcopal Conferences of various parts of the world ended a two day visit to the Gaza Strip this morning, Monday, January 13.

As bishops from Europe, South Africa and North America we came to the Holy Land to pray with and support the Christian community and the cause of peace.

In Gaza we witnessed the deep poverty of the people, and the courageous presence of the small and vulnerable Christian communities there. Gaza is a man-made disaster, a shocking scandal, an injustice that cries out to the human community for a resolution. We call upon political leaders to improve the humanitarian situation of the people in Gaza, assuring access to the basic necessities for a dignified human life, the possibilities for economic development, and freedom of movement.

In the seemingly hopeless situation of Gaza, we met people of hope. We were encouraged by our visit to tiny Christian communities, which day after day, through many institutions, reach out with compassion to the poorest of the poor, both Muslim and Christian. We continue to pray for and support the priests, religious and laypeople working in Gaza. They exercise a ministry of presence, care for disabled children and the elderly, and teach the young. Their testimony of faith, hope and love gave us hope. This is precisely the hope needed at this moment to bring peace, a peace that can only be built on justice and equity for both peoples.

Palestinians and Israelis desperately need this peace. For example, in the Cremisan valley the route of the security barrier threatens the agricultural land held for generations by 58 Christian families. The current peace talks come at a critical time.

Now is the time to ensure that the aspirations for justice of both sides are fulfilled. We urge public officials to become leaders of hope, not people of obstruction. We call upon them to listen to the words of Pope Francis, who recently said to the Diplomatic Corps: "The resumption of peace talks between Israelis and Palestinians is a positive sign, and I express my hope that both parties will resolve, with the support of the international community, to take courageous decisions aimed at finding a just and lasting solution to a conflict which urgently needs to end ".

As we leave the Holy Land, the bishops and people of the local Church remain in our hearts. They are not alone. Together with them we are people of hope. We pray that the visit of Pope Francis to the Holy Land will reinforce hope in the region. We believe a lasting peace is possible

Archbishop Stephen Brislin, South Africa,
Bishop Pierre Burcher, Scandinavia,
Bishop William Crean, Ireland,
Bishop Michel Dubost, France
Archbishop Paul-Andre Durocher, Canada,
Archbishop Patrick Kelly, England and Wales,
Bishop William Kenney, England and Wales
Bishop Declan Lang, England and Wales,
Bishop Denis Nulty, Ireland,
Bishop Richard Pates, United States of America,
Bishop Thomas Renz, Germany,
Bishop Janusz Stepnowski, Poland,
Archbishop Joan Enric Vives, Spain

Vatican Representative to UN Addresses Situation in Palestine

Friday, 25 July 2014

(Vatican Radio) The Permanent observer of the Holy See to the United Nations organs in Geneva, Archbishop Silvano Tomasi, delivered a statement during a special session of the UN's Human Rights Council on the human rights situation in the Occupied Palestinian Territory, including East Jerusalem. Below, please find the full text of his remarks in English.

Statement by H.E. Archbishop Silvano M. Tomasi, Permanent Representative of the Holy See to the United Nations and Other International Organizations in Geneva 21st Special Session of the Human Rights Council on the human rights situation in the Occupied Palestinian Territory including East Jerusalem.

Mr. President,

As the number of people killed, wounded, uprooted from their homes, continues to increase in the conflict between Israel and some Palestinian groups, particularly in the Gaza Strip, the voice of reason seems submerged by the blast of arms. Violence will lead nowhere either now or in the future. The perpetration of injustices and the violation of human rights, especially the right to life and to live in peace and security, sow fresh seeds of hatred and resentment. A culture of violence is being consolidated, the fruits of which are destruction and death. In the long run, there can be no winners in the current tragedy, only more suffering. Most of the victims are civilians, who by international humanitarian law, should be protected. The United Nations estimates that approximately seventy percent of Palestinians killed have been innocent civilians. This is just as intolerable as the rockets missiles directed indiscriminately toward civilian targets in Israel. Consciences are paralyzed by a climate of protracted violence, which seeks to impose solution through the annihilation of the other. Demonizing others, however, does not eliminate their rights. Instead, the way to the future, lies in recognizing our common humanity.

In his Pilgrimage to the Holy Land, Pope Francis demanded that the present unacceptable situation of the Israeli-Palestinian conflict be brought to an end.[1] "For the good of all," he said, "there is a need to intensify efforts and initiatives aimed at creating the conditions for a stable peace based on justice, on the recognition of the rights of every individual, and on mutual security. The time has come for everyone to find the courage to be generous and creative in the service of the common good, the courage to forge a peace which rests on the acknowledgment by all of the right of two States to exist and to live in peace and security within internationally recognized borders."[2] The legitimate aspiration to security, on one side, and to decent living conditions, on the other, with access to the normal means of existence like medicines, water and jobs, for example, reflects a fundamental human right, without which peace is very difficult to preserve.

The worsening situation in Gaza is an incessant reminder of the necessity to arrive at a cease-fire immediately and to start negotiating a lasting peace. "Peace will bring countless benefits for the peoples of this region and for the world as a whole," adds Pope Francis, "and so it must resolutely be pursued, even if each side has to make certain sacrifices." It becomes a responsibility of the international community to engage in earnest in the pursuit of peace and to help the parties in this horrible conflict reach some understanding in order to stop the violence and look to the future with mutual trust.

Mr. President,

The Delegation of the Holy See reiterates its view that violence never pays. Violence will only lead to more suffering, devastation and death, and will prevent peace from becoming a reality. The strategy of violence can be contagious and become uncontrollable. To combat violence and its detrimental consequences we must avoid becoming accustomed to killing. At a time where brutality is common and human rights violations are ubiquitous, we must not become indifferent but respond positively in order to attenuate the conflict which concerns us all.

The media should report in a fair and unbiased manner the tragedy of all who are suffering because of the conflict, in order to facilitate the development of an impartial dialogue that acknowledges the rights of everyone, respects the just concerns of the international community, and benefits from the solidarity of the international community in supporting a serious effort to attain peace. With an eye to the future, the vicious circle of retribution and retaliation must cease. With violence, men and women will continue to live as enemies and adversaries, but with peace they can live as brothers and sisters.

Thank you, Mr. President.

Gaza's Christians Trapped like Everyone Else

Vatican Radio

Gaza's 1300 Christians are made up of some 310 families. "All of them are concentrated in the city of Gaza, Fr. Raed explains. "Not in the other refugee camps or cities of Gaza. So they are in the middle of the conflict. The whole situation is difficult: no electricity, no water, day and night bombardments, missiles from both sides. So it is really, really terrible. They can't go out even if they would like to. Even if they can go out, where can they go? The Egyptian crossing is closed, the Israeli side is closed so they are trapped there."

Churches have opened their doors to displaced people, giving refuge to as many people as they can, Fr. Raed notes. "In our Holy Family school the number of refugees was days ago, 700. Today, we reached 1,100 people living there. In the Greek Orthodox church, days ago the number was 1,100 people. Now, it is 1,900 people... They have "nothing, nothing at all to offer them."

"Churches are trying to help them, providing them with food, with gasoline, with milk for their children. We in Caritas tried to provide hot meals for the whole week and this is the last day (since Caritas' most recent appeal for funds) and we are trying since this morning to get more funds for another week. Because we expected that the war will end and we didn't expect that it would last until today... I am describing the situation but to see the photos and hear these stories, it's really beyond your imagination!" says a distraught Fr. Raed. "It's like in the Second World War which means (there's) whole(sale) destruction. They are targeting everybody: civilians, women, children and hospitals."

El-Yousef praised the work of George Anton, a CNEWA team member. He "leaves his young family on a daily basis and risks his own life to visit local institutions and individuals in order to assess the situation on the ground," he said. He describes his personal experience and the stories of ordinary people affected by the war, the dozens of displaced families housed at the Holy Family Catholic Church, the hundreds of injured patients at the Anglican-run Al Ahli Arab Hospital and dozens of devout Muslim women and their children taking refuge at the ancient Greek Orthodox church of St. Porphyrios.

"Our churches and Church institutions in Gaza continue to be that beacon of hope despite all of the misery," El-Jousef wrote. "Holy Family School, the Greek Orthodox parish and the Greek Orthodox Cultural Center have all opened up their facilities to hundreds of displaced families, giving them food, clean water and above all a safe roof over their heads. The Al Ahli Arab Hospital continues to open up its facilities in this emergency crisis to anyone needing medical treatment, free of charge. Incarnate Word Father Georges Hernandez continues to risk his life every day by making home and hospital visits. The Missionaries of Charity continue to call Gaza home despite the various offers for evacuation."

Despite all of the suffering," El-Jousef writes, "the Christian mission is certainly at its best. These brave souls — who are personally risking their lives — continue to comfort the injured and displaced, and provide assistance to the weak and marginalized with the Gospel in their hearts. "Please know that your support and prayers for the people of Gaza, especially the women and children, are priceless and help to keep hope and faith alive."

Missionaries of Charity Nuns Continue Works in Gaza - 2014

A group of five nuns from the Missionaries of Charity silently continue their work for the poor in war-torn Gaza amid Israeli troops starting a ground offensive.

The nuns live in the Latin Convent in Zeiturn, Gaza City and their Superior Sister Belfina told Sunday Express that they are "not going anywhere" war or no war.

They have over 24 differently-abled children and 15 aged women to take care.

"Everything is fine... We are all safe. We often hear the bombings in the distance. It happens more frequently at night, but not so much during the day. The Israelis are bombing Hamas bases on the borders. But our Latin Convent is right in the middle of Gaza City, so we have not been hit by the war yet," she said in a soft, calm voice.

"We have taken the Fourth Vow — of giving wholehearted and free service to the poorest of the poor, no matter what the circumstances. We are privileged to serve in Gaza, which is one of the poorest places in the Middle East. As for the raids, we have got used to the sound of the bombs exploding. We have learnt to live with it," she says.

One of them Sister Liliet is from Orissa. She said she has been serving in the Middle East for a long time and came to Gaza a year ago.

"The Indian office in Ramallah has been calling often, sometimes four times a day, to check on me. It offered to arrange for my passport and papers so that I can return to India... But I don't want to go back," she says.

"The bombings have caused a lot of damage... the borders are closed. People's houses are being destroyed, especially in villages like Beit Lahiya and Khan Younis on the border.

Most of the children in our convent are from these villages. Their parents leave them here so that they are safe and are fed properly. Others who lose their homes in the air raids take shelter in UN schools which provide food," says Sister Liliet.

Source:Financial Express

Missionaries of Charity say they'll stay in Gaza with women, children - 2009

JUDITH SUDILOVSKY | CATHOLIC NEWS SERVICE

JERUSALEM (CNS) Despite the bombings and Israeli ground-force incursion into the Gaza Strip, the six Missionaries of Charity working in Gaza City say life has some normalcy and they plan to remain.

But for other Gazans, life has changed dramatically since Israeli airstrikes began Dec. 27 in an effort to stop Palestinian militants from launching rockets into Israel's southern region. Since then, more than 500 Palestinians have been killed. Israel also launched a ground invasion Jan.

The six sisters — from India, Malta, the Philippines, Rwanda and Slovakia — continue to bathe, feed and care for 10 incapacitated elderly women and 10 severely mentally and physically disabled children as well as they can, Sister Thertsen Devasia told Catholic News Service in a Jan. 5 phone interview.

"We are OK. The bombings are not so near," she said. Their home is located in the center of the city just behind Holy Family Catholic Church. "We go to Mass every day at the Latin church. Father sends his car for us and brings us back."

Some of the children have been terrified by the noise of the bombings, she added, but most do not react to their surroundings. A 1-year-old who recently began living with them screams whenever she hears the loud noises, the nun said.

"By the grace of God we are safe and we will stay here. If something happens to our people we will be with them," said Sister Thertsen.

Catholic Relief Services, the U.S. bishops' international aid and development agency with offices in Jerusalem, has been in continual contact with the nuns, said Sister Thertsen. Recently when they ran out of diapers, bottled water and cooking gas, CRS was able to coordinate through the Red Cross and the U.N. Relief and Works Agency for Palestine Refugees to have the material delivered to them.

However, a young Christian Gazan who asked not to be named sounded shaken while speaking to CNS by phone Jan. 4, the morning following the Israeli invasion. He said many Gazans had not slept all night, and as he looked out the window where some government offices had once stood he could see only rubble. In the background his mother called anxiously for him to move away from the window.

"We have lived through bad conditions here but never in my wildest imagination would I have thought that I would be living in a war situation," he said, wondering at the suddenness of how one goes from living a relatively daily mundane life, even in Gaza, to suddenly being in the middle of a war.

He was audibly distraught over the number of children who had lost their lives since the start of the Israeli attacks in late December. He said in early January that a 15-year-old Greek Orthodox girl died from a heart attack; she was unable to take the strain from the fear of the aerial attacks.

The Gazan said his family had not had any electricity for days and there was no running water. All the food in the refrigerator had spoiled, and although they had run out of bread he was too scared to go out to buy anything. The family lives in the center of Gaza City, which was targeted by Israel, and no stores were open in their neighborhood.

He still was able to have some phone contact and was aware of demonstrations around the world protesting the Israeli incursion.

However, he said, protests only created more animosity and hatred and widened the gap between the sides.

Though he was in touch with some of his friends, he had little opportunity to express himself freely, he said.

"I have to choose what to say to friends. People in Gaza are not afraid to die. There are fanatics here," he said. "I do not support what either side is doing. I hope this can be a lesson for both sides when this is finished."

Copyright (c) 2009 Catholic News Service/U.S. Conference of Catholic Bishops: Photo Andres Bergamini

Gaza's Christians and Muslims Grow Closer in Defiance of Israeli Attacks

Solidarity between the Christian minority and Muslim majority is growing in Gaza as both suffer under the Israeli offensive, with churches sheltering all religions and prayers being offered up on all sides.

Mourners gather at the funeral of Palestinian Christian Jalila Ayyad (AA)

Article: Middle East Eye, Mohammed Omer

GAZA CITY Without prior warning, an Israeli missile hit the house of the Ayyad family last Saturday. The Ayyads, who are Christian, were the first family among the tiny minority in Gaza to be targeted since the offensive began three weeks ago.

The Ayyad's home was severely damaged. Furniture was ruined and family belongings such as children's toys were strewn everywhere as a result of the missile's impact. But naturally the human cost was much greater. Jalila Ayyad was known among the people of Gaza as a woman that had nothing to do with any militia groups. "We are a Christian minority and have no links to Hamas or Fatah - we keep to ourselves and avoid problems," says Fouad Ayyad, Jalila's nephew.

Fouad is also the name of the bereaved husband of Jalila Ayyad. Standing in a white T-shirt stained with the blood of his wife and son - who was also seriously injured in the attack - he watches on as the nephew is interviewed.

Many tears were shed among the Christian minority at the service (AA)

A memorial service was held on Sunday for Ayyad at Porphyrius Greek Orthodox Church on Sunday. The church has become a haven not just for Christian but also hundreds of Muslim families seeking shelter there as the offensive drags on.

"The church has been our hosts for the past two weeks, offering food, clothes and whatever we needed, their loss is our loss, their pain is our pain," says 45-year-old Abu Khaled.

At the memorial service for Jalila, Archbishop Alexios said: "Another human being, an innocent one, has lost her life." In the pews, crowds of Palestinian Christians sobbed as first from their tiny minority to be killed in the conflict was laid to rest.

In something that surprised local journalists, Jalila's body was carried by both Muslims and Christians to the grave. It seems the shared wounds, mourning and rage are bridging past divides in war-ravaged Gaza.

Last week, Gaza's Greek Orthodox Church also sustained damage by Israeli artillery shelling. Fifteen graves were damaged and damage was also caused to the Church's sole hearse, says Kamel Ayyad, a parish member.

"The world must realise that Israel's missiles don't differentiate between Christians and Muslims," said Abu.

At the memorial service a sad young man surrounded by attendees dressed in black gave a speech on behalf of the Greek Orthodox community and questioned the position of the international community in dealing with Israel's crimes.

"Here is a Palestinian, an Arab, a Christian woman, martyred by Israeli shelling," he said. "Bombs slammed into us and killed without differentiating between civilians and combatants," he adds.

Christians and Muslims both helped to carry the coffin to the grave (AA)

Father Manuel Musallam, a former priest of the Latin Church, has always been an advocate for Palestinian unity. "When they destroy your mosques, call your prayers from our churches".

There are approximately 1,500 Christians in Gaza. Mosques stand next to churches along the thin coastal enclave. George Ayyad, a relative of Jalila, rejects the idea that Christians will leave Gaza after this incident. "This is exactly what the Israelis want, but where should we go?" he questions, before he continues "This is my homeland and we are Christians here in Gaza for more than 1,000 years and we will remain."

During the memorial, bible scriptures were recited before Ayyad's body was carried out and placed in a simple white coffin that had been decorated with a black cross. Homeless Christians and Muslims brought out her remains together in the same community where Jalila will be buried, in the town she was born: in Gaza. A Virgin Mary icon was placed in Jalila's coffin while her relatives sang "Hallelujah."

Caritas Jerusalem Director says conflict has claimed its first Christian victim.

Independent Catholic News, 2014

An Israeli missile strike on Sunday hit the house of the Ayyads, a Christian family living in Gaza "without any previous notice and we don't even know why it was attacked," says Fr. Raed. "The whole house was completely destroyed and the mother, who is 60 years old, died immediately. And her son, who is thirty years old, is severely injured. Two of his legs were cut and he has burns on 70% of his body. And damages in his head. So he is in a very critical condition."

Caritas has been negotiating with Israeli authorities to allow Ayyad's transfer from Gaza to St. Joseph's hospital in Jerusalem for treatment but so far, no authorization has been forthcoming, he says. "He is risking his life. Doctors said if he doesn't go out from Gaza immediately, he has only a 20% chance to live." A first attempt to evacuate him failed after an Israeli strike on the hospital where he is receiving care.

The mother was buried three hours after her death Sunday "because there are no places in the hospitals and because her body was torn completely. So she was buried in the Greek Orthodox church of Gaza."

The latest resumption of hostilities between Israel and Hamas in Gaza has claimed its first confirmed Christian victim: 60- year-old woman Jalileh Ayyad.

Sami El-Yousef, regional director for Palestine and Israel for the Catholic Near East Welfare Association (CNEWA), provided the Register with an update on Christians and Christian institutions in

Gaza. El-Yousef's organization provides vital humanitarian services to Christians and Muslims in the Gaza Strip and elsewhere.

In a phone interview, he said that, although the Israeli army apparently warned the family that their home would be targeted, a missile flew through their roof and into the home before they were able to flee. Ayyad was killed instantly; her 32-year-old son, Jeries, survived, but is in critical condition. He sustained extensive burns and shrapnel wounds that required the amputation of both his legs. He was transferred to St. Joseph's Hospital in Jerusalem "where he is fighting for his life," according to El-Jousef.

He said that the Caritas clinic and three clinics run by the Near East Council of Churches in Gaza "are all shut down because they operate in areas that are way too dangerous to reach."

Furthermore, the residence of the religious sisters serving the Latin Parish in Zeitoun, Gaza, was damaged by an Israeli shell.

El-Yousef provided additional details on CNEWA's blog:

I received an urgent call two days ago from Suhaila Tarazi, director of the Al Ahli Arab Hospital in Gaza, explaining the urgency for medicines, medical supplies and, more importantly, fuel to operate the hospital's generator. She reported the hospital had to make a painful decision to shut down their generator for 4 hours that afternoon in order to ration fuel. She was very upset not knowing what impact it will have on the patients' treatment and recovery.

We immediately lobbied with our connections to ensure the hospital gets the fuel supply it needs to continue to save lives.

The Holy Family Latin Church in Gaza has just received an evacuation order warning them that Israei is planning to bomb their neighbourhood tonight. In a message, a priest writes: "The church of Gaza has received an order to evacuate.. they will bomb the Zeitun area and the people are already fleeing. The problem is that the priest Fr George and the three nuns of Mother Teresa have 29 handicapped children and nine old ladies who can't move.

"How will they manage to leave?? If anyone can intercede with someone in power, and pray, please do it. We are trying.. may our impotence be taken up by his Omnipotence!!"

The House of Christ in Gaza, is a care home dedicated to looking after disabled children. The disabled children were removed from the care home into the Holy Family Church recently because Israel was targeting the area.

The parish appeal for prayers.

Caritas Jerusalem in Gaza

Photo: Andres Bergamini

Father Raed Abusahlia, president of Caritas Jerusalem who has been in contact with the parish priest, told Catholic News Service that Father Jorge Hernandez of the Institute of the Incarnate Word and three nuns who live at the parish had nowhere to evacuate the 29 severely disabled children and nine elderly women in their care.

Since Israel launched airstrikes against Gaza July 8, it has sent text messages to citizens to evacuate if they will be near a target. Israel bombed near Holy Family Catholic Church the morning of July 30.

The Vatican's Fides news agency, citing details from Father Hernandez, said the main target of the bombing was a home a few meters away from the parish. The home was completely destroyed, and the parish school, office and some rooms used by the parish were partially destroyed.

Father Abusahlia told CNS all the windows of the whole compound, as well as that of the Greek Orthodox Church, already were shattered from previous bombings of buildings around them.

"They are in a very difficult situation," said Father Abusahlia. "It is a very dangerous area."

He said the number of refugees at the parish school, some distance away from the parish compound, increased from 600 people to 1,400 in the week ending July 30, and the number of refugees sheltered by the Greek Orthodox Church had increased from 1,400 to 1,900.

Caritas has been providing them with powdered milk, diapers and gasoline, which is especially important after the attack on the Gaza electrical plant. They rely on generators, Father Abusahlia said, and the gas to run them is very difficult and expensive to obtain.

Fides quoted Father Hernandez as saying: "We had a tough night, but we are here. This war is absurd.

"Everything happens around us," he said. "The Hamas militants continue to fire rockets and then hide in the alleys. And we cannot do anything. We cannot evacuate, it is impossible with children. Their families live here. It is more dangerous to go out than stay here. We try to stay in safer places, always on the ground floor."

Many people ran away, but the evacuation was not possible for those who currently live in the church: in addition to the Argentine Jorge Hernandez, a priest of the Institute of the Incarnate Word, there are even three nuns of Mother Teresa along with 29 disabled children and 9 elderly women in their care at the parish of the Holy Family.

"We had a tough night, but we are here. This war is absurd", says Fr. Hernandez. "After destroying the neighborhood of Shujayeh, now Zeitun is being targeted. Everything happens around us. The Hamas militants continue to fire rockets and then hide in the alleys. And we cannot do anything. We cannot evacuate, it is impossible with children. Their families live here. It is more dangerous to go out than stay here. We try to stay in safer places, always on the ground floor. "

"It is an absurd spiral: both sides", says Bishop William Shomali, Patriarchal Vicar of the Patriarch of Jerusalem of the Latins to Fides Agency "must listen to the voice of reason, stop the bloodshed and begin negotiations in order to address and solve problems. Otherwise all this violence will continue to repeat itself cyclically.

Seven out of the thirteen hospitals in Gaza have severe damage and the Home for the Disabled was bombed killing two special needs women.

The El Wafa hospital was bombed (July 17) twice destroying seven million dollars worth of essential medical equipment. The major power plant was bombed. A humanitarian disaster has unfolded since July 8th when Gaza came under fire and Hamas keeps shooting rockets into Israel. The Al Jazeera News office was also attacked yesterday; 12 ambulances have been destroyed.

More than 800 Palestinians have been killed mostly women and children. Over fifty families have been entirely wiped out where all members have died. This is a slaughter. The saddest story is the four boys ages 7-11 years old killed (July 16) on the beach while playing soccer.

They were fired upon twice by air and by sea. So tragic!

Source: Catholic News Service Reprinted courtesy of Catholic News Service, copyright 2014

There is Still Hope

Pontifical Mission for Palestine - the Papal Agency for Middle East Relief and Development

Emergency Intervention Assessment - First Post War Visit to Gaza (3-5 September 2014)

The Ugly Reality on the Ground

A street in Shija'ia neighborhood, Gaza **City.**

This was one of those visits where you brace yourself for the worst, given that the Gaza Strip went through a brutal war for a period of 51 days, during which the PMP was in close contact, with our friends and partners there and intensely watched the news coming out of Gaza and thus nothing we were about to see should have been a great shock. I guess we were proven wrong!

The "Italian" residential tower hit by Israeli missiles in Al-

The moment we arrived, the damage became apparent; from the newly built and now demolished crossing terminal on the Palestinian side, stretching kilometers of badly damaged neighborhoods until we arrived at our first meeting at Al-Ahli Arab Hospital. I do not believe we drove through any street that did not have a demolished building; whether residential buildings and towers, offices, shops, factories, warehouses, mosques, schools, hospitals and clinics, and government ministries. All of this one can handle, but the human stories were the most touching of all - people losing loved ones, their property, clothes, and all personal items leaving their past and memories behind.

I will never forget some of the surreal moments during our visit of people breaking down in tears when they saw us expressing that they thought they would not live, not even to see us again. Other sad stories included the nurse who worked at Al-Ahli Arab Hospital who was killed when she went home after working tirelessly on her shift to save lives and was fatally killed when her home was shelled. The only survivor of that incident was her baby of only a few months old whom she was still holding as she was clearly trying to protect her baby and her other child from imminent danger; or the clinical psychologist who took his personal belongings to his father's house only to find out that his father's house and his house were destroyed; Or the university professor who was nearing retirement and had been putting his life savings into his own two- story apartment building only to discover that the entire building had been demolished and he is now homeless; Or the secretary whose five nephews and nieces went up to the roof of their building to feed their pigeons were hit by a missile killing 3 of them instantly and leaving two in critical condition. They are now undergoing medical treatment and rehabilitation in a Turkish hospital.

And those who lived through the war clearly feared for their lives and lived under constant threat; many said they never put their pajamas and had all their valuables packed in a suitcase if they had to evacuate on a short notice! What a way to live for two months not knowing when your turn will come, and what kind of life awaits you thereafter. They continue to worry about their jobs, whether their children will be able to go back to school and the widespread diseases that are rapidly spreading throughout the Gaza Strip.

Nothing I say here will do justice to truly describe the humanitarian disaster called Gaza. One truly has to see it with his or her own eyes, and listen to the human tragedies to comprehend the true reality on the ground.

Update on PMP's Gaza Emergency Intervention

During PMP's three-day visit, I was able to meet all of our partners in Gaza and get a personal account of the situation and the impact of PMP's emergency intervention. Here is a brief update about the program's main components:

Phase 1 - Medicines, Medical Supplies, Fuel and Covering Medical Costs

Al-Ahli Arab Hospital

Most of PMP's emergency assistance in phase 1 of the program supported the operations of Al-Ahli Arab Hospital during the war. Donor assistance procured medicines, medical supplies, generator fuel, and covered the costs of emergency medical treatment for nearly 5,000 hospital patients who suffered from war-related injuries, infectious diseases and burns. These patients were able to undergo examinations by medical doctors, tests, surgery, specialized treatment and rehabilitation. The assistance specifically treated 1,600 burn cases and supported family members of the injured and also helped provide psychosocial therapy for hundreds of children of the injured. Throughout the war and with the support of donor assistance, the hospital provided high quality, professional services on a continuous basis free of charge. The hospital also hired additional staff to cope with the influx of emergency cases, stocked the hospital pharmacy with needed supplies and medicines and ensured an uninterrupted power supply from the hospital's electric generators at a time when Gaza had and continues to have limited electrical power.

NECC Clinic in Shija'ia neighborhood

NECC Clinics in Shija'ia, Darraj and Rafah all now in operation offering services free of charge. We were only able to visit Shija'ia clinic in Gaza City due to pressed timing. Nothing short of a miracle describes how this clinic only sustained minor damages while the entire street and neighborhood surrounding the clinic was almost completely destroyed. As a matter of fact, the only other clinic serving Shija'ia neighborhood, the *Ata Habib* governmental clinic was destroyed during the early days of the war. Since the ceasefire began, the minimal fee charged has been waived despite severe over crowdedness due to the large volume of patients from Shija'ia neighborhood and significant increase in the number of cases with communicable skin diseases, malnutrition, diarrhea and respiratory tract infections. Since reopening, the Shija'ia NECC clinic's clientele has doubled averaging 200 cases per day. A mother approached me expressing her deep appreciation to the clinic, its staff and donors for the quality services provided to her and her family. She said that she lost everything during the war, and the only stability in her life is the clinic in which she has been a member for over 15 years.

Phase 2 – Home and Institutional Renovations / Psychosocial Intervention

Home and Institutional Renovations

After the ceasefire began, PMP's partners assessed the extent of the damages sustained to the various Christian institutions and its community. For institutional damages, PMP has already committed to help rehabilitate sections of the Rosary Sisters School, NECC's network of clinics and vocational training centers, as well as the residence of the Sisters of Incarnate Word. As for the Holy Family School, although it sustained minimal war damages, most of the damages occurred after it was turned into a makeshift shelter for over a thousand people for a period of a month. It now requires major renovation work to restore the building as an educational institution and we are hoping to be able to contribute to this restoration project as well.

Although the destroyed homes of the Ayyad family and the Saba family were very much in the news, there are many other sad stories of homes that were partially damaged but enough to make the homes uninhabitable. PMP is currently working with the Greek Orthodox Trustees Committee and the International Orthodox Christian Charities (IOCC) to conduct an assessment of Christian homes that have sustained damages. According to the records, there are 88 homes however the IOCC team continues to assess more damaged homes of families in need. We hope to receive their assessment in a few days so that PMP can determine the level of support based on available funds. However, just to think that 88 homes sustained some sort of damage when there are only 390 Christian households in Gaza (or 22.5% of all households) is significant in itself and the list keeps growing as more homes continue to be brought to our attention! Finally, it is important to note that we have approval from our donors to use some of the funds to help displaced families cover expensive rental costs given the extent of the damage to their homes.

Rosary Sisters School's playground awning under repair. A mosque in the background was partially destroyed.

Residence of the Sisters of the Incarnate Word which was hit by shrapnel.

Psychosocial Intervention

The psychosocial program is advancing to its implementation stage, supporting children, school staff and parents traumatized by the war. During our visit, PMP held meetings with our local partners to launch the programs as soon as funds become available. The entirety of these programs would range between six months - one year, which would have a significant impact on thousands. Our local partners include the 5 Christian schools (Holy Family School; Latin Patriarchate School; Rosary Sisters School; Greek Orthodox School; and the Lighthouse School); Al- Ahli Arab Hospital; NECC mother and child clinics and vocational training centers; the YMCA- Gaza; the Society of Women Graduates (targeting 15 kindergartens and 7 public schools in the most severely affected areas); and the Myrrh Bearers Society. Proposals have been submitted to various donors and we are hopeful that funds can be raised to implement all of these programs.

General Assessment of the Situation – What's next?

It was very clear to me that it will take Gaza a long time to recover from the latest war, and that the likelihood of another round of hostilities is still very high. The destruction in Gaza is widespread; from public institutions, the private sector (including businesses and factories), and residential neighborhoods including some 18,000 homes. As for the education sector, the Ministry of Education has asked the schools to reopen on the 14th of September and to dedicate the first week to extracurricular activities to allow students to release tension and fear from the war. Many people in Gaza doubt that the schools will open in time given the fact that 15

UNRWA and 15 government schools are asked to continue to operate as shelters for more than 110,000 internally displaced people who are homeless; 22 schools that were destroyed and 118 schools that sustained damages have not yet been rebuilt or rehabilitated.

Destroyed Al-Wafa Hospital today with banner of what it used to look like before it was shelled. Hospital beds on top of the rubble.

However, what will be expected is a mediocre quality of education in extremely overcrowded schools which will put the whole educational system in Gaza in question.

As for the situation on the ground, everyone we spoke to highlight the level of frustration and outright anger towards Hamas and Fatah's leadership. Public outrage at Hamas stems from the fact that despite all the suffering of human and physical losses during the war, the situation surrounding daily life has not changed; the blockade remains in full force, the borders are closed and Israel has not allowed building supplies into the Gaza Strip which are desperately needed to rebuild Gaza and create jobs for the unemployed. The only positive outcome has been the expanded fishing area. Gazans have also expressed anger at Fatah, the PNA and the leadership of the Palestinian President, his ministers and other government officials. They wonder if they really care about their plight and why has the leadership of the supposedly 'national unity' government been absent in the public eye in Gaza? When the ceasefire was declared, the expectation was that Fatah leadership

and representatives would immediately go to Gaza and provide aid and given the severe emergency, move their offices there!

As for the Israeli side, there is anger especially amongst residents closest to the Gaza borders that had to evacuate their homes or spend most of their time in shelters. What has the Israeli government achieved for them, knowing very well that the military capability of Hamas is still intact and they can resume firing rockets at anytime? They are tired of this never ending cycle that keeps repeating itself every few years.

Shelled residential building on one of the main streets in Gaza

Given the sacrifices and losses on both sides, the logical expectation is that both leaderships should be ready to engage in serious negotiations that can address the root causes of the conflict and come to a negotiated settlement that would end the occupation and reach the internationally recognized solution of two states for two people, based on the 1967 borders, living in peace and harmony next to each other.

Shelled Ministry of Finance in Gaza City.

However, the reality on the ground is far from it. The Palestinians are on the verge of another division between the two major political parties that will probably be deeper than the previous one, and the Israeli government is back to its same old routine of confiscating more land, the latest being 4,000 dunams in the Bethlehem and Hebron districts, for the purpose of expanding their settlement project that is already preempting the two state solution and deeming it a dream of the past! Regardless of the angle one wishes to assess the current situation, it is indeed very pessimistic. Nothing short of a miracle will divert another bloody clash in the foreseeable future!

Assessment of the Christian Presence in Gaza

During the war on Gaza, the Christian institutions were at the forefront delivering humanitarian aid to the people of Gaza. The Holy Family School and the Greek Orthodox convent complex and the Greek Orthodox Community Center voluntarily opened up their doors as shelters to the homeless and displaced, providing food (actually it was reported that the Christian institutions were the only shelters that offered a hot meal during the Ramadan *Iftar*), clean potable water, hygiene kits and other basic necessities; the Al-Ahli Arab Hospital remained open under extremely difficult circumstances, offering free quality medical services for the injured and sick. Those receiving treatment there who were referred from other medical facilities commented on the quality of care after being neglected at other institutions.

Soap and detergent factory shelled in Gaza City.

The YMCA and Myrrh Bearers Society were opened up as distribution centers to their respective communities delivering food and hygiene kits as well as clean drinking water. The NECC clinics also opened immediately after the war providing services free of charge. The Catholic Relief Services and Caritas teams were also very active in Gaza, delivering urgent supplies to the vulnerable and needy.

Al-Zafer "4" Tower that was destroyed on the 50th day of the war housed 44 families including the Saba family, a Christian family of 4 people who are now homeless.

There is certainly a renewed appreciation by the community at large for the active role of the Christian institutions during the war. These institutions are no longer viewed as "closed" institutions to their immediate communities but rather serving all those in need with the Christian values at heart and are very much respected as a result. To me, this was personally the best conclusion I came out with from this latest visit, knowing that our efforts in the past few years to work with the Christian institutions to make them stronger really paid off, and what we truly have today are vibrant, strong Christian institutions that are respected and appreciated by Gaza society. Many thanks to our back donors for not losing hope on Gaza despite the odds, and for supporting our drive to strengthen these Christian institutions. After all, the services they provide touched the hearts and souls of all Gazans, especially the marginalized and weak.

And what about the Christian community? They have uffered like the rest of the community who lived through shelling and explosions at a rate that was unprecedented; they suffered from lack of adequate food supplies, clean water and electricity, damages to their homes and institutions and continue to suffer from travel restrictions. They too were traumatized to say the least and were no exception from the rest of the community at large and they share the same frustrations and fears like the rest of Gaza's society. Many of them, as their Muslim brothers and sisters confided in me that three wars in a span of 6 years was a little bit too much, especially that the latest one was the fiercest, and that maybe, just maybe, it was time to call it quits on Gaza and look for a quieter, safer place to live for them and their family! This was discouraging, but certainly understandable given the freshness of the war in their memory and given the lack of a durable solution. However, I have heard the same from these brave souls after the December 2008 war and after the November 2012 war and most of them are still there. I pray and hope that this will be another difficult period in their lives that will be soon behind us all. Keep praying for our people in Gaza.

Sami El-Yousef

Regional Director

Pontifical Mission for Palestine

A Cry for Peace Amid the Hell of Gaza

Catholic Relief Services in Gaza City gives the Register a ground-zero view of life for Gazans caught in the Israeli-Hamas cycle of cease-fire and conflict.

by PETER JESSERER SMITH 08/19/2014

A Palestinian man reads amid the rubble of a destroyed area of housing in Gaza City, Gaza, on Aug. 16. Dan Kitwood/Getty Images

GAZA CITY, Gaza — A cease-fire begins, a cease-fire breaks down, and the Palestinians of the Gaza Strip fall, one by one, victim to the bloody maw of war waged between its Hamas rulers and Israel. Amid the nightmarish destruction of Gaza, the Catholic Church is working with fellow Christian churches and aid organizations to provide humanitarian relief and light a candle of hope for the Palestinian territory's 1.8 million people.

The death toll in Gaza has exceeded 2,000 Palestinians, most of whom are civilians, while more than 10,000 are injured, and hundreds of thousands are displaced in the 139-square-mile territory. At least 67 Israelis, mostly soldiers, have died in efforts to destroy terror tunnels and rockets that have displaced thousands of Israelis from their homes in the south.

Speaking with the Register from Gaza City, Matthew McGarry, Catholic Relief Services' country representative for Jerusalem,

West Bank and Gaza, gave an account earlier this month of the humanitarian situation facing the war-battered people of Gaza.

What's the scope of the devastation in Gaza?

It's quite widespread, but very targeted. I got back into Gaza yesterday and was driving around town in the city center. ... Every block or every second block, there is one house or one floor of an apartment building or a mosque or a clinic or a shop just annihilated. It was an F-16 strike, or multiple strikes, and completely obliterated.

So to an outside observer, it doesn't look like anything has returned to normal, because, every block, a house is gone. Whereas in other neighborhoods, the city of Rafah, itself in the south, which are in the buffer zone — a three-kilometer strip that was basically declared a no-go zone by the Israeli army and where the ground troops were largely operating — there are entire neighborhoods that are just gone. ... It looks like a scene out of Aleppo or Dresden [in 1945], where it is just rubble, for block after block. The damage is total in some places.

The people we are serving so far, coming from those neighborhoods, are families whose houses are completely destroyed. They are staying out in the open or with relatives.

Drinking water is in extreme short supply. Gaza sits on top of a contaminated aquifer: Turn on the tap water, and it comes out brackish and salty. The only way they can get drinking water is to run the ground water through the desalination process or to import your water from somewhere else. [Gaza] mostly runs on two hours of power, every two days, for ... the last month. Unless you have a generator, you can't desalinate the water.

How many people have been affected by the fighting? What are the biggest humanitarian concerns?

Recent numbers I have seen have it at half a million people displaced. It is a little bit less than a third of the entire population of Gaza. There are varying degrees of severity; people who ran out in the middle of the night without shoes [after having been] warned their houses are going to be blown up. And two seconds later, they have nothing. In terms of the humanitarian crisis, the biggest concerns are primarily access to clean water, because it is such a finite commodity. Food is generally still available, but it is getting food to the hands of the people who need it that is challenging. ... There's a great risk of outbreaks of communicable diseases, with the numbers of displaced people in schools, camps and private houses without access to hygiene items, cleaning facilities, that sort of thing.

How are CRS' relief workers holding up? What's the danger they face?

There were tremendous risks in the past month, and I have seen people perform quite heroically and getting out in the midst of active fighting ... Our office had been closed for the better part of two weeks. It was too dangerous for staff to come and go from the office. There was not much we could do, because it was too unsafe. We couldn't get herds of people together for distribution.

Starting with the [first] cease-fire, almost two weeks ago, the teams were able to get out and start distributing hygiene kits, kitchen supplies, water-storage equipment, for 500 households; 500 families as of yesterday and close to 3,000 people. If the cease-fire holds, close to400 or500 families a day. But some people took significant risks on getting out, getting people registered [for aid] and getting these items distributed while there was still active fighting.

What has been the humanitarian impact of Egypt and Israel's blockade on Gaza?

Movement and access in and out of Gaza for people and for goods has been heavily constrained, which then gave birth to the tunnel economy. Until about a year ago, there were hundreds of tunnels running between the underground between Egypt and Gaza, because that was one of the only ways to get in large volumes of a lot of commercial goods.

The impact has been disastrous for an already fragile economy. Unemployment was at 30% [2013], now [it is] closer to 40% [2014], with a spike at the times when the blockade was intensified. People normally would go three nautical miles out to sea [to fish]. Farther out, their boats were potentially sunk or they were arrested, so the waters were pretty heavily overfished and are not really productive anymore.

For a lot of people, it is basically impossible to get out of Gaza. But this only really came back into international attention last month, because of the ferocity of the fighting. Gaza was in a very difficult, potentially full-blown, humanitarian-crisis situation six weeks before the conflict. We and other organizations said [Gaza] is really kind of perched on the edge of a potential humanitarian crisis, and it wouldn't take much to push it over. And with the fighting in the last month being intense, it has emphatically pushed the situation into a full-on humanitarian crisis.

Hamas diverted Israeli concrete meant for Gazan civilians to build terror tunnels instead. Are there any proposals about how to rebuild Gaza's civilian infrastructure but with international oversight of construction materials?

From what I've heard, there are always different proposals on the table. There is still a Palestinian unity government, so there has been talk of the government from Ramallah taking a more active role in the management of Gaza again, as was the situation before 2006-2007 [before the Hamas takeover]. I've seen proposals for a protracted 10-year [United Nations] custodianship of Gaza. I've seen proposals for E.U. [European Union]and U.S. troops to man the buffer zones around Gaza and the border crossings to allow freedom of movement. There are proposals for the complete demilitarization of Gaza in exchange for a $50-billion reconstruction plan — one of Israel's conditions — but in order to rebuild Gaza, Hamas has to disarm, and Hamas said they will resist anyone who tries to take their weapons away at this stage. So there are a lot of different possibilities.

What is CRS doing to address people's immediate needs?

As far as our immediate response, we're distributing these hygiene kits, kitchen sets and water-storage equipment to 3,000 households. We've done about 600 of those so far. ... We're planning to do quite a bit of [collaborative] work to rehabilitate private spaces to potentially provide cleaning services to these public shelters where people are staying, to maintain safe hygienic conditions there. We've helped deliver USAID-funded supplies and medicines to private hospitals in Gaza, and we'll be delivering additional medical supplies to a network of private clinics here. We plan to provide some psycho-social support, because again, it has been traumatic, not only for people who participate in our programs, but also for our partners and staff. So we have a pretty sizeable response at this point, which we are looking to scale up: not just humanitarian aid, but also to be a positive influence for recovery and eventual reconstruction.

What key aspects of the Gazan situation should Catholics in the United States know?

I want to highlight how completely abnormal, unnatural and unsustainable the condition of Gaza is. There are 1.8 million people who live in this tiny little stretch of land, without the capacity to grow enough food to support itself on a tiny, contaminated aquifer. We can't get in or out or sail more than three miles off of the coast. And this is not a new situation, but one that has grown over quite some time. For those concerned about the situation here, there are opportunities, there are things we can do as engaged American Catholics to make a difference and be supportive of a peaceful, lasting solution to this conflict.

What can we do to help?

We have a joint initiative by the U.S. Conference of Catholic Bishops (USCCB) and Catholic Relief Services called Catholics Confront Global Poverty. It is not based solely on this issue, but peace in the Holy Land is one of the major preoccupations of the joint effort of the USCCB and CRS, so people can go to the Web space for that: ConfrontGlobalpoverty.org. There are prayer resources for American Catholics; there are plans where they can come as either tourists or pilgrims to the Holy Land; there are resources for people to contact their congressional representatives. They need to know what we think and that securing lasting peace for Israel and Palestine is of great importance to us.

This article is reprinted with permission from the National Catholic Register. The article "A Cry for Peace Amid the Hell of Gaza" originally appeared August 19, 2014 at NCRegister.com.

"Hope still shines in the eyes of Gazans"

Posted on Sep 4, 2014 in LPJ

GAZA–September 1, 2014 – Visiting Gaza for a day amidst its rubble, Bishop Shomali, Patriarchal Vicar for Jerusalem and Palestine, interacted with and met Gaza's Christian communities. A ravaged landscape and people, who mostly want to leave, awaited him. At the same time, life continues and the bishop could detect a glimmer of hope after the war.

1. You spent your day yesterday in Gaza. What did you see? Who did you meet?

When we arrived in Gaza with the Chancellor of the Latin Patriarchate, Father George Ayoub,; the bursar Father Imad Twal, and the Superior General of the Sisters of the Rosary, we were greeted at the Erez check point by a delegation from the parish, led by Father Mario da Silva, vicar of the parish. The priest, Father George Hernandez, had not yet returned from Rome where he had an audience with the Holy Father. Then we drove through the destruction of the Shejaiya neighborhood, and a devastated landscape greeted us: ruins, rubble, hundreds of destroyed and burned homes. We felt as though we found ourselves in the aftermath of the Second World War. We met a few families who shared their drama. Many were critical vis-à-vis Hamas since the war they thought had left them homeless and losers. We saw people suffering from water shortages, queuing to fill bottle sand containers from tanks on the street, made available by Caritas Jerusalem. We welcomed teenagers who sought iron in the rubble or anything of value in the ruins for resale.

We visited the Sisters of Charity of Mother Teresa who remained during the war taking care of thirty to fifty elderly and disabled persons. They were smiling, happy with their work One night, they were warned to flee because their house would be bombed..But thanks to the intervention of the Italian Embassy, they were able to stay home with the children and the elderly. It was the only solution because they could not find another place of protection from the bombs. Afterwards, we visited the house of the Sisters of the Incarnate Word. Their recently restored house was hit by debris from an explosion and therefore needs another restoration. Then we met with the Orthodox Bishop Alexios of Gaza, of Greek origin. Like a good shepherd, he stayed with his parish during the war. He told us how at the heart of the conflict, he opened his church to Palestinian Muslims during Ramadan, offering them a hot meal every night to break the fast. We also went to the Anglican Al Ahli Hospital that hosted 4,000 people injured in tragic circumstances. We stopped at the Rosary Sisters whose school bore the impact of three explosions, less serious this time than the previous war. The entire visit was a real marathon. It ended at2:00 pm, due to the early closure of Erez, and so we could not visit our parish school, which was open to a thousand homeless people, fed and cared for by Caritas throughout the war.

2.The damage is considerable. What is the predominant feeling among the people of Gaza? Fear, despair, etc?

This is the paradox: we expected to see people sad or crying but we were surprised to meet courageous people, resuming life with perseverance. People go back to work gradually. Fishermen have found a little hope; they go out from 6:00 in the evening and return at dawn, their boats full of fish, including species never before seen in their nets. Someone told me that after 8am, they find no more fish in the market, because the people had been deprived of it for so long...Yes, we saw hope shine in the eyes of those we met, and not the despair we expected.

3. Have you visited the schools that house the refugees? What is the future for these people? Yesterday was the start of school in the country. Could this happen in Gaza?

More than 30,000 houses were destroyed. Refugees who lost their homes number approximately 350,000. They continue to sleep in UNRWA schools, or with their parents and relatives. I also saw people sleeping in the streets on makeshift mattresses, until the tents arrive that the UN should send before winter. Tents... while waiting the reconstruction of Gaza; this will take years and cost billions of dollars. As for the new school year, it cannot take place, but I was told that government schools will resume classes first because they were not affected by the bombings. The UNRWA schools were the most affected. Some weeks are needed to rehabilitate them. In terms of our school in Gaza, we still need at least a month to restore and accommodate students. Then the schools will face serious financial problems. Because the families of students cannot pay for tuition, we have to find how to help.

4. What is the role of the Church there, of religious communities and Christian associations of humanitarian aid?

The Church was very active during and continues after the war: Orthodox ,Anglicans and Muslims were unanimous in recognizing the work of the Catholic Church and its humanitarian agencies, including Caritas, Catholic Relief Services, and the Pontifical Mission, who worked alongside other Christian agencies like World Vision. All did a wonderful job of distributing water, bread, blankets, hot meals and medicines. They also managed to get fuel to hospitals since the main power plant was badly damaged, and they are now generating engines that provide electricity.

5. What hope exists for the people of Gaza? Rebuild until the next war? Do they believe in the truce? And especially do they still believe in peace?

After three consecutive wars, interrupted by brief truces, the people of Gaza have lost hope in a truce and believe little in peace. Christians are reduced to less than 1,500, think only of leaving. Some Gazans nevertheless still believes in peace. It is those who believe they have won the war and think that soon they enjoy all the benefits of this victory: open access, creation of a port and an airport. The facts ,especially the in the future, will say who won. The victory, in truth, will be political or diplomatic because from a military point of view, all are losers. Negotiations are expected to begin in September: whoever gets the most will have "won" the war. As for us, we pray that this is the last war in Gaza and the coming of peace. This is our hope.

Remarks compiled by Myriam Ambroselli

Pilgrimages

"In my opinion it is very important for Catholics to go on pilgrimage to the Holy Land and visit places made sacred by Jesus' presence; they should also meet local Christians and know about their problems. The organization of pilgrimages should also include encounters with the local community, i.e., the "living stones" of the Holy Land: this is a way to give them hope again."

Cardinal John Foley, Inside the Vatican, 2010

Christian leaders: Pilgrimages must change to help Holy Land Peace

Cardinal McCarrick Catholic News Service *Simon Caldwell*

Catholic and Anglican leaders have challenged Christians to find new ways to establish lasting peace in the Holy Land, including changing the nature of pilgrimages.

International Christian, Jewish and Muslim delegates at the two-day Conference on Christians in the Holy Land, at Lambeth Palace in July, considered concrete steps that might be taken by ordinary people to help to resolve enduring tensions that have forced millions of Palestinian Christians to flee their homeland in the past 50 years.

Anglican Archbishop Rowan Williams of Canterbury, leader of the worldwide Anglican Communion, told a July 19 news conference at the palace, his London residence, that the delegates had looked for a "bit of a step change in Christian involvement here with the situation of Christians in the Holy Land, a step change that will allow us to identify and support specific projects more effectively."

"As this is not just for the churches in the Holy Land but for the communities those churches are embedded in, we don't see this as an exclusively Christian project," he said.

He added that the "approach to pilgrimages" needed to change beyond a "tourist venture" to allowing visitors "to engage with the reality on the ground."

More than prayer

Archbishop Vincent Nichols of Westminster, president of the Catholic Bishops' Conference of England and Wales, told the news conference that British parishes would be encouraged to work for peace and forgiveness, rooted in justice, for all the people of the region.

The plan includes charitable relief work, contact with people in the region and in the Palestinian diaspora, and the lobbying of politicians to work for change. He said he would like to see such work extend to the wider community in the United Kingdom to include leaders of other faiths.

The conference, organized by the Church of England and the Catholic Church in England and Wales, was attended by Cardinal Jean-Louis Tauran, president of the Pontifical Council for Interreligious Dialogue.

The Cardinal called for renewed dialogue among followers of the Abrahamic faiths in the region, but he also made a specific plea for the rights of the minority Christians in the Holy Land to be guaranteed and respected.

He said Christian communities were not founded by missionaries sent from Rome or Constantinople but by the apostles and were a gift to their societies because "they bring cultural openness, a sense of the dignity of the human person and particularly of women; a conception of freedom which harmonizes rights and privileges, and a conception of political society which can lead to democracy."

Among the delegates were Bishop Gerald Kicanas of Tucson, Ariz., who is of Lebanese descent, and Cardinal Theodore McCarrick, retired archbishop of Washington, who has worked for 10 years with the U.S.-based National Interreligious Leadership Initiative for Peace in the Middle East.

Peace dissipates problems

In an interview with Catholic News Service, Cardinal McCarrick said the major obstacle for progress in the Holy Land and the plight of Christians there was the absence of peace.

"Once you have peace there, many of the other problems will disappear," he said. "I think one of the reasons Christians are leaving is that they don't find peace there. . . . I think [the conference] will let people know they are not alone in striving for peace in the Holy Land.

"The main thing is that we keep trying and, in good times and in bad, we keep the search for peace going on. This is the Lord's land, and we must all work together to find a solution that is just and which is going to bring peace with justice and security in the Holy Land," he said.

Copyright © 2011 Catholic News Service www.catholicnews.com
Reprinted with permission of CNS

British Catholic Conference Commitment in Pilgrimage with 800 Christian Children

Theme of the Pilgrimage: "Do not forbid them to come to me" - Press release: 13th January 2006

The Archbishop of Liverpool Patrick Kelly led a delegation of the British Catholic Conference on a pilgrimage entitled 'Journey to Bethlehem' on Friday the 12th of January. The theme of the pilgrimage were Christ's words "Allow the little Children and do not forbid them to come to Me" (Matt 19.13-15), reflecting the state of closure in Bethlehem, the restrictions on movements of the local community and the Israeli-built wall that surrounds Bethlehem and has turned the city of Christ into a prison.

The British delegation joined the heads of the Churches of Jerusalem, world Church leaders and the local mayors in a Bethlehem city parade that gathered more than 800 Christian children from thirty parishes across Palestine: Bethlehem and its sister cities of Beit Jala and Beit Sahour, Jerusalem, Abboud, Nablus, Ramallah and elsewhere. The procession also included Christian children from the Israeli city of Nazareth which has a large Palestinian Christian community. For many children, the pilgrimage was their first trip to Bethlehem – a city only a few miles from their home towns.

Archbishop Kelly stressed his visit was part of an ongoing programme to support the Christian Church in the Palestinian Occupied Territories, reminding the congregation at an ecumenical service in the Church of the Nativity that, "The first Christmas began here in extraordinary political circumstances under Roman occupation, yet the light shone through. As Pope Paul VI said: 'If you want peace, work for Justice'. This is why we are here today."

Archbishop Kelly emphasized that his visit represented: "The third stage over the past month in the commitment by the Catholic Community in England and Wales to the Church in the Holy Land. The first stage was the ecumenical pilgrimage just before Christmas in which Cardinal Cormac Murphy-O'Connor took part." The present pilgrimage follows the second stage, the filming by the BBC of a Christmas Eve Mass in Liverpool Cathedral that was dedicated to Bethlehem, both as the city of Christ and "as it is today', which was attended by a representative of Bethlehem's Christian community.

Archbishop Patrick Kelly travelled with the newly-appointed Auxiliary Bishop of Birmingham, William Kenney. The pilgrimage 'Journey to Bethlehem' was organized by The Holy Land Christian Ecumenical Foundation (HCEF), a nonprofit organization based in the Holy Land and the US that aims at bridging the gap between Christian communities in the world and Arab-Christians of the Holy Land.

The children marched through the streets of Bethlehem, ending with an ecumenical service at the Nativity Church where they listened to sermons by local and visiting Christian leaders under the theme of Christ's words, "Allow the children and do not forbid them to come unto me; for the Kingdom of heaven belongs to ones like these" {Matt 19. 12-15]. Speeches by the church leaders spoke about the joy of life, reflected by the children, but also spoke about the wall that separates Bethlehem from the neighbouring cities. Speakers longed for a day when such a wall should not exist in the Holy Land.

Auxiliary Bishop of Birmingham William Kenney said: "Peace begins with children. They are the future. Today Bethlehem feels exactly as it was 2000 years ago. The city was under occupation and Christ was born here because of the occupation. This is a very important occasion because it reminds us that children are the same everywhere and they should be allowed to be the same."

This was the third "Journey to Bethlehem" and the aim of the pilgrimage is to keep Bethlehem open. The pilgrimage is only possible under a special relaxation of the military regulations imposed by the Israel forces that restrict the movement of the Palestinians of Palestine as well as Israeli-Palestinian citizens. The difficulties in arranging such a visit makes these events all the more important moments.

The address from George Ghattas of the HCEF stressed that this visit came in solidarity with the people of Bethlehem, through "the spirit of children who represent the future of The Christian community and the life of the living stones of the Holy Land". The term 'Living Stones' refers to the communities from which Christ drew his disciples, and who remain a living community in the Holy Land. The 'Living Stones' are also described as a 'Fifth Gospel' who keep alive the language, customs, culture and a continuing tradition from Christ's time.

Archbishop Kelly said, "I think that the living stones here are important. I think that we all believe the church will be much poorer if, for instance, we have no people who spoke Aramaic, the language of Christ. They bring it all to life."

The children represented the variety of denominations of the Holy Land: Latin Catholic, Orthodox, Copts, Syriacs (whose liturgy is in Aramiac), Lutheran, Presbyterians and Greek Catholic or 'Malakites', the indigenous church of Palestine and a Uniate church in full communion with Rome . The day ended at the Peace Centre on Manger Square were all church leaders joined the Peace Centre staff to distribute Christmas presents to the children.

Moving Forward: The Hope for Peace

"We are thinkers, we are theologians, we are philosophers, we are teachers, we are believers in the Bible and in Jesus Christ and we are rolling up our sleeves and are making a difference by shedding light in a bleak situation because nothing will stand between us and the Lord."

Fr. Firas Arideh, Catholic Priest, Holy Land, 2013

Place of Divine Encounter - The Holy See's Hopes for Jerusalem

AUGUST 13, 2007 - *America magazine*

Drew Christiansen, S.J. served for 13 years as the U.S. Bishops' adviser on Mideast affairs.

The late John Paul II's pilgrimage to the Holy Land for the Great Jubilee of the Year 2000 came as the culmination of the pope's two-and-a-half decades of religious peacemaking. The personal importance of the visit for John Paul himself was made clear when, following the closing banquet, the late pope requested an unscheduled visit to the Holy Sepulcher for private prayer. Israeli security agents spent 45 minutes closing down the narrow route through the Old City and reactivating the special vehicle they had constructed to maneuver its uneven streets. Once there, an already impaired Pope John Paul climbed the steep stairs to the Calvary altar unassisted and prayed alone for 45 minutes.

The Achievement of a Failed Dialogue

The most celebrated event of that visit was Pope John Paul's prayer at the Western (or Wailing) Wall, where like other, mostly Jewish pilgrims, he left a slip of paper with his own prayer in a crack between the stones. Another, less known event, nearly derailed the whole trip. It was an interreligious ceremony organized at the pope's explicit request and the one sour note in what otherwise appeared to be the sweet melody of the pilgrimage.

Local church officials and the pope's own nuncio had warned how difficult such a Jewish-Christian-Muslim dialogue would be to bring off, but the pope insisted. To provide musical interludes between the speeches, choirs were invited to sing, but a Muslim choir could not be arranged, so a Muslim boys chorus was hurriedly assembled from the Catholic schools they attended. The grand mufti refused to participate, so President Arafat ordered a lesser judge from the Islamic courts, Sheik Tairseer Tamimi, to speak in his place.

The fireworks began when the Ashkenazi Chief Rabbi Yisrael Meir Lau announced during his address that by his presence the pope had acknowledged Israeli sovereignty over the whole city of Jerusalem. In fact, Vatican policy was that the future of the city should be settled by negotiation in accord with international law. Then Sheik Tamimi arose to speak and delivered a political tirade about driving the infidels from the land and establishing an Islamic state under a new Saladin—Yasir Arafat. The Israeli diplomats seated behind me stood up, shouting in righteous protest. This, I thought, must be what a Friday sermon is like in the militant mosques in Gaza. Then, by pre-arrangement, the sheik left, so as not to be forced to shake the rabbi's hand.

After the pope spoke, the program called for the three men to plant and water three olive trees. Rabbi Lau stood aside, as the already infirm pope, alone, planted the three trees and, in turn, watered them unassisted. What the pope had dreamed of as a moment of religious unity in the midst of political conflict seemed to have become the very vision of disunity. But the next morning, the Israeli press saw it quite differently. In a region where religious leaders were too often embroiled in politics, they editorialized, the frail Pope John Paul showed by example how a man of God should lead and so be a force for peace.

Six Phases of Policy History

That attempt at interreligious dialogue can serve as an image of the Holy See's efforts over the last 40 years to shape international policy toward Jerusalem. The principals have often talked past one another; there has been controversy; one side or another has tried to score points, but in the end the Holy See has shown how a city sacred to three religions and two nations might become a symbol of peace for humanity.

John Paul genuinely yearned to make a pilgrimage to Jerusalem. Beginning with his 1984 apostolic letter Redemptionis Anno, in which he voiced his desire to visit Jerusalem, through the Basic Agreement with the Palestine Liberation Organization in February 2000, weeks before the trip, his pontificate made significant contributions to the evolution of Vatican policy on the future of Jerusalem. Of the six stages in the development of that policy, four took place under John Paul.

Prior to John Paul's papacy, the Holy See's policy fell into two phases: (1) following the U.N. vote for partition of Mandate Palestine in 1947, the Holy See accepted the recommendation of the U.N. Partition Plan, which made Jerusalem a separate political entity (a corpus separatum) under international rule; (2) following the 1967 Israeli capture of East Jerusalem, Pope Paul VI called for a special internationally guaranteed statute to govern the city. In the minds of most people, including many diplomats and most journalists, the qualifier "internationally guaranteed" implied that the Holy See sought an international regime for the city, as envisioned under the earlier U.N. plan, what was frequently called "internationalization" of the city. That was not the case. It meant what it said: a special statute (a treaty) relating to the historic and religious aspects of the city guaranteed by the international community, not just by the country or countries that controlled the territory or access to it.

History had taught that control by one party or another meant exclusion for others. In particular, Jews had been excluded from their holy sites until 1967 by Jordan and afterward many Arabs, including local Palestinian Christians, were later excluded by Israel from Jerusalem.

The development of Vatican policy in the pontificate of Pope John Paul falls into four partially overlapping stages: (1) in 1984 the articulation of the universal religious significance of Jerusalem; (2) from the late 80s through the 90s defense of the rights of all the citizens of the city; (3) in the mid-90s, as final status talks approached, the expansion of the concept of universal interests in Jerusalem, and (4) in 2000, backing for Palestinian aspirations for the city.

City of Divine-Human Encounter

In 1984, Pope John Paul II issued an apostolic exhortation, Redemptionis Anno, articulating a Catholic theological vision of the Holy Land. Unlike that of evangelicals and particularly of Christian Zionists, Catholic respect for the ties of the Jewish people to the Land of Israel and for the memory of the biblical promise of the land to Abraham and his descendants is not decisive in determining the church's position on the land. Rather, the position of the Holy See has been rooted in international law, which has its own theological warrants in the Catholic tradition, and the requirements of justice for territory claimed by both Israelis and Palestinians. Prevented under the Lateran Treaty, which established the Vatican City State, from entering explicitly into territorial disputes, the Holy See still reserves the right to comment on the morality of the situation. Hence it has shown a willingness to speak up for both Israeli and Palestinian rights.

The contribution of Redemptionis Anno is that it provides a universalistic religious perspective from which to regard a land sacred to three religions and to two peoples. It is universal in two senses. First, it is sacred to the adherents of the three great monotheistic religions; second, it has significance for the whole human community as a site of humanity's encounter with God. Thus John Paul wrote of Jerusalem: Insofar as she is the homeland of the hearts of all the spiritual descendants of Abraham, who hold her very dear, and the place where, according to faith, the created things of earth encounter the infinite transcendence of God, Jerusalem stands out as a symbol of coming together, of union, and of peace for the human family.

The pope went on to stipulate the need "to do everything possible to preserve the unique and sacred character of the city." He explained this meant "not only the monuments or sacred places but the whole historical Jerusalem and the existence of religious communities, their situation and future...." This last clause hints at two unfolding developments in Vatican policy: insistence on the rights of all in the city, beginning with the living religious communities there, and on a broader concept of what is to be physically preserved and protected.

From Rights of Access to Human and Civil Rights

When governments spoke in the past of rights in Jerusalem, they referred specifically to the right to worship and the right of believers of the three traditions to have "access" to their holy places. As elsewhere in its approach to religious liberty, the Holy See with regard to the Holy Land has come to promote the right to religious liberty broadly understood, rather than simply the freedom to worship. For that reason, for example, the 1993 Fundamental Agreement with Israel stipulated several rights, including rights of the church to its own means of communication, the right to establish educational institutions and operate charitable organizations.

Of course, even to exercise the right to worship in its narrow sense, people must be permitted to gather. In the Holy Land that means worshiping at holy places, like the Holy Sepulcher, the Mount of Olives and the Church of the Nativity. With growing difficulties over the implementation of the Oslo Accords during the 1990s and the struggle for territory that followed it, the Holy See insisted on the rights of movement of local Palestinian Christians to go to the holy places, access that was often denied because of security concerns. In this connection, the Vatican frequently reminded its interlocutors that the Jerusalem with which it was concerned was not just the holy places but the local communities of people who worshiped there and for whom the holy places were the historic center of religious life. To underscore the same connection, the local Christians spoke of themselves as "living stones," in contrast to the bare "stones" of the ancient monuments.

But living as a community takes more than religious rights, no matter how broadly conceived. It also requires that members of the community enjoy basic human and civil rights as well. As the implementation of the Oslo Accords stalled mid-decade and tensions grew, Vatican policy emphasized the need for equal rights for all the residents of Jerusalem. It recognized the unequal conditions that had developed since 1967, the growth of Israeli security concerns after the first intifada (uprising) in 1987-93 and the gradual collapse of the Oslo peace agreements from the mid-90s on.

Advocating for Palestinian Christians

This expanded focus on rights also coincided with the efforts of the Holy See to support the Christian communities in the Holy Land, the vast majority of whom were Palestinians. The first intifada had prompted a growth of pride and self-identification on the part of Palestinian Christians. In 1986 Michel Sabbah, a native Palestinian from the Nazareth area, was appointed Latin (Roman Catholic) Patriarch of Jerusalem. Not long after that the three patriarchs and heads of other churches periodically published joint statements on issues that concerned them in the Holy Land. These statements were significant because the various churches were putting aside ancient rivalries, which were often exploited by the authorities, to make common cause on behalf of the faithful of the Holy Land. In 1994 the church leaders published a memorandum on Jerusalem, affirming the rights of all believers dwelling in the city and supporting an internationally guaranteed special statute for Jerusalem. Common backing of the statute placed the Greek Orthodox Patriarchate and the Vatican on the same side of the issue of the future status of the city.

In 1996, with a view to the opening of final status talks, the Vatican Secretariat of State issued a special note, titled Jerusalem: Considerations of the Secretariat of State. Along with the customary proposals for the safeguarding and, where necessary, "restoring" of historic and religious aspects of Jerusalem, the memorandum added, "There must be equality of rights and treatment for those belonging to the communities of the three religions found in the city, in the context of the freedom of spiritual, cultural, civic and economic activities."

Annexation and Human Rights

Tensions also rose over the preservation of historic Jerusalem with respect to annexation and confiscation of Palestinian and Palestinian-Israeli property—confiscations that frequently affected the political geography of Jerusalem. So the Holy See began to speak out directly for broader protections for Jerusalem, embracing its historical, cultural and even ecological heritage.

The last seemed, in part, a response to the sprawl created by the growing ring of settlements surrounding Jerusalem that destroyed the urban-rural nexus, which as late as 1990 still gave one the sense of the biblical landscape. The open land, for example, that once divided Jerusalem and Bethlehem began to be gobbled up with the Har Homa settlement (called Abu Ghoneim by the Palestinians). Lest they suffer more confiscations, the Palestinians then began building to the edge of the area they controlled. As a result, the historic area known as Shepherds' Fields fell victim to competitive sprawl. Preserving Jerusalem as a common heritage became an increasingly distant hope.

The 1996 statement from the Vatican Secretariat of State took on the issue of annexation and confiscation of land in the most forthright way: "The part of the city militarily occupied in 1967 and subsequently annexed and declared the capital of the state of Israel is occupied territory, and all Israeli measures which exceed the power of a belligerent occupant under international law are therefore null and void."

Finally, in February 2000, just before Pope John Paul's pilgrimage, the Holy See signed an agreement with the P.L.O. (for the Palestinian Authority). In most respects the treaty paralleled the one signed seven years before with Israel. It made explicit, however, a common commitment to uphold the "Status Quo," the Ottoman regulations stipulating how Orthodox, Latins, Armenians and others share the principal holy places. This was especially important to the Greek Orthodox, who feared that the Vatican's agreements with Israel and the P.L.O. would undermine their historic rights. But the explosive news in the agreement was the preface, particularly its statement on Jerusalem.

Though the preface to the Basic Agreement with the P.L.O. was not legally binding, Vatican backing for Palestinian hopes for the city stirred great anxiety in Israel and in the world Jewish community. Really an application of the principle that Jerusalem is valued by two peoples as well as three faiths, the preface supported "the inalienable national legitimate rights and aspirations" of the Palestinians and rejected "unilateral decisions and actions [by the Israelis] affecting the specific character and status of Jerusalem." This stirred up a hornet's nest, because the Palestinians claimed the city they call al Quds for their capital, even as the Israelis solemnly proclaimed Jerusalem their "one, eternal" capital. The pope's jubilee pilgrimage, however, was imminent, and the controversy soon passed. It will be recalled, if at all, as one of those exercises in competitive victimhood that regularly mark the Israeli-Palestinian rivalry.

Camp David and the Second Intifada

During the Camp David negotiations in the late summer of 2000, the local church took the lead in responding to proposals of negotiators. Just before the talks collapsed, Christian leaders in Jerusalem received word that President Arafat had ceded the Armenian quarter, already a depopulated neighborhood with many Jewish renters and lessees, to the Israelis. The patriarchs and heads of churches in emergency session issued a statement declaring the Armenian Quarter an integral part of Christian Jerusalem. In private communications, Mr. Arafat pulled back and promised in the future he would consult the Christian leaders on issues affecting their interests.

Within hours, however, the Camp David talks collapsed. A few days later Ariel Sharon, guarded by more than 1,000 Israeli soldiers and police, made his visit to the Temple Mount. Young Muslim men rioted in protest, igniting the second or Al-Aqsa intifada. Prospects for an Israeli-Palestinian settlement faded and with them hopes that Jerusalem would be a symbol of peace and interreligious harmony for humanity.

According to an old saying, Vatican policy is formulated in terms of centuries. Sub specie aeternitatis, the Holy See's policy on Jerusalem, like Pope John Paul's planting of the three olive trees during the tumultuous interreligious dialogue, continues to represent a standard by which to measure the achievement of tomorrow's diplomats and religious leaders.

Reprinted from America August 13, 2007, with permission of America Press, Inc., 2007. All rights reserved. For subscription information, call 1-800-627-9533 or visit www.americamagazine.org.

UNITED STATES CONFERENCE OF CATHOLIC BISHOPS

Resolution on the Israeli-Palestinian Crisis

A Statement of the U.S. Catholic Bishops, June 15, 2001

During the last nine months we have watched with sorrow and dismay as opportunities for peace in the Middle East have been lost in a spiral of violence. This violence is clearly seen in the destruction of so many homes, in the growing number of wounded and disabled, and most of all in the number of Palestinians and Israelis who have lost their lives, including many children and youth. This cycle of violence has exacerbated an already dangerous situation and dimmed prospects for peace. In this time of darkness, we make our own the prayer of Pope John Paul II:

The terms of the Middle East drama are well known: The Jewish people, after tragic experiences connected with the extermination of so many sons and daughters, driven by the desire for security, set up the State of Israel. At the same time the painful condition of the Palestinian people was created, a large part of whom are excluded from their land.... Gathered here today, we present to the One God, to the Living God, to the Father of all, the problems of peace in the Middle East and also the problem, which is so dear to us, of the rapport and real dialogue with those with whom we are united--in spite of the differences--by faith in one God, the faith inherited from Abraham. May the spirit of unity, mutual respect, and understanding prove to be more powerful than what divides and sets in opposition." (Homily at Otranto, Italy, Oct. 5, 1980) In this spirit, we reiterate our strong call of November 2000: "The only acceptable option is an end to the violence, respect for the basic human rights of all, and a return to the path of peace." (U.S. Catholic Conference, November 15, 2000.) A way must be found to return quickly to genuine negotiations, embracing, as far as possible, the gains made in the last rounds of final status talks. We deeply regret that the negotiations last summer and fall did not achieve a lasting settlement. Despite that failure and recent, terrible events, it is not too late to embrace nonviolence, dialogue and negotiation as the only road forward.

The steps toward a just and lasting peace remain the same: real security for the State of Israel, a viable state for Palestinians, just resolution of the refugee problem, an agreement on Jerusalem which protects religious freedom and other basic rights,[1] an equitable sharing of resources, especially water, and implementation of relevant UN resolutions and other provisions of international law.[2] These steps will pave the way to a future of cooperation and accommodation rather than occupation and conflict.

As supporters of the State of Israel and a state for Palestinians, we recognize that each side in this conflict has deep, long-standing and legitimate grievances that must be addressed if there is to be a just and lasting peace.

It is necessary for all to recognize that Palestinians rightly insist on an end to Israel's three-decade-long occupation of the West Bank and Gaza and to the continued establishment and expansion of settlements. Palestinians see this occupation, maintained by force and marked by daily indignities, abuse and violence, as a central underlying cause of the present crisis. Israel has a fundamental right to security, but security will not be won by ongoing annexation of Palestinian land, blockades, air strikes on cities, destruction of crops and homes, and other excessive uses of force.

It is also necessary for all to recognize that Israelis rightly see the failure of Palestinians to demonstrate full respect for Israel's right to exist and flourish within secure borders as a fundamental cause of the conflict. Palestinian leaders must clearly renounce violence and terrorist acts against innocent civilians, take effective steps to stop them, and bring to justice those responsible. The violence undermines the trust required to make peace and weakens the Palestinian search for justice. The Palestinian Authority must show the Israeli people that it is fully committed to prepare its people to live in peace with Israel.

These times call for new attitudes on the part of all the parties to the conflict. "We all know," the Holy Father said during his recent visit to Syria, "that real peace can only be achieved if there is a new attitude of understanding and respect between the peoples of the region, between the followers of the three Abrahamic religions.... [I]t is important that there be an evolution in the way the peoples of the region see one another and that at every level of society the principles of peaceful coexistence be taught and promoted." (Remarks upon arrival in Damascus, Syria, May 5, 2001.)

In the same spirit, this is a moment that requires that more Palestinian leaders and supporters of the Palestinian cause not simply advocate a Palestinian state, but also be unambiguously clear about Israel's right to peace and security, and the imperative to end all violence. This moment equally requires that more Israeli leaders and supporters of the State of Israel not only defend Israel and her people, but also advocate for the legitimate aspiration of Palestinians to live in their own homeland with dignity. At the same time, each community must refrain from inciting hatred against the other. We pray that the voices urging respect for the rights and aspirations of both Israelis and Palestinians will be heeded by their leaders and people. **The just claims of both peoples should also enjoy the active support of Christians throughout the world.** Civic, educational and religious leaders should be challenged to refrain from fanning the flames of ethnic and religious prejudice and be encouraged to promote a process of reconciliation without which peace will never be a reality.

While peace will ultimately spring from new attitudes and new ways of acting on the part of Palestinians and Israelis, our government, as well as the entire international community, must be actively engaged, in appropriate and significant ways, in working for a just and comprehensive solution to this conflict. We expect that they will do so in a way that responds respectfully to the legitimate claims and expectations of both parties, and does not acquiesce in unilateral actions which undermine negotiations.

As Catholics in the United States, we have a special concern for the toll the Israeli-Palestinian struggle is taking on the Christian communities in the area. **The native-born Christian presence in Israel and the occupied territories, less than two per-cent of the total,** risks shrinking into insignificance, in no small part due to the present troubles and their human and economic consequences. Other developments, such as the concerns of Christians about the

Nazareth mosque, only exacerbate a sense of marginalization. **As a result of these and other factors, the future of a living Christian presence in the Holy Land is in doubt.** The Latin Patriarch Michel Sabbah, himself a Palestinian from Nazareth, has pleaded with families to remain as faithful witnesses to the Gospel in the Holy Land. Regrettably, many families have already emigrated and many more are tempted to do so. **Partnerships with Catholic parishes in the Holy Land are one way to encourage the Christian presence there.**

Mindful of our historic debt to the Church in the Holy Land and our duties of solidarity to a sister church in severe need, we ask Catholics in the United States to join in strengthening the Church there during the present crisis and supporting its work for a just peace. We urge Catholics to be much more conscious of and give much greater attention to the crisis in the Middle East, and do what they can to support a living Christian presence in the land of Jesus' birth. We urge them to be unflagging in pressing our government to play an active and constructive role in the search for a just peace. We urge them to reach out in dialogue and joint action with Jews, Muslims and other Christians in this country. Finally, we urge them to support generously the urgent relief and development work of Catholic Relief Services, the Catholic Near East Welfare Association, the Assembly of Catholic Bishops of the Holy Land, and other worthy initiatives. The efforts of these and other organizations would be severely undermined if the U.S. government were to cut off humanitarian aid for the occupied territories, as some are proposing.

We pray that the God of peace, who has called us to be ambassadors of reconciliation, will achieve what human means alone cannot. Confident in God's blessings, we ask U.S. Catholics to join us through their prayers, their fasting and their good works in assisting Palestinians and Israelis, Jews, Muslims and Christians, in securing justice and peace in the Holy Land.

[1] **The question of Jerusalem involves two aspects. Territorial sovereignty is a bilateral question for Israelis and the Palestinian Authority to resolve equitably and by negotiations according to UN Resolutions. The religious dimension of Jerusalem, especially**

the "Old City," involves the need to preserve its unique and sacred character, both the Holy Places and the living communities of believers there. In order to safeguard the religious and human dimensions of Jerusalem, the Holy See has long advocated a special statute, internationally guaranteed. This statute would secure: (1) freedom of religion and conscience for all; (2) the juridical equality of the three monotheistic religions; (3) respect for the identity and sacred character of the City; (4) protection of and freedom of access for all to the Holy Places; (5) the regime of "status quo" in Holy Places where it applies. This statute, to be negotiated by the two parties in consultation with the three religious communities, could be guaranteed by the UN, the sponsors of the peace process, or another entity, but, in any case, should be sanctioned by the United Nations.

[2] Among the pertinent UN Resolutions are nos. 242, 338, and 194.

Editors note - emphasis added

The Work of the Catholic Church in the Holy Land is tied to Hope

Welcoming speech given by Fr. Arideh - Sunday, September 14, 2014

Dear friends coming from the USA Catholics Bishops conference,

I am honored in the name of the inhabitants of the historic village of Jifna to welcome you to Palestine as you join us for Sunday Mass. Today, you will celebrate with us in this house of worship a faith and tradition which is two thousand years old. This group of believers like many all over the world are assembled to give thanks and to pray. But unlike many in the world they carry a cross which is specially heavy. but we carry the cross with Joy. We carry the cross of believing in peace when it does not seem possible, in believing in justice when we are not afforded it and in having hope when the future of our existence is at stake. Yes, we the Christians in Palestine carry in our hearts and in our homes the Joy of the Resurrection while living the sorrow of death.

It is meaningful that you all have chosen to come and visit us here, a small Christian community in the village of Jifna. As guests from the United States and as a representative of the Catholic Church of the United States you present us with hope that one day the world community will help us to bear the cross which we carry. We are enriched by your presence and we hope that we are living proof that it is possible for people of different culture to live together in one homeland, while maintaining a specific identity and having a common mission.

On the November 2012 president Mahmoud Abbas went to the United Nations, where he represented the Palestinian people, in requesting full recognition of the Palestinian state. As believers in democracy. "We saw that our dignity may be hurt, but it will be healed. We are not abandoned. People are with us. We have rights just like everyone else, and we can live in calm and peace."

The work of the Catholic Church in the Holy Land is tied to hope. Our churches, our schools, our hospitals, our orphanages and all of our social institutions function to be a light in a bleak reality. That hope which stems from the dignity of each and every person, cannot be allowed to die. Its death will mean the birth of renewed violence, destruction and occupation. The voice of the church must protect the victimized and so no one has the power under any pretext to ask the oppressed to be silent. The imposition of an unjust peace would lead to a false peace more destructive than war.

Today I'm asking you to pray for this intention: you have to continue strengthen our hope, our faith: where we can say: we are not alone. and you have to maintain our presence here in the Holy Land: in Palestine: by being present in our lives, praying for us and with us for the best future and for the dignity of the Christians in Palestine, you have to protect not only stones but the living stones.

Here in Palestine we are one people, Muslims and Christians. we are under one occupation, we are under one law. there is no persecution in Palestine as the Israeli Propaganda said.

What we are asking from God today: to never lose Hope

Yes, we are dedicated to keep the hope alive. we thank you for your presence and we hope that from this visit of yours to this small village of Jifna, from the faces you see and from the voices you hear, your vision and mission for peace and security will include our hopes for freedom and justice in your daily prayers.

Finally, I would like to say a special word of thanks to CRS whois working very hard in Palestine, who works to save the dignity of every one.

God bless you all and thank you for your visit. Welcome to Palestine.

Promoting Taybeh Beer and God's Good Humor

Maria C. Khoury, Ed. D.

ThisWeekinPalestine.com

I am sitting in the middle of the wilderness and most of the days I am sincerely happy that the whole world is willing to come to me. I clearly have nothing to do with this fame since my brother-in-law, Nadim Khoury, worked extraordinarily hard since the early 90's to make one of the best products that exist in Palestine. People from all of the world want to come and see how we make this great micro brewed beer, the only micro brew beer in the whole Middle East, Taybeh Beer. Most times I am thinking we are absolutely crazy to stay in the highest mountain region of Palestine especially when we have all of the illegal Israeli settlements closing in on Taybeh and preparing a greater Israel. Sometimes, no electricity and other times, no running water and once in a while a few army invasions. But, there is something amazing happening here in Biblical Judea where Judea is ending and Samaria begins. With God's help we are still making the Finest Beer in the Middle East and feel this is our peaceful resistance.

On one level it is seriously God expressing his humor in somehow making it possible for a minority Christian family to exist among 98% Muslim population packaging a product that the majority are forbidden to drink by the Koran. And what is interesting about God is that He has granted much strength and blessings to survive harsh conditions of occupation, closure of roads and economic daily obstacles along with all of the other usual checkpoint problems.

Recently the Israeli occupation policies are making us go three hours out of the way to a designated commercial checkpoint with a scanner in order to deliver Taybeh Beer to Jerusalem which is technically only twenty-five minutes away from the brewery. Talk about a way to put you out of business since gas on this side of the world is approximately four times higher than you might know. So day by day we are beginning to feel we are a terrible threat to Israel. We focus and concentrate on creating an excellent product in Palestine so people could select Palestinian products and help keep Palestinians at work and this is a whole different threat to Israel since they like to keep the Palestinian market flooded with Israeli products whether they are beer, ice cream, milk or chips. Palestinian people suffer from lack of patriotism and they are very divided in their opinions so supporting local products is not high on their priorities. However, in the last fifteen years of making premium quality beer we have made some accomplishments in conquering the market share and we do our best to promote pride in Palestine.

I am thinking that God has humor since He is somehow allowing through the making of beer to bring awareness to the small Christian community in Palestine. People come from all corners of the world to get a Taybeh Beer tour and at the end they realize our village has been Christian for two thousand years since Christ's visit. We are the only all Christian village that is left in Palestine. How sad? Where have the rest of the Christians gone? I guess to better places like the USA, Australia, Europe, South America and anywhere that they can give a better life to their children. Thus, we have people come for the beer and they leave with a message of love. The message is simple but so hard to implement. Love thy neighbor and Love thy enemy is the bottom line. Or at least people understand that we simply want to have the freedom to be who we are and to make beer for beer lovers since freedom, justice and peace allow for all religions, all people, all colors and ethnic groups to co-exist.

For the last six years we have gathered more Christians, Muslims and Jews for the annual Taybeh Oktoberfest than any conference in our region. Taybeh has reflected peaceful resistance by making extraordinary efforts to do simple things like celebrate life. Living in an environment of not knowing what will happen day to day, the success of the festival is that it simply takes place and its peaceful. If we are blessed as in the past maybe more than ten thousand people will attend.

Taybeh Oktoberfest has become one of the distinctive festivals in Palestine and people travel from Brazil, Japan, Europe to perform and express their solidarity. We have made huge efforts to put Taybeh on the map since Israel is doing a great job to wipe us off. We want to inspire people to travel to the Holy Land and see with their own eyes what is happening. If you think that Palestinians are not practicing non-violent action please know that millions of us are trying every day to do ordinary things like work, go to school and have a party and we view this as non violent action to the awful conditions we experience under occupation. Come and support our local products or please pray for peace and be with us in spirit. When you visit Taybeh you will also understand God's humor.

Come Taste the Revolution!

Ten Reasons to Support the Indigenous Christians of the Holy Land

1.   The indigenous Arab Christians are descendents of the first faithful. They trace their roots back to who first heard and embraced the powerful, transforming message of our Lord Jesus Christ. (Acts 2:11).

2.   They continue to live out the faith in the very land where our Savior was born and lived, died, and rose from the dead. Their presence amongst a population increasingly non-Christian in orientation maintains the 2000 year-old Christian heritage of the Holy Land.

3.   They help ensure that churches and holy sites remain places of Christian worship. Without the indigenous Arab Christian presence in the Holy Land, these places would turn into cold museums, devoid of the warmth of the living body of Christ.

4.   They ensure that the younger generation is raised in Christ. The primary means by which youth learn the teachings of Christ and the Church is through a solid education in the Holy Land's Christian schools. As the first means of apostolate, the schools also offer Christians a place in which to interact with each other.

5.   They are our brothers and sisters in Christ. Though we have many different gifts and calls, we are united by the one Spirit that is given to all.

6.   Our shared Christian faith will be deepened. As our eyes are opened to other cultures, perspectives, and new ways of worshiping the same Lord, our shared Christian faith is deepened. We learn to experience Christ in new ways, and to show Christ to others.

7.   Christian Arabs are a bridge to peace for a troubled region. They share the Old Testament with Jews and share the same culture, language, history, and national aspirations as Muslims. They bridge the distance between those mired in the political conflict in the Holy Land and offer hope for peaceful resolution.

8.   They are suffering. Living conditions in the Holy Land are dire as a result of border closures that restrict freedom of movement and curfews that confine civilians to their homes. Few can travel to work, find adequate medical care, or afford housing.

9.   Emigration from the Holy Land is on the rise. Young adults have increasingly dim prospects for the future so many are leaving the Holy Land. This further reduces their minority status.

10.   Our religion calls us to help those in need. Jesus ministered to the needs of the poor, the afflicted, and the oppressed. He calls us to do the same. It is our duty as Christians to help sustain our brothers and sisters in Christ in the Holy Land.

Holy Land Christian Ecumenical Foundation

www.hcef.org

About the Author

Sir Jeffery M. Abood, KCHS

Jeff has been knighted by the Vatican in the Equestrian Order of the Holy Sepulchre of Jerusalem. He currently serves as his Section's Education Master, as well as, Co-Chair of the Education Committee for the North Central Lieutenancy.

He has also authored and edited various articles on the Holy Land. He annually compiles a literature review on the Church's perspective, regarding the current situation of the Christians in the Holy Land.

He has also received a certificate of Special Congressional Recognition for his leadership in working on behalf of the Palestinian Christian communities in the Holy Land.

Jeff is former Advocacy and Outreach Director of the Holy Land Christian Ecumenical Foundation (HCEF), which is based in Bethesda, Maryland and Bethlehem, Palestine.

Jeff can be reached at jabood@att.net.

Made in the USA
Middletown, DE
18 October 2016